No Miracles Here

Fighting Urban Decline in Japan and the United States

Theodore J. Gilman

State University of New York Press

Published by
State University of New York Press, Albany

For information, address State University of New York Press,
90 State Street, Suite 700, Albany, NY   12207

Production by Kelli Williams
Marketing by Michael Campochiaro

Library of Congress Cataloging-in-Publication Data

Gilman, Theodore J., 1965–
    No miracles here: fighting urban decline in Japan and the United States /
Theodore J. Gilman.
        p. cm.—(SUNY series in popular culture and political change)
    Includes bibliographical references and index.
    ISBN 0-7914-4791-X (alk. paper)—ISBN 0-7914-4792-8 (pbk. : alk. paper)
    1. Urban renewal—Japan. 2. Urban renewal—United States. 3. Urban policy—
Japan. 4. Urban policy—United States. 5. Japan—Social conditions. 6. United
States—Social conditions. I. Title. II. Series.

HT178.J3 G55 2001
307.3'416'0952—dc21
                                                                            00-038771

        10 9 8 7 6 5 4 3 2 1

CONTENTS

v

ABBREVIATIONS

CETA	Comprehensive Employment and Training Act
CIO	Congress of Industrial Organizations
CDBG	Community Development Block Grant
DDA	Downtown Development Authority
EDA	Economic Development Agency
EDC	Economic Development Corporation
FACI	Flint Area Conference, Inc.
FILP	Fiscal Investment and Loan Program
GEAR	Genesee Economic Area Revitalization, Inc.
GM	General Motors
HUD	Department of Housing and Urban Development
JDB	Japan Development Bank
LDP	Liberal Democratic Party
MITI	Ministry of International Trade and Industry
MOHA	Ministry of Home Affairs
MOFA	Ministry of Foreign Affairs
MOC	Ministry of Construction
UAW	United Auto Workers
UDAG	Urban Development Action Grant

PREFACE

I received generous financial support for this research. Imasato Shigeru single-handedly made it possible for me to go to Japan to conduct my field research while teaching at Kyushu University. He also taught me a great deal about Japanese local politics. This research would not have happened without his sponsorship. The Research Division of the Long-Term Credit Bank supported a summer of data collection in Tokyo. On the U.S. side, a Ford Foundation grant facilitated my fieldwork in Flint.

Many intellectual debts were incurred during this project. Tani Satomi and the members of the Japanese politics study group at the University of Michigan Ann Arbor were instrumental in helping to shape the origins of this research. Nancy Burns, Barry Rabe, and David Methe provided crucial support and constructive criticism in discussions along the way. Their extensive knowledge of American and Japanese politics made this a much better comparative study.

Numerous officials, scholars, and professionals helped me gather information. Though most asked to remain anonymous, I want to single out Yamada Takato of the Omuta City Hall for recognition. He arranged many of my interviews, provided invaluable data, and opened many doors on the Japanese side for me.

I am grateful most of all to John Campbell whose unique combination of sensitive personal support and sharp intellectual mentoring were invaluable.

Finally, I thank my wife Stephanie for her emotional support. I convinced her to spend years living in Michigan and Japan. She took her own architectural career on some crazy detours to facilitate this research. We shared many experiences that taught us about each other and deepened

ix

and strengthened our relationship considerably. While writing this book was a privilege for me, it was a sacrifice for her. I hope we can someday combine our mutual interest in the urban environment on another book.

A NOTE ON CONVENTIONS

Japanese names are presented in their conventional order, with family name first. I use official translations for the names of government agencies and offices. Macrons are used for long vowels except in some geographic names (Omuta). I have converted all Japanese yen amounts to dollars. Selecting an exchange rate for the conversion is a problem since the current rate would badly distort comparisons during the 1970s, 1980s, and 1990s. Exchange rates have fluctuated greatly during that time—from $1 to ¥360 in the 1970s to $1 to ¥100 in the late 1990s. I decided to use $1 to ¥180 as the constant exchange rate throughout the book because it approximates purchasing power in Japan for much of the time covered by this study.

CHAPTER 1

No Miracles Here: Urban Redevelopment Efforts in Japan and In the United States

A company town slowly grinds to a halt. The factories that once employed thousands and made the city an engine of national growth slowly cut back output as their ability to compete declines. Production decreases lead to job cuts and layoffs. As the company payrolls dwindle, the supporting businesses in the surrounding municipality struggle as well. Slowly they too go out of business. Young people no longer able to find work move to other, larger cities. The population ages and declines, with those left behind unable or unwilling to move. A once thriving industrial city of two hundred thousand rusts quietly, dismantled by global economic forces far beyond its control. No longer do the *yakitori* pubs and *karaoke* bars hum with the vitality of Mitsui workers done with their shift.

Karaoke bars? A leading Japanese company? In what appears to be a familiar American industrial landscape? Though it may be surprising, this portrait describes a Japanese city suffering from the effects of global economic restructuring. In the United States, the story of urban decline is well-known. Failure to compete in the American and in world markets for consumer goods and heavy manufactured items forced the slow and painful demise of several sectors of American industry. Nationally, industrial (and thus population) growth patterns have moved away from the Northeast and Midwest, toward the South and West. The service and high technology sectors of the American economy have experienced the greatest growth, and older, more established cities have had difficulty attracting industries in these sectors. The federal government has done little to alter this growth pattern, and state and local governments have met with only limited success.[1]

1

Since the early 1960s, the same economic restructuring process has occurred in numerous Japanese cities as well.[2] Given Japan's remarkable growth in the postwar period, one might not think that economic decline and urban decay would be a problem. In fact, if one only looks at national economic statistics, claims of depression and decline seem hard to believe. After all, Japan did triple its real per capita income in the 1960s, and growth in the 1970s averaged 3 to 5 percent per year. Though the prolonged post-bubble recession of the 1990s focused international attention and awareness on Japan's economic problems, two decades before that recession Japanese industrial cities started facing the same problems confronting cities in other industrialized nations. During this era of high growth, population movement from the hinterland to the cities—especially to the Tokaido region (the area in central Japan running from Tokyo to Osaka)—drained much of the younger population from smaller industrial cities. These regional cities have struggled with economic decline for decades.

The transformation in the Japanese economy from heavy to high technology industries caused the decline of numerous small cities. In the 1950s, 1960s, and 1970s, large-scale manufacturing enterprises located in the major urban centers were already attracting young people to life in the big city. At the same time, the Japanese government was helping to phase out domestic heavy industry through an active plan of rationalization. In the postwar era, coal, ship-building, steel, and other basic industries have been slowly pushed into decline due to their inability to compete internationally and due to the government's unwillingness to support them. This rationalization process propelled more of the rural and small-city population toward life and jobs in the metropolis, crippling the economies of numerous small cities throughout Japan. Simultaneously, the industries around which these regional cities were built lost their international competitive edge. The resulting combination of population drain and economic "hollowing out" in Japan is similar to what has happened in the American Rust Belt, the region of aging industrial cities in the Midwest and Northeast.

And like Americans, Japanese residents of such communities look to the government to provide assistance and to help revitalize the local economy. Governments try to respond, but their efforts often fail to stimulate renewed growth. But governments alone are not responsible for the failure to revitalize; private sector efforts fail as well. What accounts for these failures? How is urban redevelopment conducted in these two countries? What types of projects are selected and implemented in Japan and in the United States? And what are the institutional structures that shape this policy process and power distribution? These questions provide the focus of this book.

Since my emphasis is on urban revitalization, the performance of local governments is an integral part of this analysis. I am not only interested in the question of how local governments implement good policy decisions; I also want to know how they avoid making bad policy decisions. Declining cities in both nations face the daunting task of swimming against the tide of economic forces in order to revitalize their local economies. How do they avoid making an already bad situation worse?

There is an inadequate understanding of local redevelopment efforts in both Japan and in the United States, though there have been a few efforts to document this process on the American side.[3] No such study exists for Japan. This is unfortunate, given the emphasis in both nations (and in other industrialized countries as well[4]) on the decentralization of government in the 1980s and early 1990s. The "New Federalism" in the United States under the Reagan and Bush administrations sought to move policy-making responsibility to the state and local levels of government.[5] The Japanese movement for regional decentralization (*chihô bunken*) started later than that of the United States, but powerful members of the Japanese government continue to be strongly in favor of similar efforts.[6] The increase in government decentralization makes studies of local development practice and policy-making all the more relevant.

AN INSTITUTIONALIST PERSPECTIVE

This book is a comparison of redevelopment policy and policy-making in two smaller industrial cities that experienced serious socioeconomic decline.[7] The cities studied are Omuta, Fukuoka Prefecture; and Flint, Michigan. Both are company towns (*kigyô jôka machi*) in which the company cut jobs and transferred production as a result of economic restructuring in the global economy, and both have made considerable efforts at urban revitalization. Neither has been particularly successful, although Omuta has done marginally better than Flint. How can we explain these failures, and also the differences we observe? My evidence suggests that the institutional environment within which these communities exist accounts for much of the failure to spark widespread revitalization in the community.

Before elaborating on this statement, I will first explain what I mean by "institution," and how my approach fits into recent comparative institutional analyses. I begin with the assumption that institutions matter. Plenty of research—done in response to an overwhelming focus on behavioralism alone—indicates that while studying political behavior is important and useful, institutional analysis is a complementary approach that should not be neglected.[8] While it is important to study the characteristics, attitudes, and behaviors of groups and individuals, it is also important to examine the arena in which these actors interact, a point that is sometimes neglected in behavioralist studies. Few would dispute the idea that institutions do play a role in determining politics and political outcomes. The more important question is, To what extent do they shape behavior? What role do institutions play in determining what—and how—policies are implemented?

But before discussing the role of institutions, what constitutes an institution? In general, institutionalists use a definition that includes both formal organizations and informal procedures and rules that structure conduct. Hall defines institutions as "the formal rules, compliance procedures, and standard operating practices that structure the relationship between individuals in various units of the polity and economy."[9] This broad definition is widely accepted, though there is some debate over where the line between institutions and norms is drawn. Ikenberry has a three-part definition that claims that institutions "range from specific characteristics of government institutions, to the more overarching structures of state, to the nation's normative social order."[10] The inclusion of norms in the definition is somewhat problematic, for though the normative social order may determine what policy options are perceived as proper or improper, and may thus act as a constraint on behavior, norms are not necessarily institutional constraints. But institutionalists generally agree that organizational structures such as the rules separating the branches of government, electoral rules, party systems, tax laws, and organizations of economic actors all qualify as institutions. I subscribe to the broader definition that includes behavioral norms, since much of what is called "politics" is shaped by the way in which things were done in the past.

Coping With a Harsh Environment

As just mentioned briefly, local governments must not only address the question of how to make good policies, but they must also try to avoid making bad policies. This is especially true for cities in economically declining regions. Cities are severely limited in their ability to go against larger economic forces. They cannot control local or regional trade, and they cannot regulate the migration of residents. Powerful forces external to the city act as constraints on local policy-making.[11] Of particular relevance to this book is the fact that localities compete with each other for jobs and to attract businesses. A city in a declining area is playing with a bad hand of cards.

It is interesting to note that cities occasionally come up with a winning strategy, despite being dealt such a bad hand. Lowell, Massachusetts, and

Oita Prefecture, in southern Japan, are examples of localities that rebounded despite a weakening regional economy.[12] However, the case study cities in this book were more typical in that they encountered economic obstacles.

The key question for most declining communities is not how to win big, but how not to lose too badly—how to stay in the game, continuing to try things that could pay off. In the course of this effort, cities try to cut their losses as much as possible. There is no literature on urban redevelopment from this perspective, so this study is an exploratory effort. I will try to develop some generalizations through an intense look at likely case cities. This research addresses the question of what local governments do, why they do what they do, and how good their strategies are not only in terms of possible big payoffs but in terms of avoiding big losses.

The Theory: Policy Diffusion Is Inevitable and Unhelpful

Cities everywhere deal with urban decline much as they deal with other problems they face: they identify the problem and then search for a solution. Often that solution is copied from another community that has dealt with the same problem or from national policy menus. Copying successful programs is natural for cities in many countries, including Japan and the United States. Cities often borrow the ideas of others since those ideas frequently work well.

While this approach to policy-making works well in many policy areas, I rely on basic game theoretical concepts to argue that it is not appropriate for urban redevelopment. Unlike many local policy issues that are positive-sum in nature, economic revitalization is a zero-sum game. In other words, while cities can replicate most successful policy ideas almost indefinitely because they are not competitive in nature, solutions to urban decline tend to exist in competition with policies in other cities. Overreplication of a good idea produces diminishing returns for all those implementing the program even for the innovator of the idea.

After a brief description of case selection, the remainder of this chapter discusses these theoretical issues in greater detail.

Research Methodology and Presentation

To get at the issues just outlined I look at the supply of resources—finances and ideas—available to struggling cities. Specifically, I focus on the differences between Japan and the United States with regard to the sources of funding and ideas for urban revitalization. An understanding of how a city can avoid making bad economic revitalization policies rests on understanding how its decision-making patterns and actual policies are conditioned by where its two key resources come from. The next step is to devise a strategy to discover systematic differences in these key factors. Japan and the United States are two countries where local policy-making is quite different. Japan is often characterized as bureaucratic and top-down in its decision process, while the United States is said to be more fragmented and dominated by free enterprise.

In order to get the necessary detail and depth of information, I chose one city from each country. I wanted them to be in similar situations, however I also tried to pick cases that are as typical as possible—perhaps even exemplars—of what seem to be the main characteristics of each country.

Omuta and Flint are ideal cities for this comparison, since in several ways they represent the quintessential Japanese and American cities. If differences are going to appear in a comparison of these cities, they should manifest themselves here between these two "most different" cities. Omuta is a typical Japanese city in the following ways. First, bureaucrats dominate the local policy process. Although politicians have oversight powers, they seldom veto any initiatives put forth by city hall officials. Bureaucrats, with their systemic savvy and technocratic know-how, set the agenda and dictate the direction of policy-making. Second, public sector financing is more important than private sector financing for revitalization projects in Omuta. Japan's public sector leads the way, with the private sector playing a supporting, albeit secondary, role. Finally, Omuta's coal heritage places the city firmly in the middle of Japan's national industrial policy. Omuta's decline began as a direct result of the nation's move toward imported energy, and coal was one of the most important "sunset industries" (declining, internationally non-competitive industries) targeted by the government's industrial policy. The city was "on the dole" for so long that it had a lot of top-down policy experience. Omuta depended heavily on the national government, which is typical of Japanese cities. It experienced low local autonomy for several decades.

In contrast, Flint represents the stereotypical American city in several ways. Here, politicians rule the roost, and they carry more policy-making clout than do bureaucrats. City hall officials play a minor role in the redevelopment game. Flint's revitalization efforts rely overwhelmingly on private sector initiatives, with the Charles Stewart Mott Foundation's philanthropic money and energy leading the way. Though government funds do play a role in financing Flint's projects, the Foundation and other private investors provide more of the revitalization muscle power. This private elite action is stereotypically American, and Flint's experience offers a very conspicuous example of this type of behavior. Finally, Flint's reliance on the automobile industry makes it the archetypal American city. Cars are a central part of the American economy, and Flint's fortunes rose and fell with those of the industry. My primary level of analysis is the city, however my main independent variable is the source of money and ideas chosen by each city in order to combat urban decline. The cases used to illustrate the differences in the independent variable are three types of revitalization projects that are attempted in each city: amusement parks, shopping center revitalization, and industrial parks. Each type presents different problems for each city. Amusement parks are highly competitive and definitely zero-sum, so the copy-cat issue is very important in this policy type. Because it is uncharted project territory for most localities, reliance on experts—consultants—is seen as essential. Actors within the city are thus unable to mount an effective challenge to ideas or concepts proffered by consultants since they have no previous experience with this type of project. As a result, ideas which, in retrospect, appear to have been poorly conceived are able to make it to fruition. Looking at the amusement park story in Omuta and Flint, we see two cities where economically unfeasible theme park ideas rose to prominence.

Downtown shopping centers present a somewhat different problem for cities. Competition with other cities is somewhat less important than it is in the amusement park case. However, the city must still wrestle with the issue of how to attract shoppers away from new malls and back to the downtown retail district. Cities must get access to the best information on how to do this, and local actors must coordinate the interests of those involved so that a desirable plan is implemented. The story of efforts in Omuta and Flint to revitalize their downtown shopping districts provides a striking contrast in style. Omuta coordinated the numerous local interests more capably than did Flint, which tried to use a top-down approach to achieve success.

For industrial parks, innovation and copy-cat issues seem to be irrelevant because such projects are a pure commodity product. The key task for the cities is to forecast the demand for such a commodity in their area and then to build accordingly. The comparison of the cities' abilities to build the "right" amount of industrial parks for their respective regions reveals that again Omuta did a better job than Flint, which built far too much industrial park space and was in dire straits as a result. Through some nifty political maneuvering, however, Flint managed to fill its industrial parks with resurgent automobile production facilities.

Data to support my assertions are drawn from document research and from personal interviews conducted in Japan and in the United States. Most of the Japanese case information was collected in 1992 and 1993, when I spent a year as a visiting assistant professor at Kyushu University in Fukuoka, Japan. The American case information was collected over a longer period of time, since accessing Flint was easy while doing my graduate work at the University of Michigan, Ann Arbor.

Rather than explain first one case and then the other in detail, each chapter compares one redevelopment project type in both case cities. In this way, cross-national comparisons can be made more explicitly. This introductory chapter lays out the proposed theory in order to explain local redevelopment policy behavior. Chapter 2 provides a history of redevelopment efforts in each case, including the salient institutional similarities and differences between Japan and the United States with respect to urban factors and an overview of the three-pronged revitalization strategies in each city. Chapter 3 compares the efforts to promote tourism in each city through the development of amusement parks. Both Omuta and Flint tried to make a theme park the central feature of their tourism promotion program, but neither succeeded in sparking such growth. Chapter 4 examines downtown shopping area revitalization efforts in both cities, part of the overall strategy of improving their quality of life. Chapter 5 relates efforts to create jobs and to lure new firms through the construction of industrial park facilities in Omuta and Flint. Chapter 6 summarizes the findings that these comparisons suggest and tries to strengthen the causal linkages between the theory and case material. It also contains some alternative explanations for why cities try to implement what turn out to be suboptimal redevelopment policy ideas.

Revitalization Resources: Money and Ideas

Revitalization efforts require resources, specifically money and ideas. For reasons of policies, politics, or profits, actors outside the city are often persuaded that redevelopment efforts are worthwhile. These external players—upper levels of government and private actors, as well—help to make financial resources and redevelopment ideas available to the struggling city.

In both Japan and the United States, upper levels of government fund—either wholly or partially—a substantial number of urban revitalization projects. How does this financial assistance affect local decision making and policy? In both nations, governmental monetary help from above tends to push cities toward certain types of projects and away from others. Specifically, cities aim to concentrate on projects that higher levels of government will view favorably and thus will be more willing to fund. Governments are usually more willing to fund projects and programs that have worked well in other localities. Government and private institutions encourage a "supply-side" approach to redevelopment that focuses local revitalization energy on accessing resources already available for redevelopment and on adopting existing programs from other localities; from the city's perspective, the realm of viable redevelopment options is defined largely by existing programs and resources. Cities identify problems first, then go in search of solutions. Innovation—defined as new programs that have not been part of an organization's repertory and that cannot be introduced by a simple application of programmed switching rules[13]—receives far less support from financiers and decision-makers. Problems are met not with uniquely crafted solutions tailored to the specific locality's situation, but with tried-and-true ideas from an existing supply that have worked well elsewhere first. Urban redevelopment programming in Japanese and American cities is driven by a limited supply of project ideas, not by a prevailing demand for new ideas.

Supply-side diffusion occurs when localities apply for national funds from a central government list of policy options. This system allocates resources to reward cities for replicating existing successes and puts pressure on city officials to become experienced navigators of the national policy menu system. Such programs do not encourage innovation, and by specifying uses for finite resources they actually serve to discourage it. This top-down system also produces policies that rarely lead to successful urban revitalization.

Democratic nations face a contradiction in goals that is exacerbated by their respective systems of intergovernmental grants. The United States federal polity and the Japanese unitary system both contain elaborate mechanisms for the transfer of funds from the central to the local level. Gramlich describes the internal conflict neatly:

> There are very good reasons to try to keep power close to the people by having strong and vigorous local governments. At the same time, central governments have increasingly become more ambitious in trying to establish minimum service or spending levels for different government-provided goods and services. A reasonable way to compromise these partially conflicting objectives is for the central government to give closed-ended categorical grants to local governments. This technique preserves local control over the relevant functional category of expenditures but yet allows the central government to upgrade local spending.[14]

However, the local government's freedom is constrained by the central government's need to maintain control over its own budget. Central governments maintain this control by limiting the total amount of funds available to lower levels of government. Local governments develop a certain dependence on grants.

Money in the United States.

In the United States, scholars emphasize the political nature of grant programs. Conlan argues that national government grant programs, once in place, can be highly resistant to reform and reduction efforts. He shows how the growth of the American welfare state under Lyndon Johnson's Great Society plan expanded individual legislators' control over the distribution of political pork, and that neither Nixon nor Reagan was able to streamline the expanded bureaucratic apparatus because of the fragmented nature of the American political system that evolved prior to their administrations. Nixon sought to increase local control over grants and to decrease federal involvement in local affairs. Reagan sought to decrease the role of all government in all policy areas. Conlan demonstrates that prior governmental actions shape political agendas. Fear of losing control made cuts in welfare nearly impossible.[15]

Derthick supports Conlan's conclusions. She places the blame for uncontrollable social spending firmly on the elected officials in Washington, who created a system of weak legal controls that allowed states to exploit federal willingness to provide matching grants for virtually any program that could be classified as a "social service." Furthermore, she maintains that administrative controls should have kicked in to rein in government spending. But the fragmentation of Health, Education, and Welfare bureaus (fiscal control bureaus were at odds with program development bureaus) was not brought to the attention of appointed officials who made decisions about social service grants.[16] This lack of oversight would be impossible in the Japanese system, where oversight is more rigorous and where the bureaucracy micromanages grants-in-aid.

Both of these works emphasize local government reliance on national grants, but they take a top-down perspective. They ignore the fact that localities are held hostage by national programs, since these programs comprise the viable policy universe when viewed from the local level. These systemic constraints strengthen the supply-side nature of urban redevelopment policy-making. It is difficult for cities to diverge from national goals; it is easier for localities to jump on the national bandwagon of policy offerings rather than to search for a uniquely tailored solution to their particular socioeconomic problem.

Since the United States is a federal governmental system, one might argue that states are more active in local economic development than is the federal government. Eisinger, Osborne, and Brace all demonstrate that state-level industrial policies can be an effective catalysts for economic growth.[17] My research suggests that while the state may create an environment within which a city may prosper, the effect of state efforts on local growth can be highly variable from locality to locality. For some cities, state economic policies can even be tangential. The growth rates of localities within a growth-oriented state can vary widely.

From Flint's perspective, the state played a minor role in efforts to revitalize the community; though the state was busy generating economic growth, its efforts were not aimed at Flint. Furthermore, what little state money and energy Lansing did send to Flint had little impact on the local economy. This observation supports the arguments put forth by Brace and Osborne. Michigan created a clear industrial policy and made some significant gains in modernizing manufacturing, in generating growth in high technology areas in the automobile industry, and in venture capital financing.[18] But the state funds spent in Flint were aimed at none of these goals. Michigan contributed a few million dollars to some of the larger local redevelopment initiatives, including AutoWorld, Water Street Pavilion, and other capital-intensive projects, and it also built a new state office building to house local branches of state offices and departments in downtown Flint. None of these efforts were part of the state's overall economic development effort, which had a more modern, high-tech focus.

MONEY IN JAPAN

There is an extensive discussion on the question of how money, and therefore direction from above, conditions local decision making in Japan. English-language sources reflect a vast body of literature in Japanese. Japan's central government places tight budgetary constraints on local governments. Most importantly, only about one-third of local government revenues are locally derived and completely free from central government influence. Japanese localities exist in a system often labeled "30-percent autonomy." Other constraints are explained in greater depth in the next chapter. On the flow and effect of government money, the salient points are offered by Reed:

> First, the Japanese grant system is highly systematized and coordinated. Although Japanese complain about the bewildering maze of central grants, compared to the United States the system is simple. As is not true of the United States, there is little room for creative grantsmanship and very few loopholes. . . .
> Second, trying to get more grants forces the local government to

accede to the priorities of the central ministries . . . the only way
to receive more grants is to do what the ministries want done.[19]

Most literature on the flow of government money in Japan has a negative tone, stressing how dependency on resources from above inhibits
good policy-making. However, there can be advantages to such dependency: reliance on the center can serve as a check on foolish behavior. My
findings on the Japanese side suggest that such central government oversight of local revitalization has been a good thing.

Accessing Government Money in Japan and in the United States

My research suggests that Japanese and American cities go through different channels to get grants from higher levels of government. In Japan,
urban redevelopment funds are usually the domain of bureaucrats, since
urban revitalization efforts are another type of pork barrel project. Pork
barrel projects (government benefits that may help the economy of a leg-
islator's district—as in "bring home the bacon") are sometimes—but not
usually—the bailiwick of politicians. Along with Sakakibara, Dore also
portrays the distribution of central government grants and outlays as
dominated by politicians: "Politics in Shinohata [the author's case study
village] *is* about roads and bridges and schools and irrigation channels
and the gentle art of getting central government subsidies for these
things. . . ."[20] There is certainly ample evidence of politicization in the distribution of government grants and favors, but Reed argues—and my
research supports his position—that the basic distributional system is
bureaucratic. He frames his conclusions in comparative terms:

> Tarrow . . . contrasts the bureaucratic system in France with the
> Italian system, which is more political. In Italy partisan, fac-
> tional, and personal connections at the center make a significant
> difference in the distribution of central grants and favors. In
> France, however, the mayor is well advised to ignore political
> channels and concentrate on filling out the forms properly.
> Communist mayors got maybe even more than their share of
> central grants from the Gaullist regime because they used the
> bureaucratic mechanisms of the grant process more actively and
> more skillfully. Japan is more like France than Italy.[21]

Omuta's efforts to garner central government grants for economic
revitalization went through bureaucratic channels. The mayor's experi-

ence as a Construction Ministry official was an important part of this pattern. My questions in interviews about the importance of politicians in the process repeatedly turned up negative responses. For his part, Reed actively looked for test cases in which politics should have made a difference, but his conclusion remained. Reed and I are in the minority among scholars in holding this view, but our evidence is fairly convincing.

In the United States, although bureaucrats write the applications and do the legwork for such grants, it is political clout that brings money to the local level. Dahl found this to be true in New Haven, and my findings support his conclusion.[22] Political clout matters more than bureaucratic savvy in the American system.

Money from Private Sources

Though there is no literature on how private funding sources condition local government policy choices, it seems clear from my research that, analogously to the literature on national government fiscal support, private money will structure decision making in various ways. There are three sources of private funding relevant to urban redevelopment: private philanthropic organizations, private investment capitalists, and firms looking to relocate to a new site. Private foundations latch onto successful programs and fund their replication. Venture capital investors are more likely to support replicable projects that have already worked in other areas, rather than completely new project proposals.

Firms looking to relocate will want to control site development as much as possible. From the city's perspective, dealing with big business is different from dealing with small business. Job creation and tax revenues differ considerably in each case, and small firms have far less capital to contribute to redevelopment projects than do big firms. There should be literature on this topic, but none exists as of yet.

Ideas

In addition to money, cities also need ideas—solutions or policies—to effect revitalization. Where do these come from? Policy ideas can come from within the city or from some outside source. Cities can think it through themselves by analyzing the problem carefully and by actively figuring out the best possible solution. According to Gittell, the key components and characteristics needed for local economic development efforts include local leadership, strategic development agencies, institutional arrangements promoting cooperation, regional analysis to assess city assets and liabilities, sensitivity to labor force dynamics and characteristics, a broad conception of economic development, a positive city attitude toward revitalization, sensitivity to city history and social culture, and a recognition that economic success is not forever.[23] These components allow a city to best generate its own revitalization ideas.

Often, however, ideas come from outside the city. These are usually in the form of existing solutions looking for problems. Kingdon's revised version of the garbage can model of organizational choice provides a useful description of how ideas enter the policy process from outside. He envisions policy alternatives and potential solutions floating in a "policy primeval soup."[24] Specialists in a particular policy area spawn policy ideas in this soup. These ideas float in the soup until they are linked with an appropriate problem or until they fade from existence. They represent solutions in search of problems.

With regard to local government, most of the research centers on the diffusion of ideas among localities and even between levels of government. Overall redevelopment efforts in Omuta and Flint reflect a strong institutional bias toward "copy-cat" and supply-side policy selection and away from truly innovative revitalization efforts. Copy-cat and supply-side policy-making are basically the same. In both situations the city first identifies a problem, and then goes in search of a solution. Policy ideas in response to a problem can come from other cities or can also be offered as remedies by consultants who are encouraged by the system to act as purveyors of already successful policy ideas.

This tendency to replicate past successes from other communities—known in the aggregate as "policy diffusion"—works well for some types of policies, but not for economic development. Unlike most policy areas, which are positive-sum games, economic development is more of a zero-sum game. Still, policy copying is encouraged by several institutionalized features of the policy process in Japan and the United States, and contributes to the failed efforts in both cities. The zero-sum nature of economic development will be discussed later in this chapter.

Why was this method of policy imitation used? Two systemic features pushed these cities to rely on other communities' redevelopment policy innovations. First, both localities imitate successful policies out of habit. Since cities are historically used to adopting policy ideas this way in other policy areas, it makes sense for them to do so in the redevelopment policy area as well. There are numerous examples of habitual policy diffusion in both Japan and the United States, and since it is a method that has worked in the past, such policy borrowing often seems to be the best way to do things.[25] Community residents sometimes pressure their local governments to provide programs similar to those provided in neighboring localities.[26] Policy borrowing by localities is clearly an entrenched practice in both countries.

Vertical policy diffusion occurs when ideas travel between local and higher levels of government. The flow of ideas goes both ways. Lateral diffusion occurs through informational exchanges at the local level. City officials visit other localities to observe projects and to exchange ideas. Local officials also belong to professional organizations, which help to disseminate policy ideas and to keep officials up-to-date on developments in their field. Professional journals also serve this purpose in both countries. Public and private sector players in both countries support diffusion. The following sections briefly discuss the role of national programs and private sector consultants in urban redevelopment.

INSIDIOUS NATIONAL PROGRAMS

National programs for distressed localities play an insidious role in the process. Most of these programs are competitive, and localities must demonstrate need and "reasonable" spending plans in order to receive this money. But the officials who determine what is reasonable are put in an awkward position: they must decide what is reasonable, the criteria for which are often predicated on past success or failure. This bureaucratic "standard operating procedure" approach to grant allocation makes an organization quite capable of "fighting the last war," but it is not a productive way to innovate.[27] Since the bulk of government policy does not produce competition among localities, this formulaic approach to policy replication is useful in most cases. Redistributive government funding is not doled out to localities on a competitive basis. Good ideas in the social welfare policy arena, for example, are copied and initiated widely so that more individuals and communities in need may benefit. Welfare is not a zero-sum game; anyone who is eligible for it receives it. But when intercommunity competition is added to the calculation, it means that national officials must choose between needy localities based on criteria bound to produce diminishing returns. National programs thus perpetuate the no-win situation for economically distressed communities.

A system that encourages innovation may possibly generate more successful urban revitalization, while a system that encourages diffusion will generate successful noncompetitive policy, but will hinder policies that spark intercommunity competition, such as urban redevelopment. Unfortunately for many localities, however, policy diffusion is still the method of choice for most economic development. There is no realization—at the local level or higher—that the "games" are different. And the institutions concerned with urban revitalization produce a "path-dependent" approach to this policy area that reinforces an emphasis on copy-cat policy and discourages innovative policy-making.[28] This is certainly the case in Omuta and Flint.

The Role of Consultants

Consultants peddle successful programs and projects that have worked in other localities. These roving entrepreneurs provide proven solutions to cities in need. As consultants gain renown for their expertise in a particular project or program area, the demand for their services rises and the diffusion of their ideas accelerates producing a pattern I call the "lateral supply-side diffusion of ideas." Consultants play an active role in urban revitalization in both Japan and the United States. There is a link between this lateral mode of policy diffusion and the vertical axis just described: hiring experienced consultants can sometimes increase government and private sector willingness to finance redevelopment efforts. Consultants with a proven record of success provide a boost to local applications for national grants.

Consultants further strengthen—and are in turn supported by—the systemic bias toward existing policy solutions. Cole's study of learning strategies, though focused on the private sector, addresses the appeal and drawbacks of hiring consultants. His comments about consultants and their relationship to companies are equally applicable to the consultant-city relationship. Consultants, he points out,

> offer an implementation package based on materials they have developed, purchased, or appropriated. Consultants have typically had access to the experience of many companies and can therefore provide a pool of knowledge. It is in their interest to develop a generalized package that they can then market to a large range of companies. . . . Such companies were more common in the United States than in Japan or Sweden.[29]

The salient point here is that consultants routinely market a set of (presumably successful) ideas to their clients instead of devising a unique solution to the problems facing each firm or city.

While acknowledging the widespread activity of consultants in the United States, Cole also points out the drawbacks to hiring consultants, many of which are also applicable to the experience of cities. Consultants are opportunistic; they may exaggerate their expertise. A rapid expansion of the consultancy field in the late 1970s and early 1980s brought many new firms into the business. For firms in his study, the cost of verifying the expertise of consultants was considerable. Furthermore, Cole found that those who employ consultants fear that information and materials are slanted in ways that encourage continued dependence on the consultants.[30] Cities are equally susceptible to these drawbacks.

This is not to say that consultants are inherently bad or that they cause a systemic problem for struggling cities. Rather, the consultants are merely playing the system to their advantage. Policy selection practices in the United States and in Japan favor the proliferation of policy ideas diffused through the system by consultants.

An Institutional Perspective on Local Redevelopment: Diffusion Is Bad

Looking at the American experience with urban renewal and the Community Development Block Grant (CDBG) programs, one might even argue that American national government actions since the 1950s aimed at urban redevelopment have done more harm than good. From a lateral perspective, the local inclination to borrow policy ideas from other communities often blocks successful redevelopment. Localities rely on what has been done already in other communities for their redevelopment ideas. Professional journals and organizations, conferences, and personal ties are mechanisms by which policy ideas are diffused among localities. This institutionalized behavior works well to resolve some local problems, but not necessarily to generate renewed growth.[31] It is a logical strategy for risk-averse policymakers, and it works well for certain types of policy (discussed in the next section), but evidence suggests that it is not the proper mechanism for generating economic growth.

A second prevalent institution in the urban redevelopment process is the widespread use of consultants by struggling localities to foster the diffusion of previously successful efforts to spark renewed growth. Although consultants do produce successful and innovative ideas from time to time, they then ride the wave of these successes by replicating them in other cities, where the projects often do not produce the same results. This private sector supply-side system is well entrenched in both the United States and in Japan, and my evidence suggests that localities that hire economic development consultants suffer from this process. Good ideas in one—or even several—locations are not necessarily a panacea for slow growth everywhere. Yet cities spend a lot of money for advice and expertise that ultimately does not pan out.

This supply-side system encourages policy diffusion, but my evidence suggests that such diffusion is not a reliable road to successful redevelopment. Why does this system of policy diffusion produce poor urban redevelopment results? Governments and private sector actors borrow innovative ideas from other sources and facilitate the replication of those ideas in multiple localities. This process of policy diffusion creates a "diffusion curve" whose payoff structure changes depending on the type of policy being diffused. In game theory terms, some policy types create a positive-sum game, while other policy types generate a zero-sum (or negative-sum) game. The type of policy dictates the type of game, which in turn determines the shape of the diffusion curve.

Interestingly, the diffusion of innovation is desirable in many policy areas.[32] Innovating a social welfare program, an antidiscrimination law, a professional licensing program, a park system, or another community resident service creates a program that is potentially improved upon as each community institutes that program. The innovating community claims status as the program inventor, and it can upgrade its program as other communities borrow the idea and improve upon it. The absolute last community to jump on the bandwagon is ridiculed for being so slow, even though residents there ultimately reap the benefits of the polished program anyway. Being somewhere in the middle of the diffusion curve is ideal, since refinements in other communities have ironed out some of the kinks, and the program is often institutionalized in the national agency's policy menu.[33] Diffusion institutionalizes the policy, and diffusion as a means of policy-making is further entrenched on the process.

Diffusion is a useful method of policy-making as long as the program can be replicated repeatedly without producing a diminishing return for each community joining the parade. In other words, policy-making by diffusion makes sense for both local and national governments so long as the policy does not produce competition among localities adopting the policy. Social welfare programs, antidiscrimination laws, and park systems, for example, can be replicated many times before the competitive pressure causes a diminishing return on each new facility or program. Diffusion is quite rational if local governments are not in competition in that policy area. Local and national government officials in Japan and in the United States consider such policy activity "normal."

But this model of government behavior is inappropriate for economic development policy, since such programs tend to produce a zero-sum (or negative-sum) game outcome.[34] Being first matters. Schneider and Teske note that

> [s]uccessful entrepreneurs may be flattered by the competition offered by newcomers who imitate their successes. However, over time the competition erodes the entrepreneurs' profits by turning the entrepreneurs' unique insights into routine products or commodities . . .[35]

They assert that this is true for entrepreneurs in both the public and private sectors. A locality can come up with an innovative solution to socioeconomic decline. And though the next few localities to imitate that program may profit, subsequent copycats will experience diminishing returns. In fact, if several adjacent localities copy each other and build a concentration of one type of project, they may create a negative-sum game. Take the proliferation of amusement parks (or industrial parks, or gambling casinos, the current American craze) as an example. The first community to build an amusement park reaps some reward for its innovation, since it is the only facility of its kind in the region. But if the towns on either side of it also build amusement parks, supply exceeds demand and everyone suffers from the overcapacity of available amusement park space—including the innovator who built the first amusement park. It is irrational for localities to approach economic development from a diffusion perspective, since unless they innovate they will always be on the down side of a curve and will always be losing.

JAPANESE POLITICS

The notion of policy diffusion is definitely woven into the Japanese political studies fabric. The relevant literature usually focuses on two themes: the primacy of bureaucrats versus politicians in policy-making; and the direction in which policies diffuse—either vertically or horizontally. The two themes overlap to a degree, with Johnson asserting that vertical diffusion through bureaucratic channels is the norm, while Muramatsu maintains that both vertical and horizontal diffusion occur, though through political channels. Johnson's "developmental state" has as its dominant feature the setting of "substantive social and economic goals." Economic bureaucrats, officials of the Ministries of Finance, International Trade and Industry, Agriculture and Forestry, Construction, and Transportation, plus the Economic Planning Agency, are charged with the creation and implementation of these goals.[36] Johnson argues that Japan's center-local relations follow a top-down pattern and are dominated by bureaucrats. This vertical control model is grounded historically in the prewar system of local administration. Under the Meiji Constitution, Japan had a system of appointed governors. Prefectures implemented policies generated by the central government, and municipalities operated under the strong control of the prefectures. As agents of the state, the prefectures were "truly the pivot of centralization in Japan."[37] But Johnson argues that central government bureaucrats in Tokyo dominate the governmental system.

Muramatsu challenges the conventional wisdom that "[m]unicipalities are reluctant to undertake programs not assisted by the central government and local financial officials supposedly discourage self-supporting programs, preferring that the resources come from Tokyo whenever possible."[38] He argues that "although the vertical control model may be an appropriate characterization of formal administrative arrangements, it is no longer an apt description of the actual relations because it neglects the *politics* of central-local relations."[39] Bureaucratic devices pointed out by proponents of the vertical model can be—and have been—used in the opposite way, giving more initiative to localities. Muramatsu proposes an alternative model of intergovernmental relations: the lateral political competition model. This model emphasizes lateral communication and competition among localities and their active efforts to "keep up with" their cohorts. His model is driven by politicians—primarily at the local and prefectural levels—whose electoral motivations cause them to actively assert the interests of their localities, including initiating new programs and copying ideas from other local governmental organs.[40]

Existing research on lateral contact between local officials in Japan suggests that, for municipalities, information regarding policy innovation and ideas tends to come from other municipalities, not from the central government in Tokyo. Samuels reports on two Japanese surveys of local government officials in which many respondents put "other cities" at or near the top of their list of sources for policy ideas. This was true for small-, medium-size, and large cities. Although upper levels of government also served as a source of ideas for the survey respondents, the importance of lateral diffusion was striking.[41]

It is impossible to say conclusively whether politicians or bureaucrats dominate intergovernmental relations. Nor can we easily make sweeping statements about the source and direction of policy diffusion. Japan is a complex polity, and there is plenty of variance across time and issue area. Reed acknowledges this complexity and offers some generalizations about whether politicians or bureaucrats will take responsibility for an issue or decision: "Controversy pushes the issue toward the politicians' court. Technical complexity pushes it toward bureaucratic arenas. . . . [T]he degree of interest aggregation affects the probability of central or local response."[42] Sakakibara points to several issue areas that are (or have been) particularly susceptible to politicization. These include agriculture, fishery, construction, transportation, telecommunications, and parts of finance and commerce.[43] In these areas, politicization often means pork barrel projects.

Overview of Findings

Redevelopment efforts in Omuta and Flint failed because of a lack of innovation in the revitalization process. Both cities tried to use proven policies to address their economic woes, and their efforts produced few positive results. Similar strategies emerged from distinctly different institutional structures, and these strategies focused on attracting new firms to the community, promoting tourism, and improving the quality of life in the community to retain remaining residents and to entice people (and companies) to move there. Though the general strategies themselves were not inherently bad, the projects implemented to fulfill these strategies were copied closely from other cities. Expensive amusement parks that never achieved their goals, elaborate downtown shopping facilities that failed to draw shoppers to the city center, and industrial parks with standard incentive packages all added up to a lackluster revitalization scheme in both cities. Neither city devised a truly innovative plan to spark growth, even though innovation might have provided a way out of their downward spiral.

What explains this failure to think problems through intelligently? My overall conclusion is that despite differences in the institutional structure in both nations, each system pushes cities to replicate successful projects from other communities, rather than encouraging them to innovate new solutions appropriate to their own specific problems. Supply-side government programs that reward local compliance with national government programs, a heavy reliance on private sector consultants interested in replicating their own past successes, and a local tendency to copy other cities' successes all caused Omuta and Flint to choose redevelopment efforts that faced strong odds against them from the beginning.

Neither city has achieved truly successful revitalization, nevertheless Omuta has been far more successful at avoiding the pitfalls of inferior redevelopment policies. Put more bluntly, Omuta has had more government involvement in its revitalization efforts, and these efforts, although not rousing successes, have not become embarrassing failures either. Omuta has avoided making a bad situation worse. Flint has had comparatively less government involvement in its revitalization efforts, leaving most of the funding and idea access to private interests. These private sector actors have driven two large, expensive, keystone projects straight into blatant and decisive failure. The one truly successful redevelopment effort in Flint has been so only through a bit of luck and some local political intervention.

Regarding the politics of economic development, my analysis does not dispute the field's conventional wisdom about underlying causes: political-economic context determines a large portion of the urban revitalization efforts in both nations.[44] The odds against cities being able to swim against the systemic tide seem high. In addition to general macroeconomic conditions working against the communities' goals, the entrenched patterns of policy diffusion push cities down the path to imitation.

Ironically, the most concerted government efforts serve only to make matters worse, for the more higher levels of government get involved, the more they help to create a welfare mentality that dampens hopes for truly new ideas to emerge. Despite the widely acknowledged differences between Japan and the United States, the impact of intergovernmental relations on urban redevelopment appears similar in both nations. In Japan, the recent rhetoric of local autonomy was caused by the reality of strong central government influence and local dependence on national programs. In the United States, where federalism ostensibly confers greater autonomy on localities, reliance on national programs and subsidies is also strong.

THE NATIONAL GOVERNMENT'S ROLE

The role of the national government in urban revitalization differs in Japan and in the United States. In the Japanese case, political events do not affect the redevelopment process; bureaucrats dominate the game, and they operate in and around a set of stable national policy programs that do not change over time. The government finances much of the revitalization effort through grants and loans from an array of public corporations. These public corporations control funds comprising about 40 percent of the national budget. Such enterprises perform many different functions, though this study is only concerned with how they affect urban redevelopment efforts. According to Johnson, Japan's public corporations "make loans to implement official industrial policies and to aid low productivity or declining sectors of the economy. They also spend funds to strengthen the industrial infrastructure or to develop resources. They help stabilize prices; they produce revenue; and they do research."[45] For Omuta, the Japan Development Bank (JDB) and the Regional Promotion and Facilities Corporation (Chiiki Shinkô Seibi Kôdan) are two of the more important public corporations.

On the American side, politics matters more than bureaucracy. This accounts for the variation in federal programs over time. As new administrations assume control in Washington, they change the policy environment within which cities must operate. Unlike their Japanese counterparts, whose policy options seldom change, American cities are constantly faced with updated and newly refocused grant programs from which they must extract benefits. Political connections and clout seem to count for more than technocratic savvy in the American grant system. Though federal programs are an important part of Flint's redevelopment effort, their main function is to leverage private investment. Private funding sources are even more important, and these include private nonprofit foundations and venture capital investors. Philanthropic organizations are a crucial part of urban revitalization in America, and they present an interesting dilemma for cities benefiting from their generosity. On the one hand they provide the means to implement large projects that might not otherwise come to fruition. On the other hand, they are not accountable to anyone, and they carry ideological baggage that can constrain cities and push them down one particular developmental path.

CHAPTER 2

A TALE OF TWO CITIES:
REDEVELOPMENT BACKGROUND AND STRATEGY

How can we explain the similarities and differences in governmental activity in response to industrial decline observed in Omuta and Flint? Starting with a look at political institutions makes sense. A basic understanding of the governmental framework of incentives—stretching from the national to the local level—will provide a backdrop against which we may study the actors in each community. Institutions help determine what actors in the political system can and cannot do. Moreover, the institutional structure partially determines what goals actors will try to achieve.

I will first begin with a brief description of the decline of Omuta and Flint. Both cities have fallen far from their glory days as engines of national growth and industry. This section illustrates the conditions that prompted a need for community revitalization. I will then describe redevelopment efforts in the two cities from the early 1970s to the early 1990s, using an institutionalist lens.

Institutionalist analysis illustrates the continued significance of traditional generalizations about local government in Japan: lack of fiscal autonomy, bureaucratic predominance, and dependence on the center. Though localities must apply for many national government programs, the institutions show the revitalization process to be a supply-side process, in which localities follow the national government's lead. The system forces the city government to play a role in revitalization because the city must act as a conduit for national government funds. Though city hall takes the lead in planning many projects, it has relatively little discretionary power.

There is some debate over whether the American federal system fosters a dependence on the center that appears overwhelmingly supply-side driven too. On the one hand, as in Japan, American redevelopment efforts appear to follow the national lead, for example, the 1974 community development legislation contained restrictions that required localities to focus attention on the needs of disadvantaged groups. Peterson, Rabe, and Wong note that

> [a]mendments passed in 1977 and 1978 strengthened requirements for the housing assistance plan and mandated more concentrated use of federal housing resources for the inner-city poor. Guidelines promulgated during the Carter administration stipulated that 75 percent of the block grant dollars be used on programs that would primarily benefit low- and moderate-income households and that grant applications clarify how each proposed project would benefit such households.[1]

However, local officials interviewed by Peterson, Rabe, and Wong asserted that federal guidelines do not shape local programs. They maintained that cities use federal funds that complement their own local strategies and initiatives.[2]

Localities can exercise fiscal autonomy, though they prefer to have outside sources foot the revitalization bill. Do localities care where this outside money comes from? Local governments are equally receptive to private and public revitalization assistance. As in the Japanese system, American local governments act as the conduit through which federal funds flow to the private sector. However, other aspects of the American institutional structure support the conventional wisdom about American redevelopment politics: politicians are more important players in the process than bureaucrats, and the private sector plays the largest role in planning, funding, and implementing projects. Compared to Japan, the United States is still a political system featuring small government.

Since urban redevelopment is a local problem, it makes sense to examine the institutions at the local level first. This is how the community residents view government, and this is where revitalization efforts start. As these efforts percolate up, they encounter prefectural/state structures and national institutions. So this is the order in which I will describe the institutions and their effects on redevelopment policy-making, following an introduction to Omuta and Flint.

AN INTRODUCTION TO THE CASE STUDY CITIES

Cities of all sizes face the need for economic revitalization; this study does not attempt to explain the politics of redevelopment for all types of cities. Instead, it addresses the need to examine smaller cities. Larger cities are certainly important, and most studies of urban issues focus on the larger metropolises.[3] But smaller cities must not be forgotten, since a sizable percentage of the population of both nations lives there. In addition, smaller cities make excellent research subjects because development cycles tend to be highly visible and pronounced in these communities.[4] By studying small cities, it is easier to get beyond the aggregate economic data and to uncover the attitudes and behavior of individuals in the city. Small cities are particularly useful if one wants to highlight the community psychology and the way in which individuals affect the process.[5]

OMUTA

Omuta is a Japanese city battling the effects of macroeconomic restructuring. A port city on the Ariake Sea in southern Fukuoka Prefecture on the island of Kyushu, Omuta, experienced a hundred-year heyday as the largest coal-mining center in Japan, and during that time produced much of the energy that drove Japan's rapid twentieth-century industrial growth.[6] The Mitsui Miike mine was the largest coal mine in Japan, and was the center of an extensive industrial complex that included metal smelting and processing, chemical production from coal, electricity generation, and coal mining for industrial use throughout the country. But as Japan's ability to compete with other coal-producing nations declined, demand for Miike coal declined too.

Omuta is a victim of a postwar economic double-whammy: international price competition plus a global switch from coal to petroleum energy sources. As domestically produced coal either became more expensive or held its production price per ton constant, the price per ton of imported coal fell dramatically.[7] For Japanese coal consumers—mainly heavy industry and electric power producers—it made little sense to purchase domestic coal. As a result, the domestic coal mining industry entered a period of rationalization—encouraged and supported by the Ministry of International Trade and Industry (MITI)—that continues to this day.[8] Figure 2.1 illustrates the extent of rationalization that occurred at the Mitsui Miike coal mine.[9]

The left scale refers to total annual coal production, in thousands of tons, while the right scale indicates the number of miners. The dramatic rise in coal output from 1955 through 1970 was the result of significant

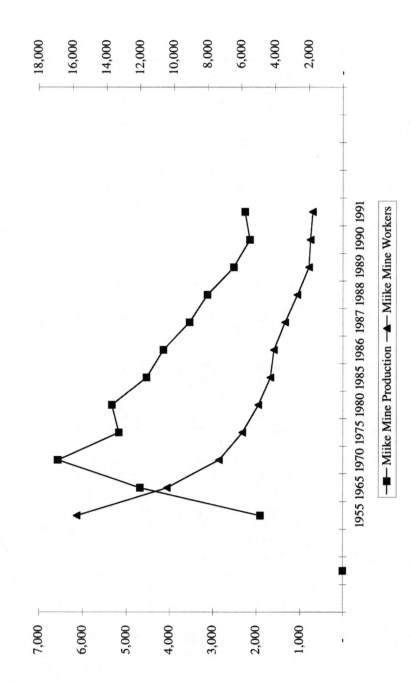

Figure 2.1: Miike Mine Production and Employment, 1955–1991

1955 1965 1970 1975 1980 1985 1986 1987 1988 1989 1990 1991

—■— Miike Mine Production —▲— Miike Mine Workers

Figure 2.2: Total Mitsui Production Employment

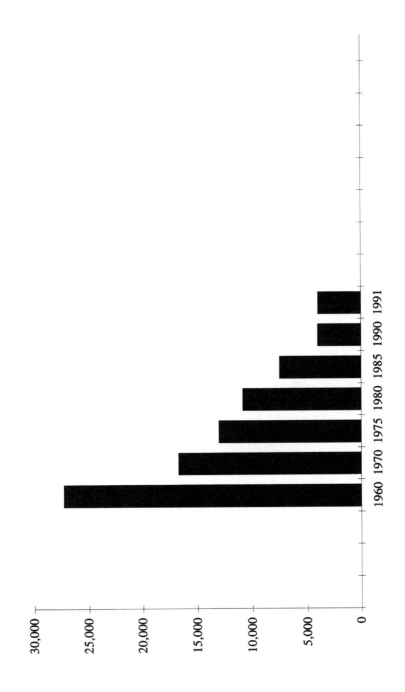

Figure 2.3: Total Omuta City Employment, by Industry Sector

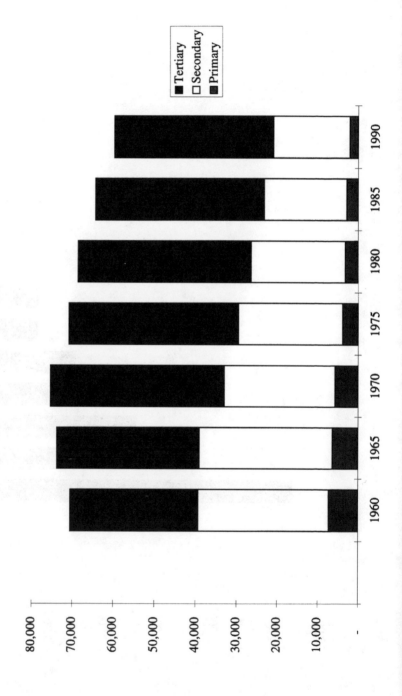

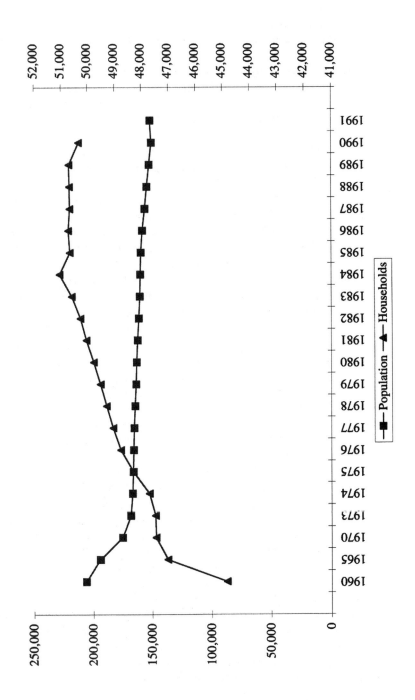

Figure 2.4: Omuta Population Trends, 1960–1991

technological advances in the 1960s and labor unrest in the mid-1950s that kept the mine closed and production levels low. For Omuta residents, the key issue was, and still is, jobs. The Miike mine was the center of a huge industrial complex—the Japanese have borrowed the Russian word *combinat*—that was built around the mine. As Miike went, so went the community. The Mitsui group combinat is made up of ten major companies, nine of which are still in existence in Omuta. All but two have experienced serious job cuts in the past thirty years.

As figure 2.2 shows, the mine and other Mitsui production facilities provided almost 29,000 jobs for Omuta area residents in 1960. By 1991 that number had dropped to around 4,500. The impact of such a steep drop in the job base was catastrophic from the city's point of view.

In addition to the steep drop in the number of jobs, the composition of jobs in Omuta changed as well. This is illustrated in figure 2.3. In the 1960s the majority of jobs were in secondary, or manufacturing, industries. This was largely due to Mitsui's presence in the city. But as coal rationalization took hold and as the combinat started to decline, tertiary industry jobs came to outnumber manufacturing, even as the total number of employment opportunities declined over time.[10]

Jobs in primary industries—farming, fishing, and forestry in Omuta—have not been a major source of employment in the postwar period, but they too have been roughly cut in half since 1960, and now account for about 4 percent of all the jobs in that city. This is in line with national trends. It is not clear why so many service sector jobs survive despite the decline in population. In 1960, the percentages of manufacturing and service sector jobs were almost equal, at 46 and 44 percent respectively. By 1970, 36 percent of the jobs in Omuta were in secondary industries and 56 percent were in the service sector. This trend continued through the 1970s and into the 1980s. By 1985, manufacturing jobs dropped to 31 percent and service sector jobs swelled to 64 percent. One possible explanation is that public sector employment picked up as manufacturing employment declined. The city of Omuta is the second largest employer in the city, after Mitsui. Another explanation is that the number of small businesses and offices has mushroomed. City statistics suggest there are more workers working in smaller offices than there were during the height of Mitsui's productive output, although it is unclear from these numbers what jobs these workers are doing.[11]

Naturally, when jobs dry up in a city, people move elsewhere to find work to support their families. This has certainly happened in Omuta. The population declined from a high of almost 209,000 in 1959 to the current level, slightly over 150,000 as of the 1990 national census. The largest drop occurred between 1960 and 1970, when the city lost 34,000 residents. There was a steady, though more gradual, decline from 175,000 residents in 1970 to 150,000 in 1990. This trend is depicted in figure 2.4.

As families have moved out of the city and as the population has declined, the composition of the remaining population has changed. Those who can move out of town do so, and those who cannot move remain. Increasingly, the population of Omuta is made up of older citizens with no children. And as the current population continues to age, with no influx of new, younger working families to offset the trend, the number of people per family drops at about the same rate at which the population ages. This trend has not changed substantially since the major job cuts at Mitsui in the late 1960s; this indicates two things. First, the population is getting steadily older. In 1965, 10 percent of the population was age 65 years or older. By 1990, that number had increased to 18 percent. These numbers are well above the national averages: In 1965, 6.3 percent of the Japanese population was age 65 years or older, while by 1990 that number had increased to 12.1 percent.[12] Second, efforts to create jobs and to attract new workers have not yet succeeded. I will explain these efforts in detail in the next section.

Another indication of the severity of Omuta's situation appears in the city's birth and death statistics. Nationally, given present trends the number of deaths is not expected to exceed the number of births until sometime after the year 2000. But as figure 2.5 shows, Omuta passed that threshold in 1988, and the trend shows no signs of reversing. Many nations are trying to halt population growth, but for Japan such a tendency is troublesome. Moreover, for a particular locality, the effects are readily visible and devastating. The population continues to age, with no indications of a more productive population developing in the near future. Omuta, like all of Japan, is concerned that there will not be enough younger citizens of working age to generate economic growth and to support the aging population through the pension and welfare systems. This is a brief summary of the socioeconomic conditions facing local, prefectural, and national officials who are trying to help redevelop Omuta's economy. It is a hard task that officials have been working on for only a few years, relative to the length of the downward decline.

Flint

The recent history of Flint, Michigan, is fairly well-known, thanks to the 1989 quasi documentary film *Roger and Me* by Flint native Michael Moore, and to numerous articles in the popular press.[13] Flint experienced a roughly fifty-year heyday as a center of automobile production in the United States. Best known as the home of Buick and as a labor union

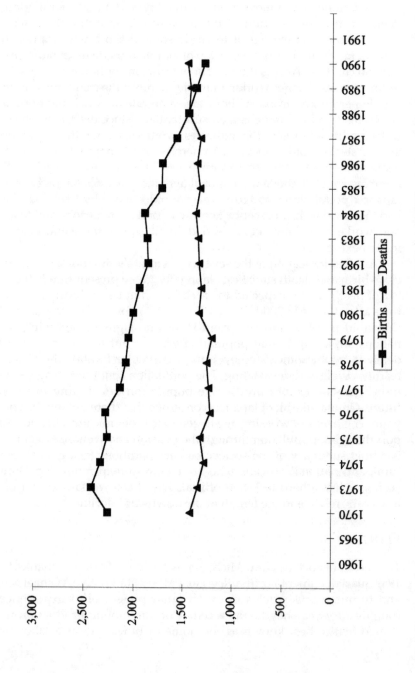

Figure 2.5: Omuta Population, Births and Deaths (per year)

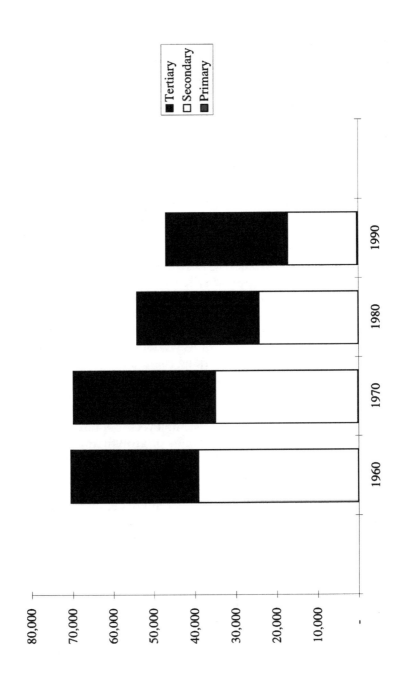

Figure 2.6: Total Flint City Employment, by Industry Sector

stronghold, Flint's history of boom and decline—and of capital versus labor—make it representative of much of America's twentieth-century industrial history. Flint's history is a good example of major trends in the politics of U.S. industrial development as well. The prosperity immediately following World War I sent production and employment in Flint and in other industrial cities soaring.

Welfare capitalism—benevolent, privately funded efforts at community support and enrichment—evolved nationwide after World War I. In Flint, this phenomenon was embodied in the Mott Foundation, the largest philanthropic organization based in Flint. Prior to the Great Depression, the leaders of the automobile industry in Flint built an elaborate network of privately sponsored welfare programs, insurance plans, and charitable organizations aimed at helping working people adjust to urban industrial life. They sought to preempt demands for public welfare programs or independent working-class actions.[14] Charles Stewart Mott, one of the founding directors of General Motors (GM), established the foundation as a philanthropic organization in 1926. Just as the local industrialists sought to control politics in Flint, they strived to control social and cultural change there as well. The 1920s was a time of improving economic conditions and expanding welfare capitalism. Though their approach was somewhat paternalistic, Mott and others showed a genuine concern for the well-being of the city and for its working people. It was in their interest to have a happy, healthy working community on which to draw.

The Great Depression catalyzed the growth of unions, which became a legitimate part of the auto industry when President Roosevelt pressured GM into bargaining with the UAW and the CIO to end the Great Sit-Down Strike of 1936–1937 in Flint. GM's employees and production facilities in Flint have undergone several cycles of growth and decline since the 1930s.[15] The automobile industry is vulnerable to the rise and fall of consumer demand for vehicles. But in addition to the cyclic rise and fall of the American auto industry, Flint gradually lost production to other communities that offered cheaper labor, lower utilities costs, better factory facilities and infrastructure, or other investment incentives. Production moved out of Flint, bound for communities in the South and West. Flint's recent past is similar to that of other cities in what is now known as the "American Rust Belt."

The oil crisis of 1973 marked a new era for Flint, just as it did for Omuta. Gas prices rose rapidly, and the demand for smaller, fuel-efficient cars made it difficult for GM to compete with imported vehicles. Over the next decade, GM cut jobs and production from its older Flint facilities, or transferred them to other sites in an ongoing corporate restructuring effort.[16]

The changes in the industry and the sudden uncompetitiveness of GM had a profound effect on the Flint populace. Auto industry jobs declined, and people were forced to find jobs outside of manufacturing. Figure 2.6 indicates the total number of full-time jobs in Flint, broken down by broad industrial sector. Although service sector jobs stayed roughly constant or even increased slightly, the number of manufacturing jobs in Flint has dropped drastically since 1970. This is due to plant closings within the city limits.

Obviously people cannot support themselves and their families without jobs, and the population of Flint has changed accordingly. Figure 2.7 demonstrates that, following a rapid rise to a peak of almost 197,000 inhabitants, the city population dropped to slightly over 140,000 in 1990. The number of households in Flint has fallen from a high of almost 61,000 in 1970 to just over 53,000 in 1990. With no jobs available and living conditions deteriorating, people are looking elsewhere for jobs and housing. The city of Flint faces a daunting challenge if it hopes to recover the prosperity of its recent past.

Interestingly, there is no mass exodus of young people away from Flint the way there is in Omuta. As figure 2.8 suggests, the median age in Flint has consistently hovered between 25 and 30 in the postwar era, though it was lowest in 1980 and has since rebounded to 1950 levels. Flint is not becoming a city of old people. However, the number of persons per household is steadily decreasing. This may indicate that people feel they cannot support larger families on their current sources of income. It is certainly not a sign of prosperity, for it does not show population growth.

This is a brief summary of the socioeconomic trends and conditions in Flint facing city officials and residents. Several interesting trends emerge from this demographic comparison. First, both Omuta and Flint started dealing with these challenges around 1970. Larger political economic issues changed the playing field for both cities, causing once prosperous company towns to slide into decline. Second, the decline in Omuta and Flint has been the result of a decline in domestic heavy industry. Though Omuta was driven by coal and Flint by the comparatively high technology of automobile manufacturing, both cities suffered from an influx of cheaper products from abroad. Japanese industrial consumers could buy coal more cheaply abroad than at home, while American consumers could buy more fuel efficient and more reliable cars from foreign manufacturers. Japan's vaunted industrial policy did no more to save Omuta than America's comparatively laissez-faire industrial policy did to save Flint. In both cases, private sector (corporate) decisions dictated the fate of the local community. Finally, all of the money and energy invested by both public and private sector players has produced little in the way of positive

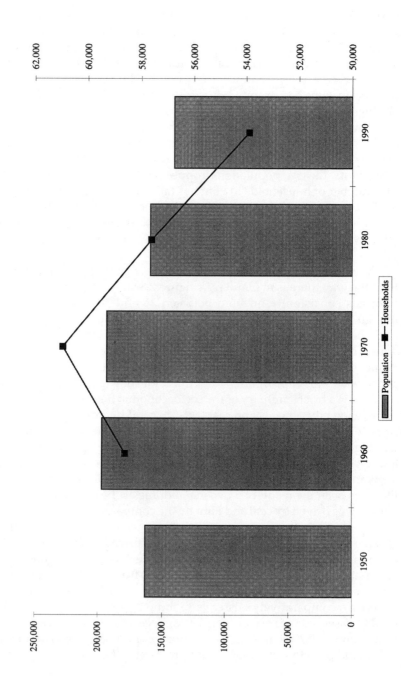

Figure 2.7: City of Flint Population, 1950–1990

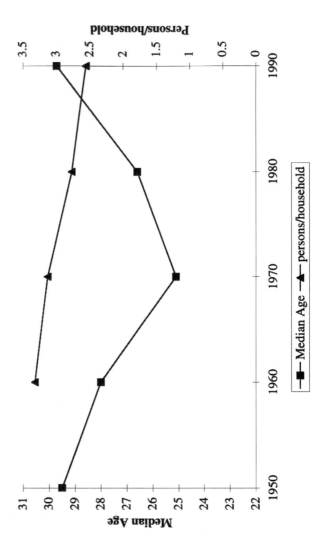

Figure 2.8: Flint Population Changes, 1950–1990

results. But city officials continue to hammer away at the problems, determined to help stimulate a renaissance in the city.

Institutional Effects in Omuta and Flint

This section tells the story of redevelopment in Omuta and Flint with special emphasis on the impact of institutions on the process and policy outcomes. A comparison of formal structures is woven into these stories.[17]

Omuta

Omuta's responses to economic decline have been late in coming, relative to the timing of the city's economic decline. While things were clearly going downhill in the early and mid-1970s, real efforts at redevelopment and revitalization did not start until the mid-1980s. The focus of policy responses in the 1970s and early 1980s was on compensation for displaced workers, rather than on new sources of jobs and economic growth. The policy focus from the mid-1980s into the 1990s was a mixture of quality of life improvement issues for city residents, and attempted innovations in economic redevelopment to create jobs and to attract people to the city. The shift in local focus was clearly due in part to changes in the national policy landscape. And the quality of life efforts were more successful than the job creation and economic growth measures: Omuta is a better place to live—it is cleaner, has more park space, and new civic facilities—than it was before the mid-1980s, but few new jobs have been created and the economy continues to sputter along.

The overall effect of institutions in Omuta reflects the unitary nature of Japan's governmental system in many ways, although there are also some distinct areas of functional fragmentation. Starting at the local level, the major institutional factors in the urban redevelopment arena are as follows. The directly elected mayor is strong, and therefore the local political system generally facilitates elite-led policy-making. The city assembly is weak, never seriously challenging the mayor or city hall bureaucrats on any of the plans generated by the administration. However, though veto points are few, they can be (and have been) used effectively by those opposed to a particular project. In addition, the primacy of bureaucrats over politicians is evident in Omuta's redevelopment efforts, *with the exception* that the mayor was the primary catalyst for the city's redevelopment efforts. Japanese local bureaucrats serve two masters. The mayor is their real superior, while national ministries and agencies are their functional superiors. Local officials must be responsive to both. The final salient local institutional feature is the lack of fiscal autonomy that constrains city budget decision making. Since the city generates only about one-third of its budget revenues directly, it is heavily reliant on disbursements from prefectural and national accounts. Above the local level, Fukuoka prefecture acts as a conduit for redevelopment funds and expertise from Tokyo. Japan is divided into fortyseven prefectures. Prefectures are headed by a directly elected governor and a prefectural assembly. The former is more powerful. Even though there is some discretionary power at the prefectural level, most participants characterize the prefecture as a pipe through which national resources flow to the localities. Prefectures are free to implement policies that are "not in conflict with the law." However, according to Reed,

> the central ministries have broad authority to interpret the law in the absence of court decisions, and they guard their authority jealously. Each time a local government has attempted to enact an innovative policy, the concerned ministry has argued that the ordinance conflicts with the law and is therefore illegal.[18]

The central government assigns numerous functions to the prefecture, and provides finances for the implementation of these programs. While these assigned functions seem to be overwhelming when viewed from an American perspective, Japanese local governments have somewhat more authority than local governments in a typical unitary state.[19]

The budgetary constraints placed on localities by the Tokyo government prompt Omuta and other cities to look to national programs for fiscal assistance. Local taxes account for roughly one-third of local revenues. Of the remaining two-thirds of the local budget, the two most important taxes are the transfer tax (*jôyozei*) and the allocation tax (*kôfuzei*). Both are collected by the national government and are returned to the locality by the Ministry of Home Affairs (MOHA). The transfer tax is a straight tax, meaning the amount collected from the locality is the amount disbursed to that locality from the central government, while the allocation tax is a form of general revenue sharing. The MOHA calculates the demand for a list of services provided by the locality, subtracts the actual revenues of the local government, and disburses the difference up to a total representing a fixed percentage of three national taxes. These three sources comprise general revenue for the locality and come with no strings attached. All other disbursements are made for specific purposes. The MOHA is arguably the most powerful ministry from the local government's perspective. All local borrowing is subject to MOHA approval.

An interesting change to note is the steady increase in the MOHA's budget through the 1970s and 1980s, depicted in figure 2.9. It grew much faster than both the MITI and Ministry of Construction (MOC) budgets, and did so despite serious administrative reform efforts at the national level. The MOHA budget more than quintupled between 1975 and 1990, while the MOC budget barely doubled. MITI's budget quadrupled in the same time span, but in absolute terms the MOHA budget was twenty times the size of the MITI's budget.[20] However, these figures are somewhat deceptive because most of the MOHA budget simply passes through the ministry to the local level. The MOHA is a key institution for localities borrowing money, but it exerts little or no control over the budget or general administration beyond the enforcement of conservative budgeting criteria and formulas. The MOC and the MITI are more important in these areas.

The programs implemented at the national level thus make up the universe within which localities must operate. From the local perspective, these programs are the most important factor determining policy choices and outcomes.

Omuta's change in policy focus in the mid-1980s did not result from any direct, immediate changes in the local political structure. In fact, Omuta's local government structure has not changed significantly in the postwar era. Since the Occupation reforms, Omuta—like every other city in Japan—has had a directly elected mayor and a city assembly. The number of representatives in that assembly is determined by a specific formula, based on the population.[21]

Rather, the threat of change in the national policy landscape prompted new policy priorities and developments. Starting in the early 1960s, Omuta benefited from a steady stream of subsidies to coal-producing areas. In the mid-1980s these rationalization subsidy programs began to draw to a close. The change in priorities at the national level catalyzed a change in priorities at the local level. I will describe the shift from coal policies to postcoal policies in the following section.

Is change in the policy environment a case of institutional change? I argue that it is. The coal policies described in the next section were backed by a series of laws passed by the national Diet. This legal framework was the institutional basis for thirty years of local government activity and routinized behavior. With the impending expiration of these laws, national bureaucrats and local officials were forced to find a new raison d'être. Omuta's local economic policy-making was habitually predicated on national laws, priorities, and directions. When these changed, Omuta was forced to change as well.

Figure 2.9: Ministry Budget Comparison

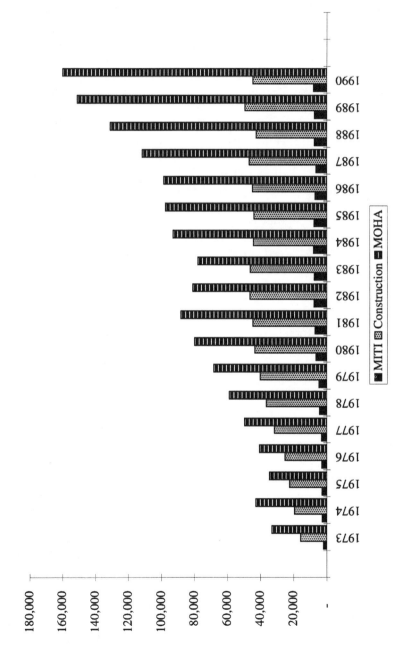

Policy Responses

This section describes the strategic change in Omuta's policy efforts from coal preservation and rationalization to coal replacement. Generally speaking, how did Omuta and Flint construct redevelopment policies? Both cities tried to revitalize using as much outside capital—both public and private—as possible. There are numerous ways to break down their redevelopment policy efforts. Policy pronouncements in Omuta and Flint each focus on seven different types. Omuta lists infrastructure development; industrial promotion; "living environment"; resident welfare; education and culture; and international cultural exchange; as well as taking advantage of regionally focused policies in its revitalization documents. Flint's Urban Investment Plan of 1993 focused on infrastructure, economic development, education and training, health care and social services, housing, law enforcement, and parks and recreation. Broadly speaking, all aim to improve either economic growth or quality of life. How can we explain the difference in focus? To a large extent, each city planned programs that it believed could be financed with outside resources. So each applied for whatever was available.

How does one rebuild a small city like Omuta? Functionally speaking, there appear to be two types of policies used to revive slumping cities. The first type is designed to improve the quality of life in the city. One Omuta official pointed out that company towns—especially industrial centers like Omuta—are often severely lacking in infrastructure and public life-style amenities like parks, roads and waterways, extensive sewer systems, and attractive city centers.[22] Government policies and plans to improve these facilities are aimed at making the former company town a better, more pleasant place to live. The words *machi-zukuri* (community-building) and *sumiyasui* (easy to live in) appear repeatedly in such infrastructure improvement plans. This type of policy is construction-oriented, with modest goals and tangible results that make them rather easy to implement.

Making Omuta a more pleasant place to live had two purposes. First, it was an attempt to raise the level of public amenities so that they were on a par with those in other communities. Omuta had less green public space than other communities its size, though it worked hard to remedy this problem.[23] Second, the city sought an image make-over that residents hoped would make it a more attractive place for outside firms. It is a widely held article of faith that firms will be more likely to locate to places where their employees will want to live, although I am not aware of any study that confirms this notion.[24] Omuta also had dreams of becoming a bedroom community for workers in Fukuoka City, an hour north by express train.

The second type of redevelopment policy is designed to attract people and job-creating firms to the city. A type of local level industrial promotion policy, these efforts target industries and even individual firms and try to entice them with "soft" projects such as participation in government projects, tax breaks, investment credits, and other industry promotion incentives, and "hard" projects such as industrial parks and transport network improvements. These projects are more ambitious, and take time to show success or failure. While they too require construction, they also demand an effective sales strategy and other elusive skills that contribute to a city's changing image.

Of course, these two types of projects overlap, support, and complement each other. Omuta had numerous projects in both policy areas, though so far the quality of life projects appear to be more "successful" than the industrial promotion efforts. Quality of life appears to be improving—there is a new city library and an improved park system, with plans for a new hospital on the drawing board—while few jobs are being created in Omuta. In addition, the city worked to improve its reputation as a destination for tourists, and toward this end developed an amusement park, city zoo, and other leisure facilities. Tourism falls into both categories of redevelopment project. Residents use such facilities during their leisure time, and tourism facilities create jobs either directly or indirectly (e.g., through increased sales by local merchants).

COAL POLICY ENVIRONMENT, 1970 TO MID-1980S

For the better part of the 1970s, Omuta's revitalization policy consisted primarily of efforts to extract compensation payments for workers who were laid off or retired early. This support money came from the continuation of the Coal Area Assistance and Promotion Policy, a national government program aimed at the long-term rationalization of Omuta's main industry. This is a long-running national government policy whose aim is to stabilize areas and communities hurt by the decline of the domestic coal industry. It is the earliest governmental attempt to control and soften the decline of Omuta and similar cities. Managed primarily by MITI, with the support of other government ministries and agencies, the policy encompasses numerous laws and policies aiding many groups and individuals related to the coal industry. There are six laws related to coal industry decline upon which coal area policy is based. The oldest, aimed at cleaning up pollution in coal regions, was passed in 1952. The most recent, which uses tax revenue from petroleum sales to help regions cope with labor, pollution, and new industry issues, was passed in 1967. One will expire in the year 2001, while the rest are slated to expire in 2002.[25]

Under these laws, a series of coal programs (Sekitan Taisaku) was promulgated by the national government for use in localities throughout Japan. The first coal program took effect in 1963, and ran for two years. Programs 2 and 3 also had two-year durations. But subsequent policies—including the final coal program, the ninth, which took effect in 1991[26]—had longer terms specified as regions became more stable and less frequent adjustment was required.

What was the local government's role in the coal program era? Local actions in the 1970s and early 1980s closely resemble the top-down, insulated system one might expect in a unitary political system. Since the early 1950s, the Omuta city government has regularly joined with related coal industry and labor groups to pressure Tokyo to keep the subsidies flowing. Throughout the 1970s the community was quite unified in its movement toward this goal. Coal was Omuta's lifeblood, and the thought of that industry no longer supporting the community was unimaginable. Until 1986, the mayor of Omuta was always a Mitsui company employee. Articulating the priorities of the city, company, and union, he would travel to Fukuoka, the prefectural government seat, and to Tokyo to push for more funds for his increasingly depressed city. Supported in his efforts by both labor and big business, it is not surprising that the city's economic policy consisted primarily of successfully extracting subsidies from the national government for so long. Business, labor, and government wanted the money, and the Tokyo government was willing to continue its largesse.

This program was a continuation of national government efforts to rationalize (downsize) the Japanese coal industry. Initial rationalization efforts—begun in 1950—were aimed at improving efficiency and corporate strength in the coal industry. Rationalization was designed to revive the industry, and its collapse was an unplanned event. Despite the government's best efforts, coal mine output efficiency did not improve. By 1955 the rationalization plans had already begun to focus on managing decline rather than on planning improvements.[27] The national government was more interested in compensating the "losers" in Japan's postwar industrial transformation than in preserving the Japanese coal industry. The government adopted this approach because of pressure from coal consumers, such as steel producers and the electric power industry. Neither wanted to subsidize the inefficient coal industry by agreeing to pay higher than market prices. These coal consumers argued that such subsidies would slow national growth, and the coal industry was not worth such a sacrifice. Government officials listened, and they made policies designed to manage the decline of coal.[28]

Nevertheless, the top priority for the local government through the mid-1980s was the preservation of the coal mine and related industry. This was still the engine driving the local economy, and the major political and economic actors worked to maintain this situation. Since public opinion was unified on this point, it was easy for the local government to set the same priorities year after year. The national government responded with subsidies for this prominent sunset industry, and it maintained a set of institutions that worked to achieve this goal. Ultimately, funds for the gradual rationalization of the industry flowed from the national to the local level for several decades, in large part because of standard programmatic inertia: such programs, once established, are difficult to disassemble. As Campbell puts it, "[i]n all organizations, participants will usually follow the rules and do today what they did yesterday, inhibiting policy change."[29]

There was no perceived need for policy innovation during this time, since the major interests were satisfied with the status quo. And coal policy implementation went smoothly because of the centralization and bureaucratization of the program. National ministry officials worked with prefectural and local officials to distribute benefits, cushioning the industry's decline for decades.

COAL POLICY, MID-1980S TO THE EARLY 1990S

As production at the Mitsui Miike mine was cut and jobs were lost, the national government provided money and advice to cushion the decline. Nationally, assistance to coal-mining areas was provided by a wide range of government ministries, although MITI and MOHA led the way in bureaucratic authority and budget disbursements, respectively. The era of job cuts, early retirements, and payments to affected former workers and families was coming to a close. The coal policy's main focus became forward-looking and developmental. Financing regional promotion plans, new coal technology research centers, symposia on clean coal technology and regional development, and overseas study missions emerged as the heart of the last two coal policies.

A change in institutional balance occurred in the 1980s. Even though there was no structural change, and the same important institutional players were going through the same institutional channels, a fragmentation of priorities occurred at the local level. Two camps developed in Omuta politics, one that wanted to preserve the status quo that centered on coal and coal-related industries, and a second that saw the dependence on coal coming to an end. The latter sought to move forward and to create a new economic era for the city, thus leaving the coal era behind.

Why did this division occur at this point in time? The institutionalist lens does not answer this question, but there are several possible explanations. From a political perspective, Mitsui employment dropped to a level that made the unions and the company less politically powerful in Tokyo. At the national level, this made it safe for Tokyo to cut back—with an eye toward eventually eliminating—the long-standing coal area subsidies. But the coal lobby had been weak for years, so this is not a likely explanation. From a bureaucratic perspective, the rationalization in other coal areas was even further advanced than in Omuta, so MITI saw a declining need to cushion this sunset industry as a whole. Smaller mines had been closed for years, and coal extraction efficiency (tons per person per month) rose steadily through the 1970s and 1980s.[30] Subsidies could not be stopped cold, but the change in economic factors prompted a change in subsidy strategy. I will describe this change shortly.

An intergovernmental perspective offers a third possible explanation. At the local level, the division between status quo supporters and progressives came to a head in the 1986 mayoral election, and the splits were visible in previously unified sectors of the community. The outcome of this local contest sent a signal to Tokyo that it was finally OK to stop the subsidy programs, although there is no solid evidence that Tokyo was paying any attention to these signals. The signal was in the form of the new mayor, who began a campaign to change Omuta's image and to initiate a postcoal era.[31] The changes in Omuta alone did not cause the change at the national level. Other coal areas experienced similar changes. But Omuta's history as the site of the largest mine was important. Other mining areas had not held onto coal as long as Omuta had.

Mitsui, the largest employer in Omuta, was also changing. Older industrial concerns were phased out in favor of new ones: metal smelting and aluminum refining moved up-scale to more high-value activities such as aluminum fiber production;[32] technologically advanced rare earth refining was started;[33] coal chemical plants retooled to produce fine ceramics and other products demanded by high technology industries;[34] and as the coal mine slowly decreased production, it increased its research and training (of miners from other parts of Asia) in the fields of coal extraction and safety techniques. The Mitsui Coal labor union experienced evolutionary pains as well. Some workers sought to keep the coal industry alive, while others argued for retraining and for the creation of new jobs within the company. Ultimately, the union split into two factions, the old union (*kyû kumiai*) and the new union (*shin kumiai*).[35] These two camps continue to exist, but both grow increasingly weak as time goes by and as membership decreases.

These local political and economic changes catalyzed a shift in the national policy environment. As just mentioned briefly, MITI decided it was time to bring the special coal policy series to a close. It made this decision based on the evidence that the coal industry was a fraction of its former size.[36] But rather than end the program abruptly, MITI changed the focus of its grants to coal areas. The ministry has a strong postwar tradition of promulgating and implementing industrial policy, and some at MITI saw a phoenix rising from the ashes of the coal industry. MITI became a sponsor of coal technology research and development in the hope that new products and technology might be developed for export to coal-producing nations. MITI began funding research into clean coal technology, and for more efficient, safer coal extraction processes. For Omuta, this change produced the World Coal Technology Center project, a research and development facility that intended to use the old Miike mine facilities. More generally, MITI developed a Coal Area Promotion Policy that included such efforts as infrastructure improvement, luring firms to former coal areas (kigyô yûchi), and aiding small and medium-size businesses in these areas. These efforts were done under the auspices of MITI's Regional Promotion and Facilities Corporation (Chiiki Shinkô Seibi Kôdan).[37] As the largest producer of coal in Japan, Mitsui jumped at the opportunity to receive further government grants. And as the site of the largest mine in Japan, Omuta cooperated in the directional shift. Perhaps there was a post-coal future that also included coal.

In 1986, the forward-looking forces scored a decisive victory when, for the first time, Omuta elected a mayor who was not from the Mitsui establishment. The election of Shiotsuka Kôichi says a lot about the changes that happened in Omuta politics. An Omuta native, who graduated from the prestigious Tokyo University, he worked in the national Ministry of Construction until he was elected mayor at age forty. During his tenure at the ministry, he spent two years on loan to the United Nations' Development Agency, working on development issues in Manila, in the Philippines. By far Omuta's youngest mayor ever, he represented a technocratic vision of a new Omuta that seeks to change the city from a coal town to a more economically diversified community.[38]

The 1986 election was ultimately a referendum about the future course of the city, and the conflict has seldom surfaced since the election. A conservative coalition based on the Liberal Democratic Party (LDP), Komeito, and Minshato all supported Shiotsuka. Although the postoil crisis unified coalition has fragmented somewhat, Omuta politics still functions much as it did in the 1970s and early 1980s, with a strong executive, high-elite cohesion, and few veto points. There are a few distinct differences, but they are mostly in the policy content rather than in the process.

Mayor Shiotsuka provided the strong executive leadership of past mayors; he may have been an even stronger leader, since he charted a new course for the city that will not show quick results.[39] The greatest change in Omuta can be seen in efforts at new policy development. Until Shiotsuka, there were none; starting with Shiotsuka, this became a central focus of local politics. Shiotsuka was clearly the catalyst for this change, and the centralized, vertically tracked institutional structure facilitated his ability to set city priorities. However, there is little true innovation in Omuta, since the revitalization and diversification policies now underway are the kinds of projects that other cities have been attempting for years, though they are new to Omuta. Shiotsuka catalyzed a change in policy direction, but the national institutional framework—including the various policies implemented elsewhere—dictated what was actually done. Omuta's new master plan of 1991 describes the general direction in which the city wanted to go. Industrial park zones and infrastructural improvement, supported by quality of life and leisure facility projects were the core of the plan. Figure 2.10 is a list of the major projects.

The idea for these projects came mainly from examinations of what other cities were doing to foster economic development.[40] Visits to other cities and consultations with prefectural and national officials prompted Omuta officials to try similar policies and projects. While none of these projects is particularly innovative, they all represent a dramatic departure from the policy inertia of the years prior to the Shiotsuka administration.

Changes in national-level programs—not statutory changes, but changes in administrative policy focus and emphasis—available to localities promoting economic development encouraged Omuta to move away from welfare-oriented subsidies and toward policies focused on growth. Even though the intent of the programs changed, the structure through which they passed, and the way in which they were managed, went unaltered. The mayor was still a central figure in the process, primarily in setting the local policy agenda. His endorsement virtually assured that a project would move forward. Though the city assembly must clear all projects, the assembly is functionally just a rubber stamp. It holds hearings and grills city hall officials on project proposals, but they have never had much input on any redevelopment programs.[41] The assembly role is purely oversight, a formality in the policy process.

As the list of revitalization projects shows, bureaucrats—from city hall up to the national level—dominate the pursuit of redevelopment project ideas. From the planning through implementation stages, they call the shots and really make things happen. One of the local officials' most important functions—given the fiscally top-down nature of Japanese government—is serving as the actual link with the prefectural and national levels. From the standpoint of Japanese political studies, this is somewhat counterintuitive. Many of the projects listed could be classified as pork-barrel appropriations. Road improvements, downtown development projects, and other upgrades to the physical infrastructure are usually

Figure 2.10: Redevelopment Projects in Omuta, 1970–1992

Project Name	sponsor/ applicant*	funding sources*	main funding source*	innovation source	early '70s- early '80s	early '80s- present	policy type	dominant player type
Farm Subsidies (cadmium problem)	3	1	1	N/A	X	X	redist	pol
Coal Policy (continuing)	3	1	1	N/A	X	X	redist	pol
Ariake GeoBio World theme park	3,4	1,2,3,4	1	lateral		X	growth	bur
Downtown Area Activity Plan (Community Mart Model Project)	3,4	1,2,3,4	4	vert./lateral		X	facil. imp.	bur/bus
Kattachi Area Development Project	3	3,4	4	vertical		X	facil. imp.	bur
Omuta Zoo Revitalization	3	3	3	self		X	growth	bur
Suwa Park Facilities Project	3	3,4	3	vertical		X	facil. imp.	bur
New City Hospital	3	planning stage	N/A	?		X	facil. imp.	bur
Area Road Improvement	3	1,2,3	1,2	vertical		X	facil. imp.	bur
Industrial/Regional Promotion and Corporate Invitation	3	3	3	lateral		X	growth	bur/bus
Omuta Central Industrial Park	3	3,4	3	lateral		X	growth	bur
Omuta Technopark Inland Industrial Park Development Project	3	1	1	vertical		X	growth	bur
Product Distribution Center	3	3,4	3	self		X	growth	bur
World Coal Technology Center	3,4	1	1	vertical		X	growth	bur/bus
Miike Port Facilities Improvement Plan	3,4	2	2	self		X	growth	bus
The Central Ariake Region Activity Promotion Council	3,4	1,2,3,4	N/A	lateral		X	growth	pol
Ariake Coastal Summit	3	1,2	N/A	lateral		X	growth	pol

*1=national government, 2=prefecture

3=Omuta, 4=private capital

assumed to be the domain of politicians—in the local, prefectural, and national assemblies—seeking electoral security.[42] But in this policy area in Omuta at least, there is little evidence to support this notion. Even though the mayor is a politician involved in many of these efforts, he is not closely connected to any local representatives. His past experience in the bureaucracy seems to account for this bureaucratic focus.

Bureaucratic primacy exists in this policy area for other reasons as well. Though money is available from various national sources, getting it can be difficult. Cities compete for funds, so having an idea of what the ministry in control of the purse strings wants in a proposal is important. The system places a higher value on systemic savvy and technical knowledge than on political contacts and clout. The application forms required for such grants are lengthy and contorted, and demand a technocratic expertise that politicians do not necessarily have. Experienced local and national career officials write books explaining the various ways of accessing national coffers.[43] Even though officials from different sections work together at the local level, this is not the case at the prefectural and national levels. The ministries are quite fragmented on a horizontal scale; MITI, the MOC, and the MOHA all have programs for urban redevelopment that functionally overlap one another. But there is little cooperation among these agencies to avoid duplication. In fact, the six coal laws required a number of agencies and ministries to each create their own plan to assist each coal area. The Prime Minister's Office, along with the Ministries of Finance, Agriculture, Transportation, Health/Welfare, Labor, Construction, Local Affairs, and International Trade and Industry were required to generate and implement such programs.[44] Each had to reach down to the local level and provide subsidies to struggling coal regions, Omuta among them.

In this policy area, bureaucrats are more important than politicians, and bureaucratic intergovernmental relations are deep. One manifestation of these vertical ties is seen in the practice of *jinji kôryû*, the "personnel exchange" system that all national agencies use. National officials are dispatched to the prefectural or local level for a year or two, where they serve as section chiefs and gain practical project management experience. During that time, they still receive their preassignment salary, paid by their ministry of origin. Upon returning to their home ministry, they usually move up a level in the bureaucracy. MITI and the Ministries of Construction, Health and Welfare, and Local Affairs all have sent employees to Omuta. Prefectural officials are sent to the local level under the same system. Personnel exchange seems to only work from the top-down. Local officials do not go to higher levels to gain experience. But localities benefit from the presence of officials from higher levels. Personal contacts in various offices, expertise at grant applications from the receiving end, and knowledge of available programs all help localities take advantage of national ministry resources.

As the tables in this section indicate, most of the redevelopment projects in Omuta are dominated by bureaucrats and receive some national funding. To get a better understanding for the effect of these institutions on a microlevel, we need only look at the way in which Omuta dealt with the end of the coal policy series.

Searching for a future, Omuta sent a study mission to Europe in October 1989—led by Mayor Shiotsuka—to see how communities in similar situations handled the decline of the coal industry. Upon their return, the mayor told the Japanese press that the British and West German governments took active measures to help unemployed workers find new jobs. In a ninety-five-page description, the mission reported their findings to the Energy Resources Agency (Shigen Enerugi-cho, a branch of MITI) in Tokyo, and to other ministries and agencies as well. In it, they recommended the establishment of a World Coal Technology Center to study mine safety and other coal technology, to serve as a dissemination point for Japan's superior technical know-how to the other coal mining nations in the Asia-Pacific region, and to help promote the Omuta region.[45]

MITI quickly jumped on this idea, and in December 1990 the first public meeting on the center was held in Omuta. Sponsored by MITI, it focused on three facets of the emerging plan: a coal technology research center, a mine safety center, and a pollution control research center. Officials from various MITI sections attended and served on the panel presenting the plan, along with representatives from the Japan Coal Association, the Coal Technology Development Cooperation Center, and Kyushu University.[46] Interestingly, no one from Mitsui Coal Mining presented a paper, and this company was not even mentioned in any of the newspapers that day.

Up to this point, the center was a good example of Omuta playing the government structure skillfully. Overseas study missions have a long history in Japan, dating back to shortly after Commodore Perry sailed into Tokyo Bay, demanding that Japan open its borders. During the Meiji period Japan sent study missions to Europe and to the United States to research such diverse subjects as national constitutions, university systems, and military and governmental structures. Though the coal area mission was organized locally and funded by the prefecture, it catalyzed government action at the national level because it took advantage of MITI's receptiveness for this type of project.

MITI became a world-famous agency because it is credited with industrial policy decisions that helped Japan achieve such rapid postwar

growth. MITI had also been working for a long time to gradually rationalize the coal industry. Omuta gave MITI the chance to turn a slowly dying
program area into a productive opportunity. Furthermore, whether inten-
tionally or not, Shiotsuka timed the study mission so that the center could
be included in the eighth coal policy being planned in 1990.

However, the project did not move forward very quickly. On
December 3, 1991, the Omuta city assembly announced its budget for the
next fiscal year, including $77,000 to study the center. Half of this money
came from MITI's "Special Coal Area Activity Project," one-quarter was a
grant from the prefecture, and the city put up the rest.[47] The good news
was that the money was approved and allocated. The bad news was that
the project was a long way from completion. Such a study is standard
operating procedure, and could not be circumvented.

In an effort to justify such a center, Omuta invited miners from other
Asian nations to study various areas of mining technology, even before the
center was built, or even approved. Chinese miners came first, for a one-
year training course, and a small group of Indonesian miners followed,
trailing a large wake of publicity.[48] All of them studied Japanese mining
techniques and took what they learned back to their home mines. But
these efforts did not speed the project to completion. Though Omuta was
able to land ministerial support for the project, once the initial study commission kicked off, little could make it move forward. The committee
members were selected and approved in mid-December 1992, and the first
basic plan for the facility was approved by the city assembly's special coal
policy committee on May 29, 1992—a mere formality, but one that was
seen as a significant stepping stone toward completion.[49]

As with all of Omuta's other projects, the city borrowed this idea from
somewhere else. A similar metal mining technology research center (this
one developed from a retired gold mine) was opened in Akita Prefecture
in northern Honshu on February 20, 1992. Omuta officials do not see this
other site as a competitor, and since such a center requires a preexisting
mine facility, it is unlikely that the supply of mining research centers will
outstrip the limited demand for mining research and development facilities. The World Coal Technology Center Facilities Planning Study Report
devotes a couple of pages to the Akita center, using it as an example of
how to construct a similar facility in Omuta. The Akita center is a modest
project, funded by MITI and built by Akita Prefecture at a cost of $6.67 mil-
lion, and has research, training, and international exchange functions. The
Omuta center looks like a virtual copy of its northern predecessor. It will
consist of five buildings: a dormitory, a restaurant, a training center, institute for visiting graduate students, and a coal industry data center. The
total cost estimate for the first three buildings is $75 million.[50]

As of the end of 1993, ground still had not been broken to begin construction on Omuta's center—four years after the coal area revitalization study mission returned from Europe. What happened to slow the project down? MITI still strongly supports the project, and has sponsored two national meetings on advances in coal technology and safety, both held in Omuta.[51] These meetings brought together leading Japanese researchers in coal technology from business, academia, and government, and received extensive coverage in the media. There is strong support for the project, and the articles and comments list many functions that the center will assume "if it is built."

Two factors seem to be responsible for the lack of forward progress on this idea. First, priorities were never clearly set for this project. The center must be built in stages, but there was no consensus on the order of construction. The latest World Coal Technology Center Report only contains a budget for three buildings, the training center, the dormitory, and the restaurant. But the eight-year time schedule in the same report claims that the coal industry data center will be built first, followed by the training center.[52] No one I spoke with can account for this discrepancy, but it seems that the planning—despite the existence of a drawing of the entire facility—is not very far along. Second, the exact site of the center was never formally announced. It will be in Omuta, and probably near the mine, but the land has not been allocated. This is not the only revitalization project in Omuta having problems with site selection. There are few desirable sites in Omuta, and most are owned by various Mitsui concerns. Wresting the land from Mitsui for a reasonable price is difficult for the city. Mitsui wants to sell high, and the city wants to buy low.[53] The result is an impasse. The land issue has stalled several Omuta projects as well.

EVALUATING THE EFFECT OF INSTITUTIONS ON OMUTA'S POLICY PROCESS AND PERFORMANCE

What effect did the institutional structure have on Omuta's redevelopment strategy? Omuta's approach to policy-making remained consistent throughout the twenty years studied here: the city looked to higher levels of government for fiscal support and ideas. This was a rational approach, since systemic constraints made this the best way for residents to achieve their goals. Supply-side policy-making was the norm for Omuta, and many of the projects in the list of redevelopment efforts—including the three largest projects, the Ariake GeoBio World theme park, the downtown retail area revitalization, and the three industrial parks—were chosen this way. Each of these projects will be discussed in the next three chapters, in comparison with its American counterpart. The central point here is that Omuta selected these projects because they represented types that had been done before in other places, and getting funding for them was feasible.

The Coal Techno-Center project is something of an exception, suggesting that cities are not barred from planning and implementing completely new ideas, and the flow of ideas and influence is not only top-down. In fact, the central government picks up the more successful local innovations and encourages other localities to try them.[54] But the bulk of Japanese intergovernmental relations consists of money and ideas flowing from the national to the local level. Such a system encourages copy-cat planning and discourages innovation. Omuta has responded to this system by attempting far more supply-side projects (either vertical or lateral) than innovative ones. Sixteen of the seventeen projects in the list were sparked by an example in another city or by a preexisting program at the national level. Only the Coal Techno-Center was locally derived.

Omuta played the policy cycle and the ministry system fairly well. But two factors contributed to Omuta's lack of successful redevelopment. First, a lack of unity at the local level prevented some of the projects from coming to fruition. The GeoBio World project, the new city hospital, area road improvements, the Coal Techno-Center, and the largest of the three industrial parks were delayed because of local resistance or obstacles. Most of these problems revolved around land acquisition, part of the project implementation process. In each case, the owner of the desired parcel of land refused or was reluctant to sell the property to the city or to the implementing agent. The refusal was sometimes a dispute over the land price, and sometimes a way of demonstrating dissatisfaction with the planned project.

These delays pushed each project further along the diffusion curve (discussed in chap. 1). For projects not intended to compete with facilities in other localities—such as the hospital, road improvements, or even the Coal Technology Center—the delays were not a serious problem. Those projects would have a positive impact whenever they were completed. But for competitive projects aimed at luring jobs and tourists away from other localities, the delay was lethal. GeoBio World was delayed because of the Japan Development Bank's (JDB) claim that the "theme park boom" had ended.[55] And the industrial park in question (the Omuta Technopark Inland Industrial Park) also did not come to fruition before similar facilities to the north (Kurume) and south (Kumamoto) of Omuta were up and running. Lack of innovation made timely completion of these projects crucial, and Omuta was unable to implement them quickly enough to make them a viable part of the city's redevelopment strategy.

FLINT

Redevelopment efforts in Flint started in the early 1970s, and have been largely unsuccessful at bringing prosperity to the city. These efforts started earlier than they did in Omuta, relative to the start of local economic deterioration. Flint's redevelopment history can be divided into three distinct periods, each prompted by changes in federal government policy toward cities. The early 1970s marked the end of the urban renewal era, which started well before the 1973 oil crisis. Urban renewal was a federally driven attempt to revive cities throughout the United States by razing whole sections of urban blight and starting over from scratch with federal funds priming the pump. It was the first federal legislation to deal with the central city, and it was no more successful in Flint than anywhere else. Urban renewal did little to change the face of cities. The procedural red tape involved in the program drove private investors away. Local officials used the program for high-priced projects rather than for neighborhood community redevelopment. In general urban renewal was treated like a real estate enterprise rather than as a social program.[56]

The second era—the focus of this research—changed the emphasis from urban renewal to locally determined downtown economic growth, which was to be sparked by winning and using federal funds in the form of Urban Development Action Grants (UDAGs) and Community Development Block Grants (CDBGs). Started during the Carter administration in 1978, UDAGs could only be awarded to urban projects financed primarily by private investments. These funds went toward big downtown projects aimed at achieving a critical mass of commercial activity to catalyze growth. Flint was very successful in winning these grants. By the end of 1984, Michigan had won a total of 112 UDAGs, with 30 going to Detroit. Flint was second with 10, and Pontiac was third with 8.[57]

From the mid-1970s through the mid-1980s, revitalization efforts consisted mostly of programs led by Flint's private sector economic elite. Large, private capital-intensive projects appeared in the downtown area, where they were supposed to lure businesses and consumers away from the burgeoning suburbs. Although private capital—provided by the Mott Foundation and by investment syndicates—paid the largest percentage for most of the projects, none moved decisively forward toward completion until they won federal grants. Most of these projects did not achieve their intended goals, and a few became notorious white elephants because the goals set for the projects were unrealistic. These goals were set by private sector consultants and by project specialists who sold the project ideas to the city. Their economic interest in the projects—they benefited, whether the projects succeeded or not—encouraged the replication of ideas from other localities and discouraged innovations that might have been more realistic and more successful.

Following this string of failures, the pattern of redevelopment efforts shifted again. This shift was caused in part by the end of the CDBG and UDAG programs in 1988. This forced city hall officials, in conjunction with smaller capital interests in the community, to change the focus of revitalization from large urban icons to small business job-creation efforts. These have been marginally successful, but their success is overshadowed by GM's decisions and by their impact on Flint; even if several smaller firms can create a couple of hundred jobs annually, these gains are often obscured by large employment decisions—either hirings or layoffs—involving thousands of workers in the automobile industry.

Redevelopment in Flint is a mixture of what we would expect to find in a fragmented federal system and in a centralized unitary system. Politicians are more important in Flint's revitalization efforts than they are in Omuta. This is an institutionalized fact of American politics, where the primacy of politicians is the norm. In this policy area at least, American congressional representatives appear more active in policy-making than their Japanese Diet counterparts.[58] At the local level, the mayor is also a central policy figure. Career civil servants are certainly players—especially at the Flint City Hall—but they do not wield the clout and authority of their Japanese counterparts. Funds for redevelopment are secured by politicians in the United States, and by bureaucrats in Japan. Both systems are quite open to citizen participation in the process, although the higher degree of local business elite involvement in revitalization planning and implementation in Flint demonstrates the lower barriers to entry into the redevelopment policy arena on the American side. In Omuta, bureaucrats take the lead on the larger projects. In Flint, private sector business people lead.

In the United States, there is considerable fiscal autonomy at the local level, which should encourage innovation. Grants from the national to the local level have more strings and control associated with them in Japan than in the United States. There is also more room for creating a system of grants in the American system.[59] In addition, there are no limits set by the federal government on local bond issues. American cities have the freedom to mortgage themselves into oblivion, and the concept of city bankruptcy is not unheard-of in the United States. The notorious case of Watertown, Wisconsin, in the 1860s is a classic case of a city floating bonds and then getting burned. Watertown issued railroad bonds for two fledgling railroad companies, using the city's credit to capitalize the railroads. In an era of rapid rail expansion, the city hoped to enjoy a growth boom that would help it capture the potential economic benefits. The railroads failed, and by 1870 Watertown's debt plus interest equaled one-half of the city's assessed property value.[60] Even though failures to honor debt have been relatively few, even large cities such as New York and Washington, DC, have flirted with debt crises in recent memory. Japanese cities float bonds, but they never approach bankruptcy, thanks to the oversight and control exercised by the MOHA in Tokyo. American local fiscal autonomy allows for more flexible use of locally derived revenues. Tax increment bonds, revenue-sharing bonds, rehabilitation bonds, and other financial instruments give United States cities a larger toolbox with which to construct redevelopment efforts.

But Flint has been caught between the fiscal freedom to do what it wants, and federal government programs that urge it to do what Washington wants. The state of Michigan has had a limited impact on Flint, and has not really helped or hindered local efforts financially. Flint might have received more state support if Detroit had not demanded so much assistance, but the Lansing government did little to push Flint in one direction or another. Ultimately, Flint has sought many grants and loans from the federal government, allowing grant availability to dictate what—and whether—projects are implemented. In this way it has behaved more like a city in a unitary state. Flint has spent less energy on innovation, and more on using the governmental system to its own advantage.

Policy implementation in Flint looks more centralized than one would expect of a fragmented political system in another way, as well. The same people and organizations were responsible for realizing policy ideas, especially in the first decade of revitalization efforts. The remarkable continuity in the names and faces involved with revitalization in Flint suggests a centralized decision-making process with few veto points and high barriers to entry into the process, and in many ways this is an accurate description of the city's redevelopment process. The fact that such centralized activity has happened highlights an interesting point about the flexibility of the American governmental structure: though localities have the freedom to go it alone to a great extent, they are not forced to exercise this autonomy. Rather, independent governmental action is but one strategy option.

The policy structure at the federal level played an important role in determining the direction of revitalization efforts in Flint. Flint was forced to change its policy strategy and responses in the late 1980s by structural changes in its environment. Specifically, the availability of federal Department of Housing and Urban Development (HUD) grants diminished, forcing Flint to find other funding sources for revitalization efforts. HUD's UDAG and CDBG programs started in the mid-1970s, but ran their course and were not renewed by the Republican administrations after 1988. While these grants were by no means the only source of redevelopment funds used in Flint, they were often the linchpin that held a project idea together and kept it moving forward.

Certain aspects of the UDAG program pushed Flint toward a reliance on developers and consultants. According to the UDAG Program Profile distributed by the city of Flint, the project selection criteria were as follows:

> Necessity of the Action Grant: projects were required to demonstrate that a financial gap existed and without the UDAG funds the project could not be implemented;
>
> Leveraging ratio: private to UDAG dollar investment (a competitive ratio was 4.5:1);
>
> Firm commitment: all parties prepared to go ahead if the grant was awarded;
>
> Recapture of UDAG dollars: demonstration that UDAG funds would be repaid to the city for reuse in the community;
>
> Alleviation of economic distress: the number of new permanent jobs to be created had to reflect $10,000 or less per job of UDAG money to be competitive;
>
> Alleviation of physical distress: renovation or new construction of houses, commercial buildings, or industries;
>
> Alleviation of fiscal distress: the amount of new taxes to be generated by the project;
>
> Impact on the special problems of minority and low and moderate income persons;
>
> Employment plans to assure that the private sector jobs created are available to minority and long-term unemployed persons;
>
> Extent of other public support for the project;
>
> Timely completion of the project: completion within four years.[61]

Though the city was charged with submitting the application and funneling funds to the project, private developers and consultants were required to provide the following information that was included in the application:

Financial documents:

Two Pro Formas for the project: One showing conventional financing without UDAG money and one showing project financing with UDAG funds. Pro formas had to include five to ten years of [predicted] gross income, minus all expenses including real estate taxes and debt service. Also, both pre-tax and after tax cash flow was to be detailed. If tax abatement was utilized, then pro formas were required with and without the tax abatement adjustment;

Project budget showing sources and uses of all funds;

Detailed construction budget;

Evidence of site control: Purchase option agreement, sale agreement, lease, or proof of ownership;

Independent appraisal of property;

Evidence of firm commitments from lender and investors (private and public). Clear statements of terms and conditions of these commitments were required on the application;

Name of developing entity and type of organizational structure (i.e., general partnership, limited partnership, proprietorship, etc.). Evidence that developers/managers had capabilities to do the project was required;

Financial statements: corporate and personal statements for the past three years;

A letter of equity commitment, indicating the source and its relationship to current cash assets and stock holder's equity. Equity must be supported by net worth three times the amount of the equity or letter of credit;

"But, for" commitment letters from all participating parties: each letter was required to contain the statement, "but for receipt of the UDAG amount requested, the investment will not be made";

Market studies to substantiate feasibility of the project;

Architectural/Engineer letter certifying construction cost estimates as reasonable and fair;

Project schedule;

List of permanent jobs to be created, including information on job categories, hourly wage rates, and methodology used to calculate the number of jobs to be created.[62]

Three requirements in particular gave experienced developers an edge and provided incentives for cities to hire developers and consultants with UDAG project experience: evidence that developers/managers had capabilities to do the project, market studies to substantiate feasibility of the project, and demonstration of the methodology used to calculate the number of jobs to be created. Flint hired nationally known developers and consultants for all of its major projects, including Recreation Consultants, which developed the Marriott Corporation's Great America theme parks in Chicago and San Francisco; Randall Duell Associates, who helped develop twenty-two theme parks, including Busch Gardens (Virginia) and Hershey Park (Pennsylvania); and James Rouse, head of the Enterprise Development Corporation, who headed the development of Boston's Quincy Market, Baltimore's Inner Harbor area, and other large retail projects. These specialists brought their recipes for success to Flint and tried to replicate them. Each of the next three chapters discusses the role of these consultants in project planning and implementation in greater detail.

The point here is that Japan has local bureaucrats who handle details such as those just listed. In the United States, though cities file the grant applications, much of the work is done by private sector consultants. Consultants also operate in Japan, although they are less common there than in the United States.[63] My research suggests that their participation in urban redevelopment may vary by policy type. Consultants were quite active in the quest for an amusement park in Omuta, but they were less involved in shopping district revitalization and not involved at all in the industrial park efforts.

The end of the federal grant program forced a change in tactics at the local level: Flint now had to fund redevelopment efforts in an environment where capital was less freely available. A multimillion-dollar surge in capital-intensive development in the late 1970s and early 1980s resulted in the $14-million Riverbank Park (opened in 1979), the $40-million Hyatt Regency Hotel complex (opened in 1981), the $73-million AutoWorld (opened in 1984), and the $29-million Water Street Pavilion (opened in 1985).[64] The result was that no large, new revitalization initiatives were started after the early 1980s. Instead, a plan composed of smaller projects was aimed at small- to medium-size businesses that emerged from local (city and county) government. Capital became tight, the large outlays of the past had not produced results, and both the public and private sectors did not want to get burned financially again.

Policy Responses

Redevelopment efforts in Flint have focused less on compensatory demands and special programs for unemployed workers than have those in Omuta. Even though workers certainly took advantage of existing federal unemployment and welfare benefits following layoffs and plant closings, there was no effort on the part of city representatives to extract any new or additional payments from the federal government for those affected. I will address the issue of why Flint sought economic development funds so aggressively in the following section.

For most of the 1970s, Flint focused on rebuilding the traditional downtown area with large capital-improvement projects. The beginning of this downtown makeover was a new University of Michigan-Flint campus. The idea was first revealed in 1972 at a meeting of Flint Area Conference, Inc. (FACI), and ground-breaking occurred in 1974.[65] Figure 2.11 lists the series of major projects that appeared downtown over the decade following the University of Michigan-Flint campus. In addition to these explicitly developmental projects in the downtown area, another industrial park was built at the city's Bishop Airport.

Sponsored by the city, it was financed with a city bond issue and money from the federal Economic Development Administration (EDA). The net effect of these projects on the economy of Flint was minimal compared to the capital expended: $568.5-million total cost for all projects combined. Buick City—which alone cost $295 million—created more jobs in the auto industry, but the other projects cost over $273 million and created few jobs, lured few new businesses, did little to stem the tide of flight to the suburbs, and did not effectively address the issues that caused Flint's decline in the first place.[66] Federal funds—allocated almost entirely from HUD grant programs—accounted for only $65 million, but were the catalyst for a number of projects.[67] Unfortunately, such comprehensive numbers were not available for Omuta.

The largest single project, Buick City, was quite different in many ways from the other redevelopment projects in Flint in that it sought to revitalize the auto industry. Most of the other projects tried to diversify the local economic base, expanding into light manufacturing, tourism, and service/retail sectors. The Buick City experience was also a political home run for the mayor (Rutherford), the kind of coup that happened infrequently in Flint's recent history. The Buick City story is told in greater detail in chapter 5.

REDEVELOPMENT EFFORTS FROM THE MID-1970S THROUGH THE MID-1980S

Much of the discussion of Omuta's redevelopment centered on the Omuta city government, but city government has played a less central role in the story of Flint. This alone highlights a significant difference in political

Figure 2.11: Redevelopment Projects in Flint, 1970–1992

Project Name	sponsor/ applicant*	funding sources*	main funding source*	innovation source	1960s- early '70s	early '70s- mid '80s	mid '80s- 1993	UDAG/CDBG- assisted	policy type	dominant player type
UM-Flint Campus	2,3	2	2	lateral	X	X			growth	bur
Riverbank Park	3	1,3,4	1,3	vert./lateral	X	X			facil. imp.	bur
St. John Industrial Park	3	1,2,3,4	1,3	lateral	X	X		X	growth	bur/bus
River Village	3,4	1,3,4	4	lateral	X	X		X	growth	bur
Riverfront Center	3,4	1,3,4	4	lateral		X		X	growth	pol/bus
State office building	2	2	2	?	X	X			growth	bur
Windmill Place	3,4	1,3,4	4	lateral		X		X	growth	bus
Autoworld	3,4	1,2,3,4	4	lateral	X	X		X	growth	pol/bus
Buick City	3,4	1,2,3,4	4	lateral		X		X	growth	pol/bus
Water Street Pavilion	3,4	1,2,3,4	4	lateral		X		X	growth	pol/bus
Carriage Factory	3	1,4	4	lateral		X	X	X	growth	bus
Schafer Square	3	1,2,4	2	lateral		X	X	X	growth	bus
Oak Tech Park	3	3	3	lateral		X	X		growth	bus
Oak Business Center	3,4	3,4	4	lateral		X	X	X	growth	bus

*1=national government, 2=state

3=Flint, 4=private capital

Largest & 2nd largest funding sources within $1 million of each other structure and function between the two cities. To compare some of the key governmental issues we must ask, What was the role of government in Flint's revitalization efforts that started in the early 1970s? In the last twenty years, Flint's city government has acted primarily as a conduit for federal funds, and has helped monitor the use of those funds for the federal government. The Omuta government did a lot of this type of activity, but whereas the Omuta government was also active in the planning and implementation, the Flint government—while in attendance on a consultative basis and as a monitor—largely left priority setting and project implementation to the private sector.

Why did Flint pursue a strategy of capital-intensive downtown redevelopment? The end product was a narrowly focused construction-based strategy. The federal government policy environment, the fiscal structure, and the existence of private consulting firms largely account for the shape of Flint's redevelopment strategy. Government structure—at all levels—was important in a passive sense: it provided the legal means for the organization of interests in a nonprofit corporate format, and it permitted these interests to operate in a quasi-official capacity with a high degree of fiscal autonomy. The foundation and the Downtown Development Authority (DDA) were central private sector players in the process, and neither could exist without statutes that permitted their creation. The policy environment at the federal level further shaped the playing field, and this is the most proactive aspect of the institutional structure. Congress directed HUD to establish programs that Flint exploited on almost every major project. Had these programs not existed, Flint's redevelopment efforts would have been quite different. But there was little bureaucratic oversight—beyond the proper allocation of funds—in Flint. Local bureaucrats made sure that HUD grant money was spent as the national government intended, but they did not conduct any program evaluation for the redevelopment projects. Planning was rooted in the private sector. And the executive branch did not evaluate Flint's projects after completion and then adjust future spending accordingly. In terms of developing a proactive strategy for economic revitalization, government did not take the lead in organizing community interests. In this regard Flint and Omuta are quite different.

An additional reason for Flint's capital-intensive redevelopment strategy was that such an approach was doable. Large sums of money were available in both the public and private sectors for urban revitalization. The cooperative federalism of the 1970s strengthened federal-city relations and made local access to federal funds relatively easy. The economic recession of the late 1970s and early 1980s made Flint an excellent candidate for revitalization efforts. Flint was one of the hardest hit cities in the country. Unemployment soared to near 30 percent, and Flint's plight was covered extensively in the media. The mayor and other local elites saw Flint as a strong candidate for redevelopment, and pushed government and private sources to help the city out of its slump. Their solicitation efforts were successful, since they attracted a lot of redevelopment capital.

Private developers—hired as consultants and project managers—also account for Flint's capital-intensive redevelopment strategy. Developers sold ideas to the city and helped Flint copy ideas from other localities. Developers, architects, and other idea entrepreneurs were active in Flint's riverfront redevelopment, shopping area revitalization, and tourism promotion escapades. Skilled grant winners, they brought successful formulas from other cities and pushed Flint to emulate the efforts of other cities. Flint followed their lead, and ended up on a one-way path to mediocrity and failure.

Both cities demonstrate a degree of centralized policy-making, but in different ways. City hall was the heart of the planning and priority process in Omuta, while Flint economic elites quickly developed a private institution to focus—or centralize—the process, simultaneously legitimizing their interests and taking an early start in generating a policy response. Organization of interests seems to account for much in the Flint case, and the leading economic elites were well organized in the early 1970s when redevelopment plans were being formed. The president and the foundation's program officers, the mayor, and executives from local banks and from local GM facilities set the tone for twenty years of development in Flint.

FACI was a crucial institution that drove Flint's revitalization. In April 1970, thirty-four Flint area executives and civic leaders met at the Consumers Power Co. lodge at Tippy Dam (on the Big Manistee River) and made plans to establish FACI. Registered with the federal government as a private, nonprofit corporation in 1971, FACI's main purpose was to plan projects and programs in the Flint area. Its tax-exempt status limited the activities in which the FACI could participate, so in May 1973 FACI established Flint Renaissance, under a different tax-exempt status. Flint Renaissance was the "action" wing of the FACI, and had broader functional powers such as the ability to obtain and preserve land, and to accept gifts and donations from the private sector. Such funds and property could be used as seed money for project development.[68] The officers of both corporations were identical, and Harding Mott—whose family established the Mott Foundation—was the first chairperson of the board. Saul Seigel, a prominent local businessperson, was president.

Through the 1970s and 1980s, FACI was a leading force in Flint's revitalization efforts. Its major accomplishment was a comprehensive ten-year plan for Flint's downtown redevelopment called "Centric '80." Five of the major projects that were undertaken to renew the downtown area evolved from this plan—the University of Michigan-Flint campus; Riverbank Park, a flood control and beautification project on the Flint River; two industrial parks—St. John Industrial Park and Bishop Airpark; River Village, a planned residential community with a market component called "Windmill Place"; and Riverfront Center, comprised of the Hyatt Hotel and a state office building. The city of Flint and the foundation cooperated with FACI to bring these projects to completion.[69]

FACI helped set the agenda for Flint's redevelopment efforts in the 1970s and 1980s. The group's board of directors met every few months, and printed newsletters updating participants on the details of projects that it had put in motion. In 1984, FACI expanded from a small group of local business elites to include a slightly broader "membership" of dues-paying participants.[70] Organizations and individuals could join FACI for on hundred dollars (or more). Conference members provided a willing pool of available local business talent that supported the organization personally and financially, contributing time, expertise, and organizational support to various projects. FACI was the coordinating arena for individuals from various local associations, including dominant players like the DDA and the foundation, and smaller (and more short-lived) organizations such as the Center City Association, the Forward Development Corporation, the Flint Neighborhood Improvement and Preservation Project, the Urban Coalition, and the International Downtown Executives Association.[71] Top city administrators and the mayor also attended meetings and were kept informed via the FACI information loop.

This description of FACI and the privatization of priority setting provides a structural explanation for the way in which priorities were set at the local level, but not for the content of those early plans. As in Omuta, policy diffusion explains much of the local decision content. But in Omuta, this diffusion occurred vertically and laterally: the city fit its ideas into the national government policy menu offerings, and the city gleaned ideas from other localities in Japan. Both types of diffusion exist in Flint. Industrial parks, amusement parks, and shopping malls were being built in other cities long before Flint caught onto them. Thus, on the issue of policy innovation Flint also resembles Omuta to some extent. Projects in both cities were innovative in the sense that they were new to the city. But they were not innovative in that they were already successful solutions elsewhere, and had been truly new ideas in other localities first. There was little innovation in Flint's redevelopment policy, in part because local institutional machinations channeled the redevelopment process into a particular groove: FACI's organization and creation of a tightly knit local in-group tied to the foundation made it difficult for those with diverging ideas to become part of the process.

However, there is a second, more compelling force that worked to discourage local innovation and to push revitalization decision making in one definite direction: the availability of federal funding and the array of subsidies proffered by the federal government. It is probable that the intent of the federal programs was not to hinder local creativity in coming up with solutions. There certainly are examples of cities generating successful revitalization solutions that are not driven or dictated by national program priorities.[72] But functionally speaking, that is exactly what happened. The funding available at the federal level solidified the priorities of local elites in Flint, and these priorities became the city's course of action. And once started down that path, the city won many grants and was thus able to implement projects. Flint became "path dependent" to the extent that other innovative options appeared too costly, and continued work in this direction seemed to be the best approach.[73]

Federal government grants are complicated to win and to administer. The paperwork involved is voluminous, and navigating the application, administration, and oversight report requirements demands special knowledge.[74] However, once a city figures out the formula, it can be quite successful in winning such grants. Flint administrators—in conjunction with several private development firms that specialized in procuring and using such grants—discovered a "path of least resistance" by which they could receive large sums of money for projects they felt were risky. In essence, the city became addicted to federal development grants and spent the 1970s on a long capital improvement high during which the city received over $65 million from Washington.[75] This helps explain why Flint pursued subsidies from the federal government so diligently, and why new innovative ideas in urban revitalization were not explored.

UDAG funds were the key to implementing the major revitalization projects, even though the amount was only around 10 percent of the total final cost. This will be illustrated in chapters 3 and 4 in the descriptions of AutoWorld and the Water Street Pavilion. Before the grants were approved, little real work occurred. After the grant approval came through, however the foundation affirmed its large financial commitments, acquired land was cleared, and the projects really began to jell. The city, state, and private developers also contributed substantial amounts, but the projects would not have moved forward without the prior votes of confidence from both HUD and the foundation.

REDEVELOPMENT EFFORTS FROM THE MID-1980S THROUGH THE EARLY 1990S

By the mid-1980s, the succession of projects just listed had finally run its course. Plans and grants were completed, and the face of downtown Flint was dramatically different from the early 1970s. Unfortunately, there were no more people living in, working in, or using the downtown area than there had been a decade earlier. Though city officials claim that 5,300 jobs were created by the $568 million in implemented projects,[76] the population indicators in this chapter suggest that Flint continued to decline. The perceived need for revitalization—or the need to keep doing something that at least seemed to be addressing the city's decline—prompted a new strategy based on smaller projects and programs. Business incubator programs and "buy local" campaigns signaled a resignation to the fact that Flint would have to struggle on in its present condition.

Having sunk substantial capital into a failed revitalization effort, local private sector elites had little financial strength left for a renewed development offensive. This time the local government—in conjunction with more moderate private sector efforts—played a larger planning and implementation role. Government efforts sought to improve the economic security of those remaining residents and businesses in Flint. Small business loans were made possible through the Flint Economic Development Corporation (EDC), capitalized in 1979 with a revolving fund made up of city, federal EDA, and leftover CDBG money. This use of leftover federal funds is one of the truly innovative uses of the institutional structure found in Flint. The city realized that the enabling federal legislation and administrative guidelines called for the allocation of grants to cities, but it did not specify that the city had to use the money for grants—funds could also be disbursed as loans. Flint officials found that these funds could be used to set up local revolving loan instruments, and could thus be used over and over again once allocated.[77] The Flint EDC made almost one hundred loans between 1980 and 1993, two-thirds of which were for business start-ups. The main point here is that these are small business initiatives: the average loan size was $45,000 and the maximum loan value was $200,000.[78]

The impact of these small business loan efforts was small in comparison to the large layoffs and cyclic employment trends of the automobile industry. But this program is part of the reshaping of Flint. Local strategists admit that Flint's goal should not be to rise to power in automobile manufacturing once more.[79] The foundation's "1983 Annual Report" states:

> Downtowns cannot be restored to their previous role as the single focal point for a city's shopping and office work. But neither are they doomed to extinction. In many cities, downtowns are developing new economic rationales and emerging as centers for specialty retailing, for retailing and dining out, and for knowledge-based professional services. . . . Thus, they are assuming different, but no less important roles in their communities.[80]

This change in Flint's redevelopment strategy, from a focus on large capital-intensive projects to an emphasis on small business support, was caused by attitudinal changes at the local level. The city government found itself controlling foreclosed property that it did not want to own—the AutoWorld facility and Water Street Pavilion complex. The companies originally set up to manage the properties defaulted on their loans, and the city was thus forced to take possession. Moreover, following the series of large and risky projects of the 1970s and early 1980s, private capital was harder to come by. The foundation suffered from its own "Vietnam Syndrome," and it was reluctant to participate in large-scale projects in Flint, having been burned numerous times. Relations between the foundation and the city remained close, but neither side initiated big projects the way they had in the previous decade.[81] Since HUD grants were to be used to leverage private capital investments, and private capital was tight, city development administrators may have seen further efforts at federal grants as having a marginal return.

Changes in the fiscal environment do not provide much of an explanation for Flint's change in strategy. Although the federal block grant program went through a transformation under the Reagan administration, these changes do not appear to have had much of an impact on Flint's revitalization strategy. The block grant application process was simplified and streamlined in the 1980s, but Flint submitted fewer grant applications in this decade. In addition to his campaign promise to get the government off the backs of the American people, Reagan also sought to get the federal government off the backs of state and local officials. The new president met these goals in the housing and urban development policy area. Block grant applications became smaller, and less detailed information was required prior to the start of a program. Even though Congress opposed the decrease in oversight advocated by HUD, the agency used a variety of administrative tactics to carry out its goals.[82] Under such a system of relaxed regulations, one might have expected Flint to apply for more federal grants. However, the city filed fewer applications.

One possible explanation lies in the political nature of the HUD grant application process. All of Flint's applications were supported by the city's most prominent congressional representatives, Rep. Dale Kildee and Sen. Donald Riegle, both of whom were Democrats. Flint's most successful grant solicitation efforts came during the Carter years, when the Democratic administration looked favorably on a city with strong ties to organized labor in a state that had a Democratic governor at the time. Michigan was a strongly Democratic state during the Reagan years as well, a fact that may have made Flint's administrators pessimistic about applying for further grants.

The emphasis on small businesses did not prohibit support for larger business concerns as well. The Flint EDC also issued tax-exempt revenue bonds of up to $10 million, but these could be used for manufacturing only. Until 1986, bonds for commercial use were also issued, but the Internal Revenue Service changed the rules for such commercial use of bonds since too few jobs were being created, and too many physicians and lawyers were using these funds to open offices.[83] The rate on such bonds is 75 to 80 percent of the prime rate, and the bond is guaranteed by the city or by the EDC. Local banks buy most of the bonds, for which the prices are negotiable; they are not set by legislation. Since 1980, roughly twenty of these bond issues have been conducted.[84]

In the immediate aftermath of the big project era, smaller ad hoc projects were conceived and implemented in Flint. The push for local business support and stabilization received a small boost in 1984 when FACI organized the first Flint Wares Fair, which generated business for area firms. The fair brought purchasing agents of area companies, school systems, and governmental agencies together at one site so that representatives of area companies with goods and services could make contact. The idea behind the fair was to keep as many purchases by area businesses and agencies as possible in the local economy. In 1985, the fair generated $40 million in contracts to area companies, and it was credited by the state governor's office with creating roughly 2,000 new jobs in the years 1984 through 1986.[85]

In an effort to learn from its mistakes, the city formulated a different approach to revitalization. FACI ceased operation in 1988, and was replaced by a new institution aimed at small business promotion. Genesee Economic Area Revitalization, (GEAR) a private, nonprofit corporation, was formed in 1989. Its stated (and apparently self-selected) purpose was "to oversee and coordinate economic development efforts in Genesee County."[86] GEAR's origins are unclear, despite the fact that it emerged in the late 1980s. In his dissertation, Dandaneau offers an extensive discussion of GEAR's economic redevelopment strategy for the Flint area. Dandaneau unsuccessfully sought GEAR's origins. He quotes Mark Davis, a Lafayette, Indiana, native who became GEAR's first executive director in 1990 as saying,

> To be honest, I've never looked, it wasn't important, and it's not important. It's only important to academics. In the real world, what is important is what are they doing, OK?[87]

Dandaneau cites a member of GEAR's strategic planning committee responding in a similar way, saying it is "hard to remember, and probably not real productive to try to sort out who started what."[88] Like FACI, GEAR was the product of local elites interested in promoting economic revitalization in Flint.

Dandaneau calls GEAR's efforts an "'enlightened' plan because no longer would Flint's elites depend upon the foundation, GM, nor any other benefactor for its progress and prosperity."[89] GEAR's earliest strategic document was the "Genesis Project," a 1989 Price Waterhouse report commissioned by GEAR and paid for with the help of a federal EDA grant. It was a vague statement of priorities that called for the expansion and diversification of Flint's economy and a clearer vision of what diversification meant. Using this document as a springboard, GEAR developed a Strategic Economic Development Plan for Flint/Genesee County in 1990. Dandaneau claims the organization then shopped this plan around to more than forty community groups, gatherings, and elected officials to solicit feedback and to generate local support for the report.[90] The final version of the strategic plan was approved by GEAR's Board of Directors on July 9, 1991.[91] Discussing the GEAR plan, Dandaneau states that the

> vision statement was originally drafted by an informal group headed by Flint businessman Dallas C. Dort. . . . The membership of this group included the heads of the GM's Flint Automotive Division, AC Rochester Division, and the University of Michigan-Flint, the Mayor of Flint, Doug Roos of the Corporation for Enterprise development (whose organization was chiefly responsible for drafting GEAR's strategic plan), as well as others who would eventually hold positions on GEAR's strategic planning committee.[92]

The plan set out four overarching goals:

(1) Develop a competitive, world-class workforce;

(2) Diversify the economy by creating new non-GM manufacturing and skilled service jobs by supporting entrepreneurship and helping existing companies;

(3) Make Flint/Genesee County a world center of applying information technology to manufacturing;

(4) Support and complement GM, UAW, and community efforts to retain jobs by understanding and responding to changing global trends.[93]

Toward this end, Dandaneau asserts, "GEAR seeks to reorganize the community's political administrative response away from what the Mott Foundation or any public sector institution might 'want it to be.'"[94] Though this strategy may look like a conscious choice on GEAR's part, in reality the city had few other options. The foundation was unwilling to lead a renewed redevelopment movement and was content to fund smaller projects while still licking its wounds from the previous decade of failure.[95] Large-scale government capital was not available for Flint to use either.

Flint did provide small businesses loans, 60 percent of which were given to small local start-up firms. But the city started following this strategy well before GEAR picked up on it. Flint started offering these loans when the federal EDA began its small business loan program in 1979.

This suggests that federal program availability—not local elite enlightenment—prompted the shift in strategy, and that it happened earlier than Dandaneau and GEAR would argue.

But the city was not ready to ignore the industry responsible for its booming growth earlier in the century. Flint was also eager to help Buick and other GM concerns and suppliers to increase production and to create jobs locally. To this end, the city still granted tax abatements and declared special industrial zones for GM facilities. Between 1977 and 1988, Flint granted twenty tax abatements for GM concerns. From 1988 through October of 1993, Flint approved an additional seventeen tax abatements for the auto maker.[96] Even though these were always disputed and mulled over by the city council—the loss of property tax revenue was usually cited by those opposed to an abatement—the council never rejected an application for such a break or designation. Flint continued to be a struggling auto industry city.

EVALUATING THE EFFECT OF INSTITUTIONS ON FLINT'S POLICY PROCESS AND PERFORMANCE

Like Omuta, Flint played the national policy cycle very well. The city landed roughly $65 million in federal assistance during the twenty years studied here. Flint's economic dire straits, coupled with the city's willingness to hire consultants who were proven successes and the foundation's

Figure 2.12: Flint Small Business Loans

strong financial support for capital-intensive projects, struck a responsive chord at HUD. Systemic fiscal constraint was a primary motivation for Flint to seek government grants, despite the fact that the government money made up a fraction of the cost of redevelopment. HUD grants served to legitimate projects selected for implementation by the local private sector elites. The system allowed the organized business elites to generate and implement several multimillion-dollar projects that did not cost the city—or these local interests—very much by comparison.

Flint and Omuta are alike in one other significant way: despite considerable support from the federal government, Flint was not very successful in revitalizing the local economy. Three of the five largest projects (AutoWorld, Riverfront Center, and Water Street Pavilion) sank into foreclosure shortly after they opened to the public. The city eventually sold Water Street Pavilion to the University of Michigan-Flint for very little money, and the university uses the facility for offices, shopping, and cafeteria space. The Hyatt closed after operating in the red, the facility sat in disuse for a while, and the hotel reopened again as part of the Radisson chain. AutoWorld still sits dormant. Flint's redevelopment efforts are thus far characterized as a series of failures in terms of creating jobs and drawing people to the downtown area.

Why did these projects fail? Flint pursued inappropriate growth solutions that cost a lot of money but did not help to turn the local political economy around. In fact, the failed projects served to exacerbate the city's problems. Some scholars attribute Flint's failure to ideological constraints within which the city had to work.[97] They blame the "city as growth machine" ideology for Flint's failure, joining other scholars who suggest that decisions about urban economic development reflect the needs of elite property interests and focus too heavily on the creation of a social and political environment conducive to commerce.[98] This ideological approach to urban revitalization is but one part of a larger institutional structure that pushes cities like Flint to develop certain strategies for redevelopment. As evidence in subsequent chapters will show, a series of professional consultants and the availability of capital (both public and private) funding for such efforts encouraged Flint to try these projects. But the simple replication of successful projects from other localities in an effort to promote growth did not work for Flint, and the predictions of success by developers and consultants turned out to be wrong.

The decision to attempt capital-intensive, growth-oriented redevelopment—the strategy that Flint opted to follow—was quite process-rational. In its search for ideas to replicate, Flint found an abundance of successful models to choose from. These successes stretched from the former manufacturing centers in the Northeast (e.g., Boston, Lowell, and Baltimore) to the industrial Midwest (Pittsburgh), and the Sunbelt cities (Miami, Charlotte, and Los Angeles). It made good sense to try to copy projects and approaches of cities that were successfully sparking growth, and Flint hired consultants and developers to help them do just that.

CONCLUSION

Actors respond rationally to their environment. Local officials consistently take advantage of programs offered by national agencies. They use the existing system to the best advantage possible (meaning they extract as much as they can from the national government), and adapt local goals and plans to fit national policy frameworks. From the 1960s through the early 1980s, Omuta consistently capitalized on Tokyo's willingness to subsidize the rationalization of the coal industry. But this institutional environment did not encourage or facilitate conversion to other industries or to any growth-oriented activities. And from the mid-1980s through the present, Omuta used national program incentives to implement projects focused on growth. From the early 1970s through the late 1980s, Flint used the federal block grant programs to catalyze and legitimate large-scale projects intended to spark growth. Just as coal subsidies dried up for Omuta, the block grant programs ended for Flint and the city was forced to change to a different strategy, this time based on small-scale capital and small business promotion.

CHAPTER 3

A TALE OF TWO THEME PARKS:
THE GEOBIO WORLD—AUTOWORLD COMPARISON

When one thinks of urban redevelopment in a coal or automobile industry town, amusement parks do not automatically come to mind. Yet Omuta and Flint incorporated expensive theme park plans into their revitalization efforts. Why did they opt for this type of program? The answer to this question ties some of the central themes of this comparison together. A heavy reliance on development consultants, supply-side policy-making, and an effort to finance revitalization efforts from sources other than the city budget are all readily apparent in their efforts.

This is a comparison of the evolution and implementation of theme park ideas in Omuta and Flint. Flint's AutoWorld theme park was eventually constructed more than a decade after it was first conceived. Omuta's GeoBio World theme park opened six years after concrete planning commenced. Both cities decided to build tourist attractions based on their previously dominant industry, and they promoted these facilities as cornerstone projects in the plans to revitalize their respective economies. Though both received huge amounts of publicity during planning, neither became the success that project planners hoped they would be.

Consultants played a significant role in the evolution of amusement park ideas in Omuta and Flint. Omuta went so far as to hire some of the designers of Tokyo Disneyland during their planning process, while Flint hired the developers from Busch Gardens and Marriott's Great Adventure parks. Consultants pushed Flint toward the amusement park idea forcefully; the city was looking for a museum-type attraction to honor the developers of the automobile. Omuta arrived at the theme park concept largely on its own—by looking at other cities in the region that successfully planned and built such attractions—and then hired the consultants to make it a reality.

Both cases present clear evidence of supply-side, copy-cat policy-making. Rather than develop innovative responses to economic decline, Omuta and Flint copied successful ideas from other cities that could be achieved with minimal local capital expenditure. In this context, "successful" theme parks refers to parks that were able to turn a profit at best, or at least to break even at worst, while creating new jobs in the community and attracting visitors to the park. Both cities generated revitalization strategies incorporating the best of what other cities had already done and what the national government had to offer in the way of assistance programs. As the discussion of revitalization strategy in the previous chapter suggests, quality of life improvements, job creation through the luring of businesses from other locations, and tourism promotion were central themes in Omuta and Flint's redevelopment efforts. The projects discussed in this chapter were central to the strategy of tourism promotion.

These projects represent policy imitation in several ways. First, the idea of using theme parks to spark redevelopment was already well established in Japan and in the United States. Examples of new parks built at the initiative of local governments are found in both countries, though the theme park "boom" was more pronounced in Japan. In the United States, successful amusement parks have largely been the domain of large firms specializing in such enterprises. Marriott, Six Flags, and Disney are three of the best-known purveyors of such fantasy facilities. All manage multiple parks across the country. In Japan, successful parks have not been owned and operated by large firms. Except for Tokyo Disneyland, Japanese theme parks are relatively small mom-and-pop operations. Kitakyushu's Space World, Nagasaki's Holland Village and Huis Ten Bosch, Miyazaki's Sea Gaia, and other examples are each independent entities.

Second, consultants specializing in theme parks were active in both nations, where they generated and sold such plans even though their cost and attendance estimates were often grossly inaccurate. Park construction costs rose substantially during construction, and attendance rarely rose to meet expectations. Still, the ideas were pushed and sold aggressively. Third, the availability of funding for these projects pushed Omuta and Flint toward the idea of theme parks. Public and private capital was willing to support theme park development in both cities because such parks had been successful in other locales. Both cities secured the majority of project funding from sources other than the city budget, effectively putting the economic risk on other entities; the city had nothing to lose and thus could forge ahead on their theme park quest with a less critical eye. Unfortunately for investors, citizens, and city officials, both park projects are remembered as significant failures.

Plans for both theme parks were multifaceted. Omuta's theme park was to center on the history and natural science issues surrounding the Miike coal mine. In addition, there were plans to combine the park with Omuta's proposed World Coal Technology Center, the coal technology research and development facility discussed in the previous chapter. It was hoped that bundling these two projects together would broaden their support at the national level, thus increasing the likelihood that they would be built. Flint's theme park planners sought to incorporate historical and educational themes as well, although AutoWorld was ultimately focused on entertainment.

OMUTA'S GEOBIO WORLD FRUSTRATION

Theme parks were a popular economic development tool in the 1980s in Japan, and the spread of these facilities to the most rural regions is due entirely to policy diffusion supported by both local and national governments. However, Omuta started its theme park development efforts on the downside of the "theme park boom," and thus had trouble generating government support for construction of the facility.

ORIGINS OF THE PLAN

It is difficult to pinpoint the origin of the idea for GeoBio World. However, for the purposes of describing what Kingdon calls "predecision processes," knowing the exact starting point of an idea is not important.[1] Ideas—whether problems or solutions—can exist in the minds of policymakers for years before they are acted upon. They may simmer for an unspecified period of time in the "policy primeval soup." Then, sometimes suddenly, an idea's time comes and it is coupled with energy; a decision to change current policy is made. Such is the case with both GeoBio World and AutoWorld, though the latter simmered longer than the former. With GeoBio World, the idea first surfaced publicly in 1988, but apparently percolated for a few years prior to that. The absolute earliest conception of the idea can probably be traced to the early 1980s, when Tokyo Disneyland was built.

Tokyo Disneyland provided inspiration—or perhaps an idol—for GeoBio World planners. It inspired park planners throughout Japan as well. The planning office walls in Omuta are sprinkled with Disney maps and posters, and souvenir dwarfs sit on the desks. The Tokyo park was mentioned several times in interviews with planning officials, and at one point they even hired some of Tokyo Disney's former ride designers to create attractions for the Omuta park. But from the beginning, the park also was to incorporate research and training facilities for biotechnology and coal-mining industries. Mayor Shiotsuka and local economic elites presented these goals, even before official plans for the attraction were started.

The most likely origin of the theme park idea in Omuta is a study commission that was convened in 1988 to examine possible uses for the large tracts of Mitsui land in Omuta. The city organized and funded the study group, which included senior representatives from the Mitsui firms, major regional banks, transportation companies, and the Japan Development Bank (JDB).[2] The idea was certainly discussed in this committee, although there is no evidence of any consensus being reached. Some thought such a park was a good idea, while others—notably the JDB—were less sanguine about its prospects.

Mayor Shiotsuka was an undisputed early champion of the project. In 1989 he made numerous public appearances in support of the project, always preaching local unity, city government support, and a can-do spirit for GeoBio World that emphasized the need for urban revitalization to be undertaken by the local people.[3] However, as the project efforts dragged on and changed, his cheerleading became muted because he did not want his name linked too closely to a plan that looked likely to fail.

EARLY PLANS FOR GEOBIO WORLD

The GeoBio World idea was first announced to the public in February 1989. Trumpeted as a new "leisure facility" aimed at increasing tourism in the city, the announcement featured a sketch of an amusement park and a description of some rides that would be built. The article openly stated the intent to use GeoBio World as the core of Omuta's rebound in the postcoal era, just as Kitakyushu City built Spaceworld (to be opened in 1990 in Kitakyushu, a one and a half hour drive north of Omuta) to kick off the poststeel era. Like Tokyo Disneyland and Spaceworld, GeoBio World was divided into "zones," each with a different theme to be conveyed through buildings, characters, rides, and concessions. The "Geo Zone" focused on Omuta's coal history, and on underground themes in general; the "Bio Zone" used Omuta's coastal location on the Ariake Sea to celebrate the ocean, and to promote knowledge of marine environmental issues.[4]

These themes have deep roots in Omuta's recent history. Omuta's Miike mine extracted coal primarily from deposits under the seabed. The mineshaft was on the coast, but the tunnels snaked out in various directions under the ocean floor. Miners worked more than a thousand feet below sea level, with the ocean pressing on the rock above their heads. In addition, the interaction of the mine and the sea periodically caused problems in Omuta's history. As coal deposits were removed and as sections of the mine were closed and abandoned, older tunnels collapsed and the seafloor above them settled. This caused some parts of the shallow Ariake Sea to deepen, which changed the ecology of those areas. Places that were once used for aquaculture—mainly seaweed cultivation—became useless for the purpose. Mitsui was forced to pay damages to the farmers and fishermen whose livelihood was affected. These early, historically derived themes were clouded and changed in later iterations of the plan. They became silly, overly cute ideas about gnomes and other creatures of fantasy. I will explain these changes shortly.

From the beginning, GeoBio World was envisioned and touted as more than just an amusement park. Biotechnology and coal technology research facilities were also part of the plan, and early drawings always included laboratory and education facilities. The initial total project cost estimate was $83 million, and the target date for opening was sometime in 1992. The first-year attendance was projected to be sixty thousand people, and by the fourth year of operation attendance forecasts predicted one million visitors annually.[5] Even though the coal connection was easily made, the biotechnology link was more tenuous. But it was also an emerging technology and a buzzword in local economic development efforts throughout Japan. To demonstrate Omuta's commitment to the biotechnology idea, the city sponsored the "Omuta Bio-Symposium" in November 1989. Featuring a panel of distinguished science professors from top regional universities, the symposium kicked off with the mayor's call to increase the appeal of "Bio-City Omuta."[6] As the theme park idea foundered, the biotechnology momentum decreased as well. A coal research and development facility is still in the works and looks quite likely, though it has been separated from the GeoBio World plans.[7]

NAVEL LAND

GeoBio World was supposedly the centerpiece of Omuta's redevelopment effort. It was planned and executed by Navel Land, a third sector (*dai-san secta*) local development company established and capitalized jointly by the city of Omuta, Fukuoka Prefecture, and by major companies from Omuta and from the northern Kyushu region. Such public-private joint ventures have also been used in other Japanese theme parks. A similar company was established to build and manage Space World in Kitakyushu, for example. The name "Navel Land" was selected for three reasons: first, its end product—the GeoBio World theme park—was seen as the *heso jigyô* (belly button project) in Omuta's revitalization plan, the project around which all others would revolve; second, Omuta's history is focused on coal, a rock that comes from the belly of the earth; third, Omuta is located in central Kyushu, and planners hope to draw people from all over the island to the park.[8] The coal theme figures prominently in the park's attractions, and the development company sought to carry the theme from the mine to the opening of the tourist attraction.

Navel Land, was officially established in September of 1989, with capital assets of $7.2 million. The city started the capitalization ball rolling by committing just over $1.1 million in March of 1989, and in April the city submitted a request for planning funds to the national government's Industrial Basic Facilities Fund (Sangyô Kiban Seibi Kikin), administered by MITI. Fukuoka Prefecture matched the city with an additional $1.1 million in August of that year, and in September the city received a $1.1-million grant from the Industrial Basic Facilities Fund. Mitsui Mining and Mitsui Tôatsu Chemical contributed $1.1 million each, and the remaining $3 million came from Fukuoka Bank, the Nishitetsu Railway Co., JR Kyushu (a rail and transportation company, formerly part of the Japan National Railway system), the Kyushu Electric Power Co., and several other private sources.[9]

On the day Navel Land, was established, the company commissioned the Japanese advertising giant Dentsu to do a commercial feasibility study and to produce the basic park plan and proposal. In the following nine months, the city and Navel Land worked hard to publicize the GeoBio World idea, sponsoring a large Bio Symposium and then a series of five Tourism Promotion symposia in the city. These were aimed at increasing community awareness of ongoing efforts and at generating public support for the projects. The city also spent about $11,000 producing and printing a color brochure explaining and promoting GeoBio World.[10]

Navel Land was a firm with a narrow mission: the construction and management of GeoBio World. Company employees were provided on a two- or three- year personnel exchange basis by city hall and by the original investing companies. The company president's seat was filled on a rotating basis by a senior management employee from one of the investing firms. Hoshioka Morihiko, the first Navel Land president, was previously head of the Mitsui Tôatsu Chemical plant in Omuta. Navel Land was controlled jointly by the city and by the firm's officers.

THE PROFESSIONAL PLANNING CARROUSEL

While the GeoBio World promotions went well, the actual facility planning did not. More precisely, generating plans was not a problem; the problem was getting them accepted by prospective funding sources.[11] All of the visions of the park included research and development facilities for biotechnology industries, coal mining technology, and mine safety to some degree, but the amusements and rides were clearly the focus of the hired consulting company presentations. In 1989, while Dentsu continued work on its commission, Navel Land hired a second Japanese company, Imagica, to generate another GeoBio World plan.[12] Dentsu presented its final plan in the fall of 1989. Imagica presented its final proposal in the spring of 1990. The park became rather ridiculous in the Imagica version, when it was announced that its theme character would be a gnome, and that all rides and construction would incorporate this theme. "GeoBio World's Weird Gnome Nation" was intended to give the park a more international feel, since the gnome comes from European fairy tales and children's stories, not from any Japanese lore.[13] The plans had different budgets and attendance estimates, with Imagica's version being larger on both counts. It is my impression that in theme park plans produced by consultants, attendance figures and operating cost estimates always balance out. This is true in both Omuta and Flint. One wonders which figure was generated first.

After both proposals were rejected for various reasons (which are discussed in the next section) by the JDB, Navel Land hired the American firm Futurist Light and Show—whose staff had also worked on Tokyo Disneyland—in May 1990, to come up with a third proposal. They presented their final plan in early August of 1990, and it also failed to win JDB approval.

A fourth firm, Sun Consultant, was hired in November 1991, to try and meet JDB expectations. It failed too. Following this fourth failure, Navel Land officials decided they would try to construct a proposal on their own.[14] Meanwhile, publicity efforts and public relations events continued, with biotechnology fairs, Kyushu Coal forums, and tourism symposia occurring annually.

Even though the GeoBio World idea surfaced in the media periodically, little of the revolving door consultant process was revealed to the public. There was brief mention of hiring Futurist Light and Show in the last paragraph of an article in the *Mainichi Shimbun*, though it was mainly due to the novelty of hiring an American firm.[15] The media never reported the problems Navel Land had in pleasing the JDB staff, and were never critical of the process or of the time and money that GeoBio World invested in the project. Other than this instance, none of the newspaper articles ever mentioned the fact that consultants were hired.

The Financial Support Issue

Why did the JDB repeatedly reject plans for GeoBio World? Promises of financial backing were in place for several years, but this funding was contingent on JDB approval. Most of the financial support was slated from various sources at the national level, while some was promised by private sources. The capital supply data were as follows:

Table 3.1: GeoBio World Financing Summary

Source	Amount	Interest Rate	Term
NTT Interest-free Financing	$8.6 million	0%	15 years
Regional Industrial Promotion Facilities Capital (Chiiki Shinkô Seibi Shikin)	$3.01 million	0%	15 years
Industrial Structural Adjustment Finance (Sangyô Kôzô Chôsei Yûshi)	$3.40 million	5.15%	15 years
Coal Area Special Use Finance (Santan Chiiki Tokuri Yûshi)	$8.20 million	4.35%	10 years
Private Bank Financing	$9.01 million	7%	15 years

Source: Internal Navel Land, documents, data as of April 1993.

The Nippon Telephone & Telegraph (NTT) money was the result of the privatization and of the public sale of NTT stock. It is managed by the Ministry of Finance, and is used for long-term, interest-free financing of public works and social capital infrastructure projects.[16] The Regional Industrial Promotion Facilities Capital is part of the Ministry of Home Affairs' (MOHA) Hometown Fund (Furusato Zaidan). This is just one of 112 such funds that make up Japan's public policy corporations. These companies do not implement policy. However, once a ministry sets a policy, these corporations are often the chosen instruments of the government for administering it. This public finance corporation was established in 1972 and given its current name in 1974. It spends funds from the Coal Special Account, but its primary duties are land-use planning, new town development, infrastructure improvements, and lending funds to firms that want to relocate outside of the Tokyo-Osaka area. It is an important government tool for social engineering that still plays a role even though the coal industry is virtually dead.[17] As for the remaining funds, the Industrial Structural Adjustment Finance is a nationwide JDB program.

The Coal Area Special Use Financing is overseen by MITI. In addition, Navel Land has already amassed—and is collecting interest on—$19.2 million, all of which will be used for the construction of GeoBio World facilities. This is money allocated from city and prefectural budgets since 1989, and capital contributed by various private companies in exchange for the right to participate in Navel Land activities.[18]

The JDB was the linchpin in the financing syndicate. All the other capital sources agreed to finance the project, pending JDB approval of the Navel Land plan. But as just mentioned, the JDB rejected four plans, for various reasons. The JDB was involved in the Navel Land project from the earliest stages. And from the very first, the JDB advised Omuta that it thought GeoBio World was a bad idea.[19] One of the biggest concerns was that there were already enough theme parks in northern Kyushu: Nagasaki is home to Holland Village and to the newer Huis Ten Bosch; Spaceworld in Kitakyushu is quite close; and Mitsui Greenland in neighboring Arao (Kumamoto Prefecture) is a fifteen-minute taxi ride from Omuta Station. The competition was too fierce and the regional population not sufficient to support another theme park.

Second, in the JDB's estimation the theme park boom was over, and Omuta was trying to enter the market too late in the game.[20] Related to this issue was the fact that the Omuta plans were not sufficiently unique to draw the crowds necessary for profitability. The JDB was not willing to fund yet another run-of-the-mill theme park. It was looking for something new and different—something innovative. The JDB saw GeoBio World's lack of innovation as a severe liability, but Omuta did not present it with any innovative plans because the "normal" method of implementing policy was not conducive to such innovation.

Third, the JDB believed the effects of such a park on community redevelopment were overrated. Although they produced no numbers or reports to support this opinion, they made this assessment based on anecdotal evidence and on the bank's experience in partially funding more than ten other theme parks in Japan.[21]

A fourth reason for JDB reluctance was the bank's assessment of the condition and commitment of the project's backing at the local level, especially corporate support in Omuta. A bank official's assessment ran as follows: Mitsui had no strength for this project in the early 1990s. Unlike New Japan Steel (Nihon Seitetsu), which built Spaceworld, Mitsui's fiscal prospects for the future—at least for the near future when GeoBio World would need lots of help if it is to succeed—were pretty weak. This was not the time for Mitsui—especially for the companies in Omuta—to be taking such risks. Also, the corporate backing for this project—in terms of pure enthusiasm—was weak. When Mitsui built Mitsui

Greenland in neighboring Arao, it was clearly a Mitsui-led affair. And Spaceworld was likewise a New Japan Steel-led project. But no one company took the GeoBio World lead. It was a hodgepodge of companies and city employees with a randomly rotating leadership that did not give off an air of stability and security.[22]

The land issue was an indication of Mitsui's real feelings on the issue. Mitsui Coal Mining agreed in September 1990—after much haggling—to sell the land to the city at a fairly low, though undisclosed, price.[23] According to those privy to the deal, Mitsui Coal Mining wants some money for the land, although the price was pretty reasonable. But in the JDB's opinion, if Mitsui really wanted to undertake this project it should have given the land to the city for free or for a token sum.

The JDB also saw weakness in the commitment of community political leaders. Bank officials maintained that the mayor was not really committed to the project. Mayor Shiotsuka's general lack of participation beyond publicity was perceived as a lack of interest or commitment.[24] Though the JDB saw the mayor this way, the mayor himself put a slightly different spin on his inaction. Mayor Shiotsuka said he would not intervene in the financing process until it looked likely that GeoBio World would get JDB approval.[25] Each waited for the other to support the project, and a lack of communication made the situation increasingly difficult. Mayor Shiotsuka and the main decision-makers at the JDB never met face-to-face. One bank official suggested that perhaps the mayor would be more earnest if he were up for reelection in the near future, or if his support base were weak.[26]

Besides the mayor, no other local elected representatives—from the local, prefectural, or national level—ever approached the JDB. Usually such approaches happen, and it seems odd to at least one JDB official that such contacts, ties, and pressure did not occur in this protracted struggle to get the project off the ground. Perhaps politicians did not want to get near a potential hot potato involving lots of risk, and thus were not really committed to the project's success. Or perhaps politicians privately shared the JDB view of GeoBio World's prospects. Either way, Navel Land, was the only force lobbying on its own behalf, and this was seen as a weakness by the JDB.

GeoBio World's Short Existence

Omuta took the initiative in 1994, and the city secured sufficient public sector loans to build GeoBio World, which finally opened in July of 1995 after eighteen months of construction. It cost just over $100 million to build, and expected attendance was 600,000 per year. Featured attractions included a simulation theater showing a four-minute film entitled *The Ultimate Roller Coaster*, a coal industry science museum, an aquarium, and a botanical garden. The 4.8 hectare park (with a 6-acre parking lot) never came close to attendance projections, and it went bankrupt and closed less than two years after it opened. GeoBio World left Omuta with a per capita debt of $160, to be paid down over the years.

FLINT'S WILD AUTOWORLD RIDE

AutoWorld was designed as a cross between a theme park, a science center, a festival marketplace, and an automotive museum. AutoWorld's 300,000 square feet of exhibit space contained the following major attractions: a replica of old Flint, built beneath a 70-foot high dome and animated with holographic images telling visitors about AutoWorld; an Imax theater presentation of AutoWorld's film, *Speed!* intended to spark excitement about automobiles; a ride called the "Humorous History of Automobility," in which visitors rode in miniature Model T cars through a fanciful version of automotive history; and a ride called the "Great Race," in which visitors rode in race car replicas through a history of the great races in automotive history; classic cars and mock-ups of car assembly lines past, present, and future were also on display. Restaurants and shops rounded out the facility's features.

ORIGINS OF THE PLAN

The origins of the AutoWorld project are somewhat clearer than those of GeoBio World. Two plausible explanations for the birth of the idea exist. Neither seems more likely than the other. One version says that the first mention of the idea came in 1969. Joseph Anderson, the retired general manager of AC Spark Plug, recalled that Harding Mott, president of the Mott Foundation, was angry because of a news story from California about students burying a Chevrolet to emphasize their antagonism toward cars. In the *Flint Journal* Anderson claims that Mott said, "We've got to do something to show how important the automobile has been in improving society."[27] But former Flint mayor James Rutherford attributes the concept of AutoWorld to Anderson himself.[28] A second version has Harding Mott

> standing in the office of a foundation vice president, Homer Dowdy, and commenting, "You know, what this community really needs is something to get its pride together. It's fading. We need to restore it. We ought to be able to do something about

what we've got right here. After all, we're one of the main centers in the history of automaking."[29]

The original idea, however, was quite different from the end product that was finally constructed. Originally, Mott wanted to do something to commemorate the importance of cars and to pay tribute to the founders of General Motors (GM). The earliest versions of AutoWorld did not intend for the facility to be self-supporting; it was to be funded by the auto industry.[30] Harding Mott's father, Charles Stewart Mott, was a philanthropist and one of the pioneers of the automobile industry. He was in his nineties when the idea was proposed, and he opposed the plan on the grounds that the idea's backers had some sort of tribute to him in mind.[31]

A contextual point should be made here. The mood of the city was important at the time. In the late 1960s and early 1970s, civic leaders sought to begin the redevelopment of downtown Flint. Harding Mott's proposal was one of a number of proposals for redeveloping the downtown area put forth when a group of city officials and civic leaders met at the Consumers Power Co. lodge at Tippy Dam on the Big Manistee River on April 2, 1970.[32] Other projects took precedence over Mott's automobile hall of fame. A downtown campus for the University of Michigan-Flint, Riverfront Center (a convention and hotel complex on the river), River Village (a middle-income multiracial housing development on the river), and Riverbank Park (a flood control project that doubled as a park and summer concert space, built by the Army Corps of Engineers) were all funded and constructed before AutoWorld.

Mobilization of Actors, Early Plans

The meeting at Tippy Dam marked the creation of the Flint Area Conference, Inc. (FACI), a nonprofit corporation designed to redevelop the central city. FACI's stated purpose was "that of an organization of civic and business leaders working with public officials in an effort to meet unfilled physical and economic needs of the community.[33] FACI was funded by the foundation, and consisted of five or six people at any given time. Made up of the leaders of business and industry in Flint, it always included foundation representatives. It was an elite organization, and all of its members did not reside in Flint.[34]

After the Tippy Dam meeting, a committee headed by Anderson was established to study the hall of fame idea. At the same time, the foundation began to hire consultants. In 1970 the architect Minoru Yamasaki was commissioned by the foundation to design a hall of fame for the automobile in Flint. Yamasaki and Associates, of Troy, Michigan, produced a plan for a "hall" to be built on an island in the Flint River. The architect submitted a bill of about $75,000 for his consulting work, but the plan was dropped when it was decided to develop the downtown campus of the University of Michigan-Flint in the same area. Yamasaki's was the first commissioned plan for AutoWorld. From 1970 to 1980 numerous consultants, developers, and designers were hired, and they played roles of varying importance in the evolution of AutoWorld. The final architect, responsible for the plans up until construction, was Randall Duell Associates of Santa Monica, California. Duell has helped develop twenty-two major theme parks, including Busch Gardens in Virginia and Hershey Park in Pennsylvania.[35]

At this point, in late 1970, the members of Anderson's committee had no firm idea of what would be exhibited in the hall. Some imagined a historical museum; others wanted a hands-on science museum. Anderson wanted to commemorate the increased mobility that the car brought to society.[36] Meanwhile, the foundation continued to hire more consultants. In 1976, the foundation hired Donald Zuchelli of Zuchelli, Hunter, and Associates, a Baltimore consulting firm. Zuchelli was hired as the predevelopment packager for Riverfront Center, the $32-million Hyatt Regency convention center begun in the late 1970s. Flint also hired the Zuchelli firm to do a market analysis of the demand for industrial park land in 1976.[37] Zuchelli became the acting head of the FACI, and he put together a study team of architects, financial experts, exhibit designers, and attendance experts to create a master plan for AutoWorld.[38] The foundation gave the FACI $250,000 for the development of new plans by this team.[39] The head of the study team was David L. Brown, president of Recreation Consultants of Santa Clara, California. Brown previously developed the Marriott Corporation's Great America theme parks in Chicago and San Francisco.

An important aspect of the planning for AutoWorld was projecting accurate attendance during the early years of the park. Projected attendance figures were 750,000 the first year, and roughly 1,000,000 the year after that.[40] According to Brown, these figures were generated using "standard industry practice" by Hammer, Siler, George and Associates, a Washington, DC-based consulting firm specializing in these types of projections. Brown said there is a "standard statistical approach" used in the industry to project attendance, and when his firm authenticated the study they arrived at the same projected figures.[41]

INITIAL FISCAL SUPPORT

Despite the fact that other redevelopment projects took priority over AutoWorld, the idea continued to simmer and planning progressed at a slow pace. In 1977, the estimated price for the completion of AutoWorld was $28 million, of which the foundation said it would consider paying $6 million. In June of 1977, foundation president William White (Harding Mott's son-in-law) said the foundation trustees had decided informally that they could commit up to $6 million if there was enough interest from GM, other automakers, and suppliers, and if bonds could be issued to pay part of the cost.[42]

The fact that other development projects had priority over AutoWorld may have helped to sustain interest in the theme park. Civic leaders, especially supporters of AutoWorld, argued that the attraction could have a positive effect on other projects. White argued that it could attract tourists and conventions to Flint. He cited consultants' studies that showed thousands of new visitors coming to Flint each year. "If we do a good job with AutoWorld, I don't see how we could keep new hotels out [of downtown]," White said.[43] The perception in Flint was that the AutoWorld project was "close to the heart of William White." This was another factor in AutoWorld's constant, if slow, progress.[44] The Bicentennial was another event that kept alive the notion that Flint's automotive and labor history was unique and important. AutoWorld was portrayed as a way to preserve this history.[45]

Once the facility planning was underway, and the initial price tag was made public, raising money to build AutoWorld began. In 1977, Jim Sheaffer was hired by the foundation as the new president of FACI. His job was to manage several of the major development projects in the downtown area.[46] In June of 1977 Sheaffer was quoted as saying, "we'll be walking around in AutoWorld in two or three years."[47] The fund-raising began in earnest. In meetings with GM executives, White lobbied for their financial support. As of January 1978, GM showed interest, but had made no financial commitment, citing hard times in the industry.[48]

The Site

One major obstacle to the realization of AutoWorld was the lack of a site on which to build. The initial site had been given to the University of Michigan-Flint in 1979, as an incentive to move downtown. When the IMA Auditorium—just across the river from the old site—became available in that same year, the foundation took out an option on it as a potential site of AutoWorld.[49] The site was supported by downtown merchants and by the Flint Area Chamber of Commerce because it was close to the commercial area of the city, and it would require only minimal disruption of downtown traffic patterns.[50] This is where AutoWorld was built.

THE FUNDING DRIVE

With a site and a plan in hand by the start of 1980, the primary task at hand was financing the construction. The goal was to finance AutoWorld without the city having to fund any part of it. On June 9, 1980, the foundation board voted to approve spending $11 million for the project.[51] By this time the projected cost of building AutoWorld had risen to $38.5 million, and discussion had begun with the federal government, specifically with the United States Department of Housing and Urban Development (HUD), about applying for federal funding for AutoWorld. Mayor Rutherford said the funding plans included $11 million in HUD grants. He and other officials predicted success in winning the grants, citing Flint's 17.4-percent unemployment for April 1980. "This is the kind of project they [HUD officials] love, especially with the level of unemployment here."[52]

In order to generate more funding, greater community support needed to be shown for the project. Although the city was not footing the bill, it contributed to the project in other ways. The city council quickly approved site plans, rezoning applications, land acquisitions, and tax-increment financing.[53] The director of the Flint Area Tourist and Convention Council said that AutoWorld could be responsible for about $16.5 million per year in increased tourism spending, assuming that only 20 percent of the projected visitors spend one night in a Flint lodging. Tourists who only spend the day would spend roughly $6.6 million annually, she said.[54] One of the city council members, Kenneth Sarginson, visited the Indianapolis Motor Speedway Museum and was impressed with the number of visitors there on a Tuesday morning. He expressed hope that Flint's AutoWorld could do as well.[55]

In 1980, the grant from HUD was seen as the key to the AutoWorld financing.[56] An Urban Development Action Grant (UDAG), local officials, and AutoWorld developers hoped it would cover almost one-third of the costs. The application for a UDAG for AutoWorld was filed simultaneously with two other smaller UDAG applications. Riverfront Place, a private office building, sought a $3-million grant, and a proposed industrial mall in eastern Flint sought $600,000.[57] Although developers desire UDAG grants, only municipalities can apply for them. The city of Flint functioned as a conduit for several UDAGs. The HUD application deadline was July 30, and decisions were made by early October. Once HUD awards a UDAG, the designated city has a limited (though extendable) amount of time in which to accept or release the funds. Flint has shown considerable skill in winning UDAGs. Between January 1979 and June 1980 alone Flint received $7.25 million in UDAG funds—$6.5 million for Riverfront Center, and $750,000 for a shopping center to be part of River Village, the housing development near the IMA site.[58]

AutoWorld's chances of getting UDAG funds looked good for several reasons. First, Flint had demonstrated past success in developing application packages for UDAGs. Second, the city's high rate of unemployment made it a prime candidate for federal assistance. Third, AutoWorld had already secured private sector grants—most notably from the foundation—that gave the project more credibility in the eyes of HUD officials.[59] The stated purpose of a UDAG is to match a minimum amount of government money with a larger share of private money for projects that help upgrade a city's economic base, provide jobs, or help rebuild neighborhoods. In the past, midwestern and northeastern cities like Flint have received the largest allocations.[60] A fourth reason for AutoWorld's probable success was that one of the key companies involved in developing AutoWorld, Appletree Enterprises of Bloomington, Minnesota, had helped win other HUD grants: a $10.3-million UDAG in Lansing and a $4.5-million award in Lynchburg, Virginia.[61] Given these assets, on July 28, 1980 the Flint City Council authorized application for a $13.6-million federal grant to fund the development of AutoWorld. At the same meeting, the council also voted to allow the developers of the park to use the city's tax-exempt bonding authority to float a $7.5-million tax-increment bond.[62]

By late summer 1980, AutoWorld was a well-known project in Flint. Support was strong, though some opposition existed. I will discuss this dissension in the next section. Even among supporters, anxiety existed over the pending UDAG funds. In late August, Mayor Rutherford, Sen. Donald Riegle Jr. (D-Mich. and a Flint native), and Rep. Dale Kildee (D-Flint) went to Washington to meet with officials from HUD and from the Department of Transportation (DoT), to whom Flint had also applied for a grant. Although no firm commitments were due until October, Riegle's state economic development coordinator, Marya Sieminski, said that "certainly HUD is being optimistic about this. . . . The grant people take a realistic view. They want to make sure the project has enough money to be successful. But they also know there is a lot of competition for grants and want all the details wrapped up in the grant application."[63] The meetings at the DoT were less optimistic, due largely to departmental budget cuts, but DoT undersecretary William Beckham suggested that the department might have exhibits in AutoWorld on such issues as auto safety.[64] In October 1980, Flint was awarded a UDAG worth $8.6 million, contingent on the city officially receiving the grant and closing on the project. The deadline for receiving or releasing the UDAG was extended to July 31, 1982.[65]

Flint and the AutoWorld developers also sought grants from the state budget. Flint asked the state for $4 million over three years to help build what was now predicted to be the $43-million AutoWorld. The request narrowly survived a challenge in the House of Representatives, as part of the regulatory budget passed by the House 60–38. Supportive legislators argued that AutoWorld would do the Flint area at least as much good as the state's annual $800,000-Pontiac Silverdome subsidy does for Oakland County.[66]

Opposition to the state subsidy came from representatives with other agendas, and also from Republican governor William Milliken. Milliken briefly lobbied the Senate to defeat the AutoWorld subsidy, but changed his position to one of support less than one week later. The governor changed his position in response to pressure from several sources. First, Milliken held a conference call with Robert Gerholz, former president of the United States Chamber of Commerce, a prominent Flint businessperson, and head of the private sector fund-raising drive; Harding Mott; Mayor Rutherford; and Arthur Summerfield Jr., an active fund-raiser for the Republican Party. Second, Roger Smith announced that GM was seriously considering contributing to the financing of AutoWorld.[67] Third, the AutoWorld subsidy was tied to a $33.4-million aid package for the city of Detroit. Sen. Harold Scott (D-Flint), a key voter on the conference committee, agreed to support an extra $3 million for Detroit as long as the AutoWorld grant was assured. Detroit mayor Coleman Young lobbied for the deal, and both appropriations were passed.[68]

With $11 million committed by the foundation, a $7.5-million tax-increment bond, $4 million from the state, and an $8.6-million UDAG, Robert Gerholz had considerable credibility when he kicked off the private sector fundraising drive for AutoWorld on March 26, 1981. The goal for the AutoWorld Foundation Capital Campaign was $4 million in local contributions and $4 million from donors outside of Flint.[69] In June of 1981 AutoWorld's stock continued to rise when former president Gerald Ford endorsed and contributed (an undisclosed amount) to the project. Along with the announcement of Ford's donation came a revised estimate of the total cost of the project: $50.1 million.[70] The single largest chunk of private funding came from an investment firm called CRI of Rockville, Maryland, in the form of $7.5 million in syndicated equity. In order to attract this private investment, the investors at CRI were guaranteed a $275,000-payment in the first year, but with no guarantees after that.[71]

This constant rise in the cost of AutoWorld continued. In November of 1981 FACI reevaluated the cost at the time of financial closing to be $60 million.[72] The financial closing was set for April 1, 1982. In order to keep costs as close to preconstruction estimates as possible, a guaranteed maximum price (GMP) was agreed on prior to the completion of all construction documents. Any cost overruns were designed out prior to the initiation of construction, in order to make the construction firms responsible for the orderly and accurate management of the construction process.[73]

The Closing Round

Fortunately for the developers, anticipated revenues kept increasing as well. Throughout 1981 and into the summer of 1982, costs and revenues continued to spiral upward like a double helix. Private investors continued to commit capital to the project. On March 3, 1982, the Flint Journal reported that $2 million had been spent since 1970 on designs, concepts, and legal work.[74] The April 1 closing date came and went, with no contracts signed and with no firm commitment to receive the UDAG money. Updated cost projections put the bill for AutoWorld construction and initial operation at $60 million. The Mott Foundation Board of Trustees was still not certain that AutoWorld could be built for that price. White was not even certain whether the park, if built, would be open year-round or only part-time.[75]

By late April, AutoWorld was very close to being a done deal, but was still tantalizingly out of reach. An editorial in the *Flint Journal* summed up the feelings of many residents:

> The Mott Foundation has committed $11 million to AutoWorld. . . . State and federal governments have seen the economic usefulness of AutoWorld. . . . The city of Flint and the state have approved raising $21 million from revenue bonds and a special tax process. . . . All this would seem to provide a firm base for AutoWorld . . . but the Mott Foundation's present concern is with . . . what kind of problem projected operating costs are likely to present. . . . Mott Foundation trustee Joseph Anderson . . . has said cancellation of AutoWorld plans would be calamitous. That may be too strong, but we hope figures warrant go-ahead. It is time for a little progress in this town, a little satisfying of the hunger for the positive.[76]

People wanted AutoWorld even if it had to be a smaller project than the plans dictated.

On May 1, 1982 the foundation board meeting was held to discuss the fate of AutoWorld. The board was not a rubber stamp, and the vote was very much in question. There were four decision options: (1) decide to go ahead with the full project and try to open by the latest announced target date of Memorial Day, 1984; (2) vote to cancel the foundation's involvement in the project on the grounds that not enough financing could be raised or that the project is not economically feasible over the long term; (3) decide that AutoWorld be built on a reduced level, cutting items from the plan to get the cost down to about $54 million; and (4) postpone a decision until closer to the deadline for receiving or releasing the $8.6-million UDAG.[77]

After a six-hour meeting, White gave the project an 80-percent chance of construction. The board decided to continue minimal funding of the AutoWorld design staff and to wait several more months before making a final decision. The foundation had already poured $8.59 million into AutoWorld since 1969, but the board refused to start construction prior to the acceptance of the UDAG. "Once you start construction, the money really starts pouring out. And we didn't feel we could take that risk until we . . . have a closing," said White. White also said the foundation had only identified $54.3 million in potential capital sources. This was $9.3 million short of the $60-million projection, with a $3-million contingency fund added in.[78]

The hesitation of the foundation board seems to be warranted. White asked rhetorically, ". . . if you spend $9.50 on a ticket in 1984, will you, one, wish to repeat the experience again and, two, will you tell your neighbor to go and see the park? That's a judgment call. Do we have the entertainment that's worth $9.50 for an adult?"[79] Throughout the decade spent planning AutoWorld, the theme of gambling and risk turned up repeatedly. The head of the firm calculating the attendance projections acknowledged the fact that despite all the planning, expertise, and money invested in the project, AutoWorld was "still a gamble for the city."[80] "If I were a betting man," said White in early 1978, "I don't know how I would bet on its [AutoWorld's] future."[81] Now the stakes were high, and the foundation board was gambling with a $60-million project.

Finally, on July 8, 1982 the foundation decided to go ahead with the project, and to begin construction in August. The foundation upped its contribution to $14 million—almost one-quarter of the total projected cost—while simultaneously acknowledging that AutoWorld remained a high-risk investment. White said the project would drain money from the foundation, and would thus reduce future foundation projects in the Flint area. In addition, he said about $4.5 million of the costs would be cut by eliminating or postponing some attractions. White also said to break even, the park must draw 830,000 visitors a year, at $9.50 per person. "It's a new business venture," he concluded, "and any new business is a risk."[82] Construction had to begin by early August at the latest, in order to make the opening day in May 1984.

Representatives from six of the financial backers—the foundation, the city of Flint, the Historic Flint AutoWorld Foundation, the Downtown

Development Authority (DDD), CRI, and HUD—met on July 20 in Washington, DC, to close the deal.[83] A ground-breaking ceremony was held, complete with ceremonial shovels, on October 15, 1982, two months behind schedule.[84] The final cost of construction was $68 million, according to figures provided by Flint's economic development administrators:[85]

Source	Amount
State of Michigan	$ 3.99 million
Federal UDAG (HUD)	$ 8.60 million
Federal CDBG (HUD)	$ 4.50 million
Tax Increment Bond (City)	$ 7.60 million
Downtown Development Authority	$10.00 million
Private Investors	$19.70 million
Mott Foundation	$14.00 million
Total Cost	$68.40 million

Opposition to AutoWorld

Opposition to AutoWorld was limited and largely ineffective. Other than Charles Stewart Mott's modest objections and the quick about-face by Governor Milliken, isolated incidents constitute most of the anti-AutoWorld sentiment in Flint. When the IMA auditorium site was officially chosen to host AutoWorld, some residents of the new River Village residential development, located across the street from the site, were unhappy with the choice. Concerns about traffic, noise, litter, construction, lower property values, and parking were all voiced by residents. In addition, some residents were taken by surprise when the site was announced. "It came as kind of a surprise. I'm not against it, but it's always kind of funny when you have to read about it. We've always hoped we could move out," said one resident. In response, James Sheaffer, director of FACI, admitted that those who would be affected should have been told earlier. "I guess you can look back at things and it would have been a good idea (to better notify people). I guess there was an oversight," said Sheaffer.[86]

Opposition also arose over the use of UDAG funds to build AutoWorld. The Urban League of Flint said it was disappointed that the UDAGs were not being spent in the neighborhoods, where they claimed the need was greater. But a HUD spokesperson claimed that their grants are distributed fairly, saying 34 percent are commercial, 32 percent are neighborhood, and 34 percent are industry grants.[87]

When asked about any opposition that he could recall, former mayor Rutherford did not mention the Urban League, local residents, or even

Governor Milliken. He said the greatest opposition came from Michael Moore, a Flint native who was then editor of the city's "alternative" newspaper, the Flint Voice.[88] Through his newspaper, Moore focused on the uncertainty surrounding the decision to build. He quoted White saying, "It's a flip of the coin . . . it may or may not be built. . . . The budget has grown beyond what we hoped for. . . . It seems like once a problem is solved, you get another one." Moore also questioned the project's ability to draw visitors, since it was to contain only two rides, one of which would take you through the "humorous history of the automobile." Moore also criticized the lack of new jobs to be created—only sixty-seven full-time and numerous seasonal minimum wage positions—and the lack of labor history in the "humorous history of the automobile."[89]

THE END

During the first month of operation, AutoWorld hit its turnstile target. From July 4 through August 4, 1984, 139,970 people visited the park.[90] But through the fall of that year, AutoWorld ran a deficit. Under the complex arrangement under which AutoWorld was financed, the head of development for CRI, Fred Burchill, was the person really in charge of the theme park. Burchill sent a mail-o-gram, received at AutoWorld on January 11, 1985, directing the officials who ran the park to shut the doors at the end of business the following Sunday, January 13.[91] This closing was the first of several and only temporary, but the park never became the successful attraction it was intended to be.

AutoWorld closed for good in 1986. High ticket prices and unappealing attractions were credited with its demise. It sat dormant for a decade, when it was eventually razed. The Flint DDA turned the land over to the University of Michigan-Flint. In a final indignity, the foundation pledged $4 million to cover the cost of demolition and transfer of the property. Even though locally the park was widely seen as "the Edsel of theme parks," Mayor Rutherford, a driving force behind AutoWorld, regretted its demise. "It's a pretty darn nice facility," he said. "It seems like somebody should be able to figure out some way to use it."[92]

COMPARATIVE ANALYSIS

These theme park cases demonstrate a clear lack of innovation and a reliance on supply-side policy-making in Omuta and Flint. Institutional factors such as grant programs and private sector consultants in both systems encourage cities to attempt projects that have been successful elsewhere. Government subsidies were readily available for these projects

precisely because they had been successful ideas in other cities. And consultants—from planners to developers and contractors—were already
skilled at winning grants and at peddling their ideas. It is perfectly reasonable that these cities chose to try theme park development, since an
easy path was laid for them and they were encouraged to follow it.

A number of the central themes of this study are supported by the
amusement park comparison. The different roles played by national governments is evident in this comparison. In the United States, politics matters more than bureaucracy, while in Japan the reverse is true. Japan's
national government played a larger role in urban revitalization, both in
project financing and in oversight. The JDB and other public corporations
were the primary players in determining whether Omuta's theme park
dreams would be realized. City officials and park planning staff had to
satisfy officials at these agencies before the project could move forward. In
contrast, the American federal government contributed less money and
advice, instead leaving responsibility for AutoWorld in the hands of the
private sector: the foundation, private developers, and venture capitalists.

Omuta and Flint lost out because they copied successful ideas from
other cities. Unfortunately for these late arrival cities, theme parks
proved to be an ill-advised path to revitalization, despite what those selling the projects claimed. Flint never recouped its losses—or its image—
after the failure of AutoWorld. And Omuta was plunged into a seemingly
endless loop of plan proposals and rejections when the money and effort
might have been directed toward other ideas. Both cities held weak
hands in a zero-sum game. Both sought to implement risky policy ideas
at great expense.

Returning to the original question, Why did these cities opt for what,
in retrospect, were bad policy ideas? In short, policy diffusion and institutional environments explain why they did what they did. Both cities
copied successful policy ideas from other localities, but they did so too
late. Japan's strict fiscal system hindered Omuta's ability to pull the trig-
ger, while America's more laissez-faire system allowed Flint's project to go
forward with disastrous consequences.

The interesting differences in the policy process highlight several of
the differences in Japanese and American urban policy-making. Key differences include the following points:

The conventional wisdom argues that American cities enjoy greater
fiscal autonomy than their Japanese counterparts, and the theme park project comparison supports this generalization to some degree. National
government funds made up a larger percentage of the project budget in
Omuta than they did in Flint. Central government grants and loans
accounted for slightly more than 72 percent of the GeoBio World budget,

while federal grants only amounted to just under 20 percent of total AutoWorld costs.

Despite this fiscal disparity, national government influence in one respect appeared roughly the same: funding from the national level proved to be the go-ahead signal for project implementation in both cities. Grants from HUD catalyzed financing commitments from the foundation and from other private sources. Of course, the obvious difference is that the Japanese governmental agency (the JDB) was more deeply involved in the project planning process, while the American government agency approved a vague idea early in the game, and left the details of the actual theme park to planners at the local level. In short, the federal government disbursements came with fewer strings attached.

A second significant difference is the role of big business in each project. Large economic interests were far more important in Omuta than they were in Flint. In Omuta, various Mitsui concerns, the two regional railway companies, regional banks, and the power company all provided start-up capital and contributed personnel and public relations support. Mitsui Coal sold the land for the park to the city at a reduced price, and major regional banks provided funding commitments (pending JDB approval). The major Japanese firms were far more involved than their American counterparts. In Flint, GM gave little monetary support, and played no planning or other role in the AutoWorld effort. This was particularly painful for project planners, given the fact that GM contributed an estimated $40–$60 million to EPCOT Center in Orlando, Florida.[93] GM subsidiaries and suppliers in the area also avoided participation in the project, leaving AutoWorld organization and management to local business groups like FACI and the DDA.

Why did Japanese firms participate in GeoBio World, while American firms opted out of AutoWorld? There was no apparent government coercion in the Japanese case, nor was there much in the way of reciprocal consent or other "advice" offered to the firms by the government. Rather, the companies apparently saw corporate benefits that they might achieve by participating. Mitsui Coal sold idle land at a time when its balance sheet was far from healthy. Liquidating unused assets was a smart move on its part, and may have even been encouraged by its creditors. JR Kyushu and Nishitetsu, the two regional railway companies, envisioned increased ridership, since both provide frequent train and bus service between Omuta and other regional cities. Private banks—Fukuoka Bank and Nishi Nihon Bank, in particular—would earn interest off their promised loans to Navel Land, assuming the park was ever approved by the JDB. The other Mitsui firms, Mitsui Metals and Mitsui Tôatsu Chemical, had nothing apparent to gain. But since they were part of the Mitsui group, they may have felt some obligation to participate. Or they may have been pressured into participating by the other Mitsui group firms.[94]

The tradition of large-scale private philanthropy must be evaluated. Money and participation from philanthropic organizations was not solicited in Japan, while the foundation played a key role in planning and funding Flint's theme park. This is not to say that such corporate philanthropic organizations do not exist in Japan; they do, for example, the founders of Bridgestone Tire and Rubber—the Ishibashi family—are from Kurume, a city one half hour north of Omuta in Fukuoka Prefecture. The Ishibashi family has built museums, libraries, and other facilities in Kurume. But such family philanthropy is less common in Japan than it is in the United States. The Carnegie, Mellon, Rockefeller, Ford, Kresge, and other industrialist-turned-philanthropist families have no counterparts in Japan. And no such foundations are based in Omuta. Flint was fortunate to have the foundation headquartered there, and one wonders what would have happened to Flint if no such organization had existed. Though the AutoWorld project funded by the foundation was a failure, the foundation has funded many smaller community social welfare initiatives that have proved quite beneficial. The existence of the foundation in Flint makes the city something of an exception among cities its size: most do not have a major foundation headquartered within their borders.

On the other hand, Japan has far more public sector institutions and corporations charged with supporting various aspects of economic development than the United States. The JDB is one such finance corporation (kôko), but there are many others. These finance corporations and their public corporation brethren (kôdan) play a critical role as conduits for funds from Tokyo to the local level. Budget data analyzed by Ostrom suggest that investment by these organizations "tends to favor sunset industries at the expense of more dynamic industries."[95] These corporations are used to combat economic decline and to support uncompetitive economic sectors. There are no comparable institutions in the United States with commensurate fiscal power and resource control.

Politics plays a role in both cases. The mayor is a central player in redevelopment in general in both cities. The difference in their roles is more idiosyncratic than systemic. Omuta's mayor carefully steered clear of involvement in GeoBio World, while the Flint mayor was heavily involved in AutoWorld's development. What explains the difference? Omuta's mayor Shiotsuka was initially active in the project, but cut back his participation when JDB objections became evident. Shiotsuka enjoyed a solid public support base, and was not challenged or otherwise electorally threatened. He could avoid the risk of association with GeoBio

World, and instead focus his efforts on other projects that were more likely to succeed. Also, his hands-off management style made his distance from GeoBio World seem natural. Shiotsuka put a lot of effort into attracting publicity and local support for projects, but he rarely came down to the level of hands-on planning. This was a wise political strategy that allowed him to take credit for project successes and to avoid blame for project failures. Shiotsuka's background as a Ministry of Construction official seems to have taught him how to play his political cards. His experience at a higher level of government allowed him to step back and to evaluate local events from a more removed perspective.

In contrast, Flint's mayor Rutherford operated in a more politically fractured and contentious environment. He never enjoyed as broad a support base as Shiotsuka, and thus might have felt the need to take on a large project with a high potential payoff, and a high eventual cost. Rutherford was the first mayor elected after Flint changed from a council-manager system (with a weak mayor) to a strong mayor system, which probably put more pressure on him. AutoWorld happened in Rutherford's second term, at a time when a recession was gripping the United States, and Flint in particular. Although he did ultimately have some positive achievements to his credit, the biggest of these—the Buick City coup—came after AutoWorld was completed.

Rutherford's background as Flint's police chief probably made it difficult for him to see local events from a more distant plane. His rough, scrappy, Flint-born-and-bred style did not lend itself to objective evaluation of projects like AutoWorld. And his vulnerability to pressure from the foundation, coupled with the desperate imperative to do something to improve Flint's situation, made it unlikely that he could have avoided participation in the AutoWorld fiasco, even if he had wanted to avoid the project.

Finally, one similarity stands out above all others: the reliance on consultants in both cases to come up with a project that would work, and the failure of those consultants hired to do so. Private sector consulting firms specializing in theme park development repeatedly told local officials that a theme park was a good idea, and that it could succeed.

CONCLUSION

A heavy reliance on development consultants, supply-side policy-making, and an effort to finance revitalization efforts from sources other than the city budget are all readily apparent in this section.

Consultants played a significant role in the evolution of amusement park ideas in Omuta and Flint. Omuta went so far as to hire some of the designers of Tokyo Disneyland during their planning process, while Flint hired the developers from Busch Gardens and Marriott's Great Adventure parks. Consultants pushed Flint toward the amusement park idea force-fully; the city was looking for a museum-type attraction to honor the developers of the automobile. Omuta arrived at the theme park concept largely on its own—by looking at other cities in the region that success-fully planned and built such attractions—and then hired the consultants to make it a reality.

Both cases present clear evidence of supply-side, copy-cat policy-making. Rather than develop innovative responses to economic decline, Omuta and Flint copied successful ideas from other cities that could be achieved with minimal local capital expenditure. In this context, "success-ful" theme parks refers to parks that were able to turn a profit at best, or at least to break even at worst, while creating new jobs in the community and attracting visitors to the park. Both cities generated revitalization strategies incorporating the best of what other cities had already done and what the national government had to offer in the way of assistance pro-grams. As the discussion of revitalization strategy in the previous chapter suggests, quality of life improvements, job creation through the luring of businesses from other locations, and tourism promotion were central themes in Omuta and Flint's redevelopment efforts. The projects dis-cussed in this chapter were central to the strategy of tourism promotion.

These projects represent policy imitation in several ways. First, the idea of using theme parks to spark redevelopment was already well estab-lished in Japan and in the United States. Examples of new parks built at the initiative of local governments are found in both countries, though the theme park "boom" was more pronounced in Japan. One substantial dif-ference stands out in comparing the two cases, however. Flint's AutoWorld was built precisely because of the credibility of its experienced designers, while Omuta's GeoBio World was delayed by the JDB because the financial institution saw the plan as just another run-of-the-mill theme park produced by experienced private consultants. For those evaluating the theme parks and backing them financially in each city, imitation of success meant very different things: in the Japanese case, it was seen as a liability, while in Flint it was clearly an asset.

Second, consultants specializing in theme parks were active in both nations, where they generated and sold such plans even though their cost and attendance estimates were often grossly inaccurate. Park construction costs rose substantially during construction, and attendance rarely rose to meet expectations. Still, the ideas were pushed and sold aggressively. Third, the availability of funding for these projects pushed Omuta and Flint toward the idea of theme parks. Public and private capital was willing to support theme park development in both cities because such parks had been successful in other locales. Both cities secured the majority of project funding from sources other than the city budget, effectively putting the economic risk on other entities; the city had nothing to lose and thus could forge ahead on their theme park quest with a less critical eye. Unfortunately for investors, citizens, and city officials, both park projects will likely be remembered as significant failures.

An interesting feature of both theme park plans was their multifaceted nature. Omuta's theme park centered on the history and natural science issues surrounding the Miike coal mine. In addition, there were plans to combine the park with Omuta's proposed World Coal Technology Center, the coal technology research and development facility discussed in the previous chapter. It was hoped that bundling these two projects together would broaden their support at the national level, thus increasing the likelihood that they would be built. Flint's theme park planners sought to incorporate historical and educational themes as well, though AutoWorld was ultimately focused on entertainment.

CHAPTER 4

DOWNTOWN RETAIL RENEWAL

L uring shoppers to the downtown area was a central part of the revital-ization strategies in both Omuta and Flint. Once-thriving commercial districts had fallen into decline and disuse, and merchants had abandoned their stores in the downtown areas. Both cities sought to reverse this trend, breathing new life into the downtown retail and entertainment sectors. Such projects aimed to create jobs in the declining areas, and to improve the quality of life by sprucing up the retail zones through significant capital improvements. Though both cities made concerted efforts in this direction, neither was particularly successful in stimulating this sort of revitalization.

Shopping district redevelopment occurred in Omuta and Flint much as the promotion of tourism had happened: innovation was notably absent. Is innovation even necessary in shopping district revitalization? I argue that it is, since cities in the same region compete explicitly for shoppers. In both Japan and in the United States, this competition exists primarily between downtown and suburban retail facilities. In both nations, the suburban shopping centers and malls seem to be winning the battle for consumers' attention. But Japan is a more densely urbanized country than the United States, so cities there also compete with one another, pitting downtown areas against each other. Omuta did not seek to lure shoppers away from suburban strip malls so much as it sought to entice them away from big, glitzy high-rise malls in downtown Fukuoka City.

Competition with other cities was somewhat less important than it was in the amusement park case. However, the city still wrestled with the issue of how to attract shoppers away from newer malls and back to the downtown retail district. Downtown retail area revitalization required a lot of detailed work on numerous aspects of the community. Local actors had to coordinate the interests of those involved so that a feasible plan could be implemented. The story of efforts in Omuta and Flint to revitalize their downtown shopping districts provides a striking contrast in style. Omuta coordinated the numerous local interests more capably than did Flint, which tried to use a top-down approach to achieve success. This evidence goes against the traditional images of Japanese and American politics—Japan is usually characterized as top-down, while the United States is more fragmented and egalitarian.

Both cities ended up taking a supply-side approach to some degree because institutional environmental constraints pushed the cities to behave in certain patterns. Successful ideas were copied from other cities, and the combination of private consultants plus national programs and finances determined the realm of possible choices. The city of Omuta took advantage of a national government program offering generous funds for retail area revitalization. Even though Omuta received funding and some planning ideas from the central government in Tokyo, it also copied successful retail development ideas from Fukuoka City, fifty miles to the north. Flint also applied for and received national government funds for downtown retail revitalization. However, its plans were not formulated by the federal government but by private developers and development consultants peddling formulas that had succeeded in other cities.

Three other striking differences between Omuta and Flint paralleled events in the promotion of tourism. First, large-scale private sector shopping mall projects were planned in both cities. Omuta's big project languished in the planning stages for several years and was ultimately never built, while Flint's big project was constructed and quickly went bankrupt. There seems to be a pattern in the differences in oversight and attitudes toward risk in the two cities. Second, private foundations—the Mott Foundation and the Enterprise Development Corporation—played a central role in retail area revitalization in Flint. There were no such private sector philanthropic organizations or venture capitalists in Omuta. The foundation's efforts in this project were counterproductive, however. Instead of supporting an innovative approach to retail area redevelopment, the foundation conservatively backed a proven successful developer and his stock idea that he was replicating across the country. A recent study of foundations and of their impact on health care reform policy concludes that foundations are in a position to do good because they are accountable to almost no one and they have the funds to act on innovative ideas. Yet their behavior in the health policy arena suggests that foundations do not push innovation and instead act rather timidly, only rarely pushing the frontiers of policy.[1] These conclusions apply to the foundation's behavior in Flint's redevelopment efforts as well. Third, despite the fact that numerous local actors have an interest in downtown retail revitalization, only in Omuta was there a serious attempt to involve merchants in the project planning and implementation process. There are both cultural and structural reasons for this last difference, and I will elaborate on them after recounting the stories from each city.

OMUTA'S SHÔTENGAI

National policy offerings played a large role in shaping downtown shopping area redevelopment in Omuta. The city consciously sought out national programs it could use for downtown redevelopment. It was particularly reliant on the Ministry of International Trade and Industry (MITI) for funding and guidance. But the city also helped to institutionalize a redevelopment process that became standard operating procedure in the community and beyond: the study, planning, and construction of revitalized shopping streets (*shôtengai*) in Omuta. Omuta's shopping areas were organized into eight shôtengai associations, each of which used the same procedure to plan and implement its revitalization plan. Shôtengai are an integral part of every community in Japan, and virtually every neighborhood in every city has such an agglomeration of small shops running through it. Shôtengai merchants sell anything one might need on a daily basis including clothes, fresh and processed foods, household goods, and appliances. These stores are usually small mom-and-pop operations, though a larger store may sometimes anchor one end of a shôtengai.

The bulk of Omuta's retail area redevelopment revolved around a national program: MITI's "Community Mart Plan" (Komyunitî Mâto Kôsô). Although this was not the only national program from which Omuta received funds, it was the largest. The Community Mart Plan, first implemented in 1984, was aimed at the long-term revitalization of Japan's shôtengai. Though I was unable to determine the origins of the idea for this program, it is a top-down effort whose goal is to stimulate urban redevelopment. Through this plan, MITI sought to meet the anticipated changing needs of communities by expanding the function of the old shôtengai from simply a place where people only shopped to more of a community nexus or village square (*kurashi no hiroba*). Modernization was the focus of the program.[2] MITI designated twenty-eight model cities for this program, Omuta among them. The first four cities designated in 1984 were

Chitose, Takasaki, Maebashi, and Nagoya. The following year MITI designated fourteen more cities. The final group of ten model cities was designated in 1986; Omuta was selected as one of the final cities in this third
year. Cities from all over the Japanese archipelago were represented,
including Hakodate, Kitakami (Iwate Prefecture), Akita, Ota (Gunma
Prefecture), Kawagoe, Sagamihara, Taitô-ku (Tokyo), Kawasaki, Komatsu,
Daitô (Shizuoka Prefecture), Okayama, Kumamoto, Otsu, Fukui, Toyama,
Kanazawa, Saga, and Kagoshima.

The selection process was one to which Japanese cities are accus-
tomed: The ministry called for proposals from any interested city, and the
cities responded by submitting applications to MITI for consideration.
The application included a demonstration of need for revitalization plus a
detailed long-term plan for shôtengai redevelopment. The program's
vague goal left plenty of latitude for innovation at the local level, but
Omuta demonstrated little creativity in its shôtengai revitalization
schemes. Instead, it copied shôtengai in other cities. MITI obviously
approved of Omuta's approach, because the city was selected from among
more than one hundred applications.

Why was Omuta's application approved by MITI? Mayor Shiotsuka
maintained that demonstrating an ability to get a project done easily was
the key to getting approval from the national agencies.[3] He referred to
the excellent application assembled by various community participants
including the city hall staff, the Omuta Chamber of Commerce, and
the shôtengai merchants' associations. The application was indeed clear.
It portrayed a strong sense that the city knew what it needed to do
and knew how to go about implementing the project. The proposed
revitalization was broken down into stages, and a detailed plan of attack
was provided for each shôtengai section. A brief history of each of
the eight shôtengai was recounted as part of the effort to demonstrate
the need for revitalization of the area. Flow charts, schedules, and
step-by-step schemes outlined each subsection of the shôtengai redevelopment program.

But the city's planning process took organization of the project to an
extreme, especially when one considers that this was only one part of a
redevelopment plan in a city of only one hundred fifty thousand. There
seemed to be far more administration involved than was really needed.
Figure 4.1 diagrams the organization. Responsibility for the whole process
was divided among four types of committees, each of which operated at a
different level of detail. The duties of each committee were vaguely
spelled out in a few sentences in the Model Project Report.[4] From the
broadest level to the most detailed level they were the Community Mart
Promotion Committee (Suishin Iinkai), which oversaw the overall flow of

the plans and appeared largely ceremonial; the Specialist Sectional Meeting (Senmon Bukai), which oversaw the actual progress of efforts surrounding each shôtengai and served as a troubleshooter for problems that might arise in all the redevelopment projects; the Management Committee (Kanji-Kai), which served primarily as a conduit for information between the higher committees and the actual working level subcommittees implementing the plans; and subcommittees (Bunka-kai, numbered one through four), which handled the actual implementation of the plans.

Figure 4.1: Omuta Shôtengai Planning Committee Structure

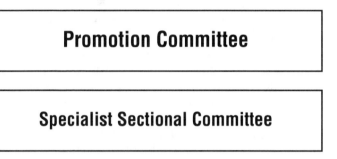

There was considerable membership overlap among the committees, which served to blur the distinctions between them. In addition, one person chaired the Promotion, Specialist Sectional Meeting, and Management committees simultaneously. Three of the four subcommittees were chaired by men who also sat on these three committees simultaneously. Even though the formal structure appeared inclusive and aimed at consensus, decision-making power was concentrated in the hands of a few individuals. The actual actions of the committees are described in the following planning section.

What was the purpose of this highly developed mechanism for administrative consultation? It seems to have been aimed at legitimating decisions made by the local small business elite. Shôtengai redevelopment was potentially very conflictual. Although everyone agreed on the need to revitalize the shopping areas, there was no consensus on how that should be done. Each shôtengai consisted of a number of shop owners who had different ideas about what would work. Most Omuta shôtengai had three factions.[5] The centrist faction was usually the insiders, those closest to the city government and to the Chamber of Commerce. The centrists often had experience in dealing with the bureaucracy and usually proposed and carried out the projects. The other two factions usually took positions of wanting either more or less radical change or development.

The potential conflict was managed through *nemawashi*, an informal consultation with participants before any real decisions are made, and the committee system was the arena in which this consultation occurred. Getting many small businessmen to agree on anything is difficult. The Chamber of Commerce and city hall officials played central roles in getting faction leaders together to work out any disagreements.[6] City, prefectural, and national officials were involved in redevelopment planning and had their own ideas. Though the committee structure seemed excessive, it created veto points for local participants to have some input, and helped to minimize the chance of a minority being quickly railroaded into a decision they did not like.

From MITI's perspective, the application and local unity were less important than the mere presence of Shiotsuka as mayor. MITI looked for an activist *jinzai* (person of talent) in an influential position at the local level who could shepherd a project to fruition.[7] There was no such leader in Omuta prior to Shiotsuka's election in 1986. Previous mayors were Mitsui products who focused on coal industry subsidies instead of thinking about moving Omuta away from coal. MITI liked Shiotsuka for two reasons, according to one official. First, the mayor was capable of sparking the creation of a regional identity for Omuta, something the city has lacked in the past. He was a visionary mayor rather than a hands-on administrator. MITI officials liked this. They saw him as a stark contrast to mayors who only focus on handouts that come down the pipe from Tokyo. Second, in MITI's eyes Shiotsuka was a leader from the same mold as Governors Hiramatsu (Oita Prefecture) and Hosokawa (Kumamoto Prefecture). These governors in prefectures adjacent to Fukuoka were known for their innovative ideas. In addition, MITI officials admired their personnel management skills. Hiramatsu defined his broad goals for Oita, then he chose the youngest and most capable people he could for his staff. He also sought out younger talent at the local level from the private sector to work with. At least one MITI official believed Shiotsuka operated in a similar manner. He even hinted that Shiotsuka might eventually run for governor in Fukuoka.[8]

Though Shiotsuka may have impressed MITI officials as a visionary and as an innovator, the policies generated under his administration were not new ideas. They were ideas that worked elsewhere, and were therefore likely to please officials in any bureaucratic agency. Shiotsuka himself came from such an organization. The mayor's image and his administration's activities do not appear to have been closely related. It is possible that MITI officials liked Shiotsuka simply because they saw him as one of their own.

The fact that Omuta was designated as one of the twenty-eight "model cities" does not necessarily mean that the city and national ministries were undertaking a truly innovative approach to urban redevelopment. Instead, they copied a successful idea already in operation in at least one Japanese city. The notion of a retail area serving as a multi-functional community center was already under development in Fukuoka City 50 miles to the north. The IMS Building, in the heart of downtown Fukuoka, was viewed with envy by those in Omuta who sought to revitalize the downtown area. IMS was a twelve-story multiuse facility that was jammed with patrons from its opening in 1989. It contained plenty of stores, restaurants, and movie theaters like any mall. But it also housed art galleries; automobile dealerships (on the seventh floor!); classroom space for community education programs such as cooking and computer skills; a radio station that holds interactive activities with IMS patrons; and a nonprofit, very active intercultural exchange organization called "Rainbow Plaza." Officials in Omuta had a strong desire to copy this facility.[9]

IMS was not a traditional shôtengai, since it included car dealers and the regional utilities companies (Saibu Gas and the Kyushu Electric Power Co.), but it was primarily an association of small merchants—clothing, boutiques, restaurants, and other retail operations. It was built in an area adjacent to more traditional shôtengai, and pedestrian traffic patterns made it an integrated part of the downtown shopping area.

Omuta had eight shôtengai, each defined by a merchants' association. They were connected to one another by a maze of narrow streets and alleys. A central focus of the shopping street area was the large Matsuya department store, which abutted several of the shopping streets. Though fundamentally different from the shôtengai, Matsuya was a central part of the downtown shopping district. First opened in 1936, Matsuya had 250 employees in 1987 and did $533 million in business in 1987.[10] In addition to the renewal of the shôtengai, Omuta's Community Mart plan called for the conversion of Matsuya into a large, multiuse retail facility modeled after IMS in Fukuoka City. Matsuya was committed to the project, and agreed to become part of the integrated shopping area revitalization scheme. Together, these nine projects were lumped together under the Japanese-English catchphrase "Area Nine."

Details of the Planning

Area Nine was not surprisingly divided into nine administrative subsections corresponding to the eight shôtengai and Matsuya. The whole shôtengai area was anchored by two foci of activity: Shinsakai-machi shôtengai to the north and the Ginza-dôri shôtengai (including the Matsuya department store) to the south; four hundred meters of shôtengai district running north-south connected the two anchors. The whole area was cut in half by the Miike Railway and by the Omuta River, both of which run east-west.

After winning the Community Mart model city designation in late 1986, shôtengai planning shifted into high gear at the local level. The planning process was notable for its formality and openness. Committee meetings were held frequently to facilitate input from local residents. In addition to formal committee meetings, extra sessions were held with relevant neighborhood associations (*chônai-kai*) to convey intentions, to get feedback, and to generally keep everyone informed about the progress of the project.

The real planning for the Community Mart program in Omuta started in the Management Committee in November of 1986, after the city received approval from MITI. The committee commissioned a survey of local merchants and residents to determine the needs of the community. An analysis was undertaken by the Chamber of Commerce and officials from the Omuta City Hall Economic Bureau on the condition, problems, and activities in each of the subdivisions. The study was funded by a $110,000-grant from MITI and by a matching $110,000 from Fukuoka Prefecture.[11] The resulting report focused on the most serious problems facing the planners. Vehicular traffic patterns were dangerous and/or inconvenient for pedestrians, for example, the Central Ginza Shôtengai (one of the nine) was bisected by the now defunct Miike railway, the private railroad that used to carry coal from the mine to various local factories; the Honmachi Shôtengai was divided by the Omuta River, which lacked a good bridge to link the two sides. Several areas had too many stores that had gone out of business. Dingy, dark, and old store facades were unappealing to shoppers, and some of the buildings were too decrepit to use. The overwhelming image of decay was not conducive to a prosperous retail sector.

In December of 1986 the Management Committee met again, this time in conjunction with the Specialist Sectional meeting, reviewed the survey results, and started work on a plan and schedule to redevelop the shôtengai area. The Management Committee also established a working group at this time to handle most of the routine work. Two days later the four sub-committees met for the first time—all together—to discuss the project schedule (long- and short-term). Ten days later the Management Committee meet again to formalize the schedule and general plan of attack. On December 24, 1986, an overview of the project and a tentative schedule for completion was presented, along with the results of the survey, at a neighborhood association session at the local workers' hall (*shokuin kaikan*).[12]

The plan generated to address Omuta's retail area problems was loaded with capital-intensive projects. It called for streets to be repaved, widened, and in some cases closed to vehicular traffic. It called for streetlights to be replaced with brighter and more stylish fixtures, covered shopping promenades with motorized roof sections to be constructed, trees to be planted, and bridges to be rebuilt and strengthened. It also called for more parking facilities and for more open public space to be created. Certain private sector improvements were required to better the image of Omuta's retail district, such as new store facades.

The mix of public and private projects suggested that although the government was involved in the process, the costs and responsibilities for much of the revitalization effort were borne by private actors. As figure 4.2 suggests, the planned division of labor placed a large chunk of the work required firmly on the local private sector actors.[13] Though road, pedestrian space, and park area improvements were done by the city, they were integrated with new covered arcade structures that were paid for by the shôtengai associations themselves. Several of the shôtengai associations also funded "pocket space" facilities, smaller public spaces in addition to the city-funded park facilities.

There are several points worth noting about this plan. First, despite all the publicity and fanfare given to the fact that Omuta was selected as a model city for a nationally sponsored project, the national government was only directly responsible for one small portion of the entire city shôtengai redevelopment scheme: the repair and improvement of sidewalks along the national route that runs through the middle of Omuta and that abuts the shôtengai district. And even this part of the project was done in conjunction with the Chiku-machi shôtengai merchants' association. Despite the fact that some funds from the national ministries were used in the overall effort, local business leaders emphasized the fact that shôtengai redevelopment is primarily a private sector effort.[14] The official division of responsibility seems to support this assertion.

Second, a number of the projects composing the revitalization plan that one might expect to fall under the purview of the city were in fact

Figure 4.2: Section Plan, by Shôtengai

Shôtengai	Improvement	Financially Responsible Entity
Chiku-machi	Arcade improvement	Shôtengai Association
	Route 208 improvement	City
	Kinhira Shrine Facilities	Shrine
	Kinhira Shrine Park Facilities	City
	Chamber of Commerce parking structure	Chamber of Commerce
	Rail bed greenery project	City
	Individual store remodeling	Individual stores
Ginza St.	Arcade improvement	Shôtengai Association
	Sidewalk improvement	Shôtengai Association
	Rail bed greenery project	City
	Individual store remodeling	Individual stores
Central Ginza St.	Arcade improvement	Shôtengai Association
	Sidewalk improvement	Shôtengai Association
	City street improvement	City
	Individual store remodeling	Individual stores
Hon-dori	Arcade entrance color block paving	City
	Individual store remodeling	Individual stores
Miyamae St.	Street facilities	Shôtengai Association
	Omuta Shrine facilities	Shôtengai Association
	Private "pocket space" facilities	Private firms
	2-chrome facilities	Shôtengai Association
	Foot bridge construction	City
	Individual store remodeling	Individual stores
Sakae St.	Arcade improvement	Shôtengai Association
	Entrance gate	Shôtengai Association
	Rail bed greenery project	Private firms
	Private "pocket space" facilities	Private firms
	Foot bridge construction	City
	Individual store remodeling	Individual stores
Dai-ichi	Parking facilities	Shôtengai Association
	City road improvements	City
	Prefectural road greenery project	Prefecture
New Ginza	Arcade improvement	Shôtengai Association
	Individual store remodeling	Individual stores
Matsuya	Parking facilities	Matsuya
	Storefront area	Matsuya

Figure 4.3: Overview of Budget for Ginza Area Arcade Projects

Shōtengai Association (S.A.)	Project	Total Cost (¥1,000)	S.A. contribution (¥1,000)	Govt. contribution (¥1,000)
Chiku-machi	Arcade improvement	328,800	246,704	82,096
Ginza St.	Arcade improvement	204,215	203,744	471
Central Ginza St.	Arcade new construction	129,899	129,899	0
Miyamae St.	Open mall facilities	35,991	21,658	14,333
Sakae-machi	Shopping promenade	63,202	18,599	44,603
Total		762,107	620,604	141,503

done by the private sector. Some sidewalk repair and improvement, pocket space facilities that provide quiet corners for public use, and some of the parking facilities were done by the private sector. Yet other sidewalks, pocket spaces, and parking were under the jurisdiction of the city.

Finally, in reality the distinction between public and private was more blurred than this plan overview indicates. Planning for each shôtengai was done in the four subcommittee (*bunka-kai*) meetings made up of landowners, residents, and store owners and proprietors. Each of the subcommittees met separately in January 1987, to generate plans for their own specific shôtengai area.[15] However, Chamber of Commerce and city hall officials sat in on these sessions to make sure that planning went smoothly and that laws and guidelines were followed.[16] These official ex officio committee members played an important role in three respects. First, they helped mediate differences of opinion among private sector participants. By suggesting which options might be more feasible, they were able to influence the committees' decision processes. Second, by virtue of the fact that the same officials attended meetings for all nine project subdivisions, they had a better sense of the overall direction of the redevelopment efforts. Their oversight helped to ensure that all the decisions about details would fit together into a coherent whole. Third, they smoothed the permit process required for all the construction and changes. This last role was a potentially contentious area, in that city and prefectural officials held potential veto power over all construction through the granting or refusal of permits. But all of the differences were apparently hammered out in the secrecy of committees, and there was no evidence of serious conflict at the local level.

In addition to consulting with all the local players on the committees, planners also sought outside support for their ideas. In February 1987, the city sponsored a meeting with academic specialists in the urban redevelopment field at a top Fukuoka hotel. The participants included professors from the top three universities in the region and from the Fukuoka city planner. A fifth participant was from the regional development research section of Japan Consultant Group, a private Tokyo consulting firm. Central private and public sector players from Omuta presented the overall scheme, intentions, and piece-by-piece plans for each of the shôtengai. In turn they received comments from the assembled scholars. No major changes resulted from these consultations, and plans continued to evolve on the local level.

Committee meetings at all levels happened frequently in late 1986 and early 1987. Between November 1986, and April 1987, the Management Committee met seven times, suggesting that most of the important work was being done at that level. During that same period, the Community

Mart Promotion Committee only met three times, the Specialist Sectional Meeting met five times, and the four subcommittees—each headed by a member of the Management Committee—each met six times.[17] Not all consultations happened in Omuta and Fukuoka, however. In early March 1987, the Management Committee, along with representatives from the Chamber of Commerce and city hall, made two site visits to inspect shôtengai in other cities. First they went to Yamaguchi City, on the western end of Honshu, where they toured several shôtengai and sat through a presentation at the Yamaguchi Chamber of Commerce office. They then went to Tsuyama, a small city in neighboring Okayama Prefecture, where they were treated to the same routine.[18] These visits were made to discuss ideas, to exchange views on shopping area redevelopment, and to give Omuta planners a chance to see how revitalization is done in other cities.[19]

FINANCING SHÔTENGAI REDEVELOPMENT

Financing was primarily done through the Small and Medium Enterprise Project Organization (Chû-Shô Kigyô Jigyô Dantai), another of Japan's public corporations that specializes in small-scale cooperative projects like this. Even though grants from the national ministries were received, they were small relative to the total cost of the projects. The grants mainly served to demonstrate government support for the project, a sign of encouragement to private sector financial institutions. Data on actual financial packages for all the shôtengai were difficult to acquire, though fairly detailed cost figures were provided by the Omuta Chamber of Commerce for the five sections completed in 1992.

As figure 4.3 indicates, the total cost of the five arcade rehabilitation projects completed through 1988 was over $4.23 million. Of this total, the national government provided only $800,000, and the rest was financed privately by the various shôtengai associations. This accounts for only a small portion of the public outlay for the Ginza Area revitalization strategy, however. Including road improvements (local, prefectural, and national routes), bridge construction, park areas, and planting new green space, the total public spending rose to $5 million. Private spending for the projects, including the Matsuya project, was $29.4 million, almost six times the amount of public money spent.[20]

The operation of the Chû-Shô Kigyô Jigyô Dantai reinforces the image of Japanese intergovernmental relations as vertical and formulaic in nature. The flow of money from the national to the local level always goes through the prefectural administration. The loan comes down to the local level via the prefecture, and loans are repaid upward via the same path.

The types of projects that can explicitly be financed this way include shopping arcades, colored street and sidewalk paving, public parking facilities, small public parks, streetlights, and anything else that can be considered community facilities. Omuta financed all these things through the Chû-Shô Kigyô Jigyô Dantai loan program.

This program is part of the government's Fiscal Investment and Loan Program (FILP). According to Johnson, it is

> called a plan both because it includes a large measure of central direction of the economy and to disguise its status as a budget. It is popularly known as the "second budget." Almost 50 percent of the size of the official national budget, its funds are used to finance the national policy companies and public corporations of Japan. From its origins in 1953 until early 1973, . . . the FILP was totally under the control of the economic bureaucrats and was used to promote the plans they approved. Today it is submitted to the Diet along with the General Account Budget for parliamentary approval, but it is still a major fiscal planning institution of the Japanese government.[21]

There are three formulas for financing local projects, depicted in figure 4.4. The first is the standard financing formula, while the other two require special permission under section 4 of the Medium and Small Retail Trade Promotion Law (Chû Shô Ko-urishôgyô Shinkô-hô). Financing under this ordinance was provided only for projects that would otherwise not occur, for projects that would serve a public good, or for projects undertaken by a group of private actors. Seventy-five percent of the public funds came from the Small and Medium Enterprise Project Organization at the national level, and the prefecture contributed the remaining 25 percent.[22] Omuta was permitted to use the most favorable third option.

As the cost figures show, the national government was not a major contributor of outright grants to the actual shôtengai revitalization effort. But substantial public funds were allocated for five projects aimed at supporting the redevelopment plan. An estimated $5 million was committed to national and prefectural route (road) improvements, Chiku-machi Park construction, Omuta River improvements, and bridge restoration. Plantings and greenery were a large part of these improvement plans.[23] There was a lot of coordination required to pull together all the small pieces of the overall revitalization scheme.

The Matsuya project was the largest part of the overall plan. The new facility was planned to house all of Matsuya's current departments plus a number of nonaffiliated retail tenants. The entire shopping center was to

Figure 4.4: Project Financing Formulae

<table>
<tr>
<td>A</td>
<td>Publicly Financed loan

65%

2.7% interest for 15 years</td>
<td>Privately Financed

35%</td>
</tr>
</table>

<table>
<tr>
<td>B</td>
<td>Publicly Financed loan

80%

0.0% interest for 20 years</td>
<td>Privately Financed

20%</td>
</tr>
</table>

<table>
<tr>
<td>C</td>
<td>Publicly Financed loan

80%

0.0% interest for 20 years</td>
<td>Privately Financed

13%</td>
<td>7% as grant from city</td>
</tr>
</table>

Options B and C are possible only if awarded permission under Part Four of the Small and Medium Enterprise Promotion Law.

be managed by Matsuya. The total projected cost of revitalizing the Matsuya department store complex was $29.4 million, of which only $4 million was expected to be covered by grant money. The remaining sum was to be financed privately with local and regional banks, paid back over twenty years with an annual interest rate of 8 percent. For this price, construction at Matsuya included 11,300 square meters of retail space, 10,900 square meters of parking structure, 4,000 square meters of housing, and 400 square meters of a multi-use annex.[24]

IMPLEMENTATION OF THE PLAN

Shôtengai redevelopment is a long-term project that Omuta pursued in small steps. One reason for the cautious approach was the air of experimentation surrounding the cooperation of the private sector, city hall, the prefecture, and national bureaucracies. The traditional vertical administration (*tatewari gyôsei*) has been modified in Omuta's *shôtengai* efforts. Specifically, interministerial cooperation occurred at a very fine level of detail, something the agencies usually do not do. This modification was apparent in the implementation of the city's redevelopment plans. The level of detail to which national bureaucratic jurisdiction and involvement extended was remarkable by American standards. A second reason for the slow project implementation was the fragmentation at the local level. Even though all shôtengai were part of the same national grant, each was planned and implemented by a different group of people. Smaller projects were completed quickly, while the larger projects took more time. The earliest segment was finished in 1988, while the largest, the Matsuya effort, had yet to break ground in 1994.

The first stage completed under the Community Mart program was part of the Miyamae-dôri Open Mall project. Finished in the spring of 1988, the project included such minor amenities as paving two sections of street with color blocks and putting in new streetlights. Colored paving blocks replaced the plain asphalt surface of a 136–meter stretch of Miyamae Street (Miyamae-dôri). This section of road is in the heart of the thirty-one shops that make up the Miyamae-dori Cooperative Association (Miyamae-dôri Kyôdô Kumiai), one of the eight merchants' associations in the city. Miyamae-dôri runs through the Ginza section (Ginza-chiku) of Omuta, which has been a retail center since before the Second World War. Interspersed with decorative tiles made from Miike Coal, the total cost of the project was $12,000.[25]

Although Miyamae-dôri is officially a street, it is used mostly as a pedestrian walkway in this area. To put colored pavers down correctly, the road bed needed to be regraded and modified substantially. These modifications were paid for by the city, since roads are city property. Roadbed changes require Ministry of Construction approval and supervision. But the money for the color blocks came from MITI's Community Mart project, so the road surface construction came under MITI's jurisdiction. This is a rare division of labor in Japan, according to Omuta Chamber of Commerce officials. The Ministry of Construction and MITI cooperated at a very fine level of detail. This cooperation was the most novel aspect of shôtengai redevelopment in Omuta. Beppu city hall representatives from neighboring Oita Prefecture came to visit twice and to observe the process—the administrative process, that is.[26]

Chamber of Commerce officials commented on the fact that there were so many details to handle. In addition to planning and financing, permits were required for each physical change made. Strategic agreements made along the way among shôtengai merchants were hard to maintain. Construction permits and variances were done individually, and getting these took time and expertise. Again, the Chamber of Commerce and city hall officials helped work out rough spots. Many meetings were held at the prefectural head office and police headquarters, city police office, city fire department, and city hall. Expertise, special knowledge, and contacts were the keys to getting these projects underway. The Chamber of Commerce functioned as a coordinator between the private and public sectors.[27]

The Miyamae-dôri project was completed in April of 1988. Several smaller projects in the district were started and finished in 1989.[28] On September 28, 1990, the Ginza Street Shôtengai Promotion Association broke ground on the largest of the cooperative projects in the shôtengai revitalization plan, the Ginza Street Arcade and color-paving project. The last major upgrade of this shôtengai was done in 1968, and it was due for an overhaul. This was finished just three months later, and opened to the public on December 6, 1990. The total cost of the project was $1.42 million.[29] How was it completed so quickly? The paving was done by the same firm and in the same manner as the Miyamae-dôri project, which made the process essentially a repeat of the earlier project. Also, the arcade they erected was a prefabricated structure that only required bolting into place. The orange- and red-colored paving blocks contrasted with the white and glass arcade structure, creating what observers saw as a "bright mood" for the old arcade.[30]

Sakae-machi started its construction on a new covered arcade and colored paving block scheme in September of 1991. This merchants' association waited until the private Nishitetsu Railway Company opened a new station abutting the shôtengai. The station provided direct access to express trains to Fukuoka City to the north, and ensured a larger volume of potential customers passing through the area. Another reason for the delay involved negotiations with the city on sewer pipe construction in the area. Only about 40 percent of homes and businesses in Omuta are connected to city sewer lines, and Sakae-machi is one of those areas with sewer service. But the grant from MITI did not cover sewage system construction, and the merchants' association was not willing to assume the cost. The city was willing to finance the sewer improvement, so the merchants received permission to revitalize the shôtengai. Except for the train station and the sewer service, Sakae-machi is pretty much like the other shôtengai. Finished at the end of April 1992, the Sakae-machi revitalization project cost $1.4 million. The city had to allocate an additional $460,000 in additional funds to cover the sewer construction.[31]

COMMUNITY MART'S LOOSE END: MATSUYA

At the end of my stay in Fukuoka, the Matsuya project was still on the drawing board. Though it was part of the original Community Mart plan, it did not come to fruition along with the shôtengai projects for several reasons. First, it was a much larger project in terms of capital commitment and area. The plan went through several iterations, but never gelled into a firm strategy on which everyone agreed. The earliest version estimated a total cost of $5.2 million.[32] But a year and a half later the plan called for a four-building complex costing an estimated $9.3 million.[33] In 1992 the plan had grown further still, with the total cost estimated at $10.4 million, despite cutting the plan back to a three-building complex.[34]

Second, the players were different from the other Community Mart segments. Matsuya is a large national corporation with a huge store in Fukuoka City, and smaller branches around the region. It is not clear that the Matsuya company wanted to sink as much capital into Omuta as they initially promised. Although periodic announcements of construction plans demonstrated unity among the initial late-1980s Community Mart players, the lack of progress on the project indicated otherwise. Matsuya, like the various Mitsui concerns, probably saw the writing on the wall vis-à-vis Omuta's future. The company expressed concern that they would have trouble finding tenants to fill the space in the proposed Omuta complex.[35] This was a valid concern, especially given the Japanese national recession in the early 1990s.

OTHER PROGRAMS

Community Mart was not the only national program that Omuta tapped for benefits. The city also received assistance from MITI's "New Commercial Consolidation Construction Planning Assistance Project" (Shin Shôgyô Shûsekinado Kôzô Sakutei Hojô Jigyô) in 1989. MITI created the program to respond to a perceived need in older, inner city shôtengai. Older shopping areas were losing business to suburban stores with large, American-style parking lots. These modern "roadside shôtengai" were meeting a demand for shopping that was easily accessible by car. The project sought to improve traffic patterns in shopping areas and to provide more customer parking in inner city areas. The biggest problem in achieving this goal was land acquisition, and the grant money was to be used in part to purchase downtown land for parking.[36]

Administered by MITI's Small and Medium Business Agency, the program selected six sites from across the country to serve as model project sites. Omuta's Yoshino area was chosen, the only such site in Kyushu. The city received $50,000 in grant money, half of which came from the prefecture and half from the national government.[37] Subsequent planning and development of the Yoshino area occurred in the same way the central shôtengai areas were revitalized. A local planning committee was established, and it worked in concert with city hall and Chamber of Commerce officials to compile ideas. Road improvements, commercial promotion, and regional development themes forced cooperation along the lines of that seen in the larger projects. Yoshino revitalization went smoothly, in particular because the local leaders followed the path cut by other shôtengai redevelopers before them.

FLINT'S WATER STREET PAVILION

Revitalization of the center city shopping area was a priority in Flint, just as it was in Omuta. The big difference was that the shôtengai project was a revitalization of existing shopping areas led by the stores themselves, while the Flint projects ultimately became a developer's attempt to construct a new downtown specialty mall from scratch. The focus of revitalization efforts in this area was an elaborate shopping mall project ultimately called "Water Street Pavilion." It was built between the Hyatt Hotel complex and the University of Michigan-Flint campus, on the south bank of the Flint River just across from Auto World. Opened in 1985, it cost $29.5 million to build. Like Auto World and the Hyatt, it failed to turn a profit. Water Street Pavilion went into receivership in 1986, becoming city property when the owners could not meet loan payments.

The story of Water Street Pavilion is much like that of Auto World: energy for the project was provided by local economic elites and politicians; early financial support was provided by the foundation and by grants from the federal government; and well-known private sector consultants and developers were hired to design and build the project, based on successful ideas they had implemented elsewhere.

Downtown development in Flint was dominated by private sector actors and local politicians. Politicians provided the energy to get the project rolling, while businesspeople raised most of the project capital, planned the project, and implemented the plans. In March 1978, Flint mayor James Rutherford announced a proposed plan for a new downtown shopping plaza—called "City Center Plaza"—to the city council and to downtown business managers. Rutherford had been working on and pushing the plan for more than a year, but this was the most public exposure the plan had received to date.

EARLY EFFORTS AT RETAIL REVITALIZATION

Rutherford maintained that the plan could be financed with few local tax dollars, one of the key selling points when the plan was revealed. The mayor went to Washington in April for meetings with officials in the

Departments of Commerce, Transportation, and Housing and Urban Development. Lawrence P. Ford, president of the Flint Area Chamber of Commerce and James Sheaffer, president of the Flint Area Conference Inc. (FACI), were part of the local group that traveled to Washington with Rutherford. Sen. Donald Riegle (D-Michigan) and Rep. Dale Kildee (D-Flint) scheduled the meetings at the federal agencies.[38]

The Flint delegation was optimistic about getting federal grants for several reasons. First, Rutherford argued that City Center Plaza would be a unique approach to downtown redevelopment. The early plan called for a new structure that would completely enclose existing downtown businesses. No other city in the nation had tried that type of project. Plaza proponents claimed it was the answer to the shopping problem downtown for cities in northern climates. Second, Rutherford held high hopes of getting federal assistance because of the timing of Flint's request. Flint, a Democratic party stronghold, was asking a Democratic administration for aid. President Carter was aware of Flint because it was his final stop on the campaign trail prior to the 1976 election. While this sounded good in the abstract, it is unlikely that Carter's Flint visit had much to do with the city's access to federal development assistance for this project. Third, and perhaps most important, Rutherford had lined up local representatives at the state and federal level to pressure federal and state agencies to meet Flint's requests for assistance. In addition to Riegle and Kildee in Washington, Rutherford won the support of Michigan State House speaker Bobby Crim, a Democrat from nearby Davison.[39] Political support for the project was in place. Next the city had to present a credible plan for the plaza.

The initial proposal was designed by MacKenzie, Knuth, and Klein, a Flint firm. It called for an elaborate system of covered walkways, plazas, and elevated crossovers for the downtown area. The estimated cost was $14.6 million, though one member of the design firm acknowledged that the plans could be scaled down. The city council responded with cautious optimism. Although they were impressed with the plan, they were also unwilling to see the city get overextended financially.[40]

Though the political timing for governmental assistance requests may have been a positive factor, the local retail climate was dismal. Commercial atrophy in the downtown area accelerated, and the Center City Plaza idea changed as more retailers closed their doors. Project champion Rutherford and the Plaza designers altered the plans to accommodate the closings. Ironically, as downtown conditions worsened, the plan grew bigger.[41] Numerous smaller merchants closed their shops in 1978 and 1979, unable to wait for the "new" downtown to become a reality. Larger retailers—such as the J. C. Penney and Smith-Bridgeman department stores—were unwilling or unable to maintain their presence downtown.

J. C. Penney closed its downtown store and opened two new stores in suburban Flint malls. Smith-Bridgeman, which might have been able to survive if its desired renovation grant from the foundation had come through, simply went out of business when the foundation balked. The larger City Center Plaza scheme briefly grew to a large retail-office-convention-apartment district that proponents hoped would attract visitors on its own merits.[42]

THE PLAN BECOMES A REALITY

During the recession of the early 1980s, the project languished. The city could not justify a major investment in mass-merchandising store facilities for the downtown area. In 1983, the idea resurfaced and picked up momentum again. In 1983 Peter R. Gluck, an urban studies professor at the University of Michigan-Flint and the secretary-treasurer of the National Urban Affairs Association, came out in support of the downtown plaza:

> I hope Center City will be pursued, and that it will contain more than mass-merchandising stores. I have no objection to those kinds of stores, but we have plenty of them already [in the suburban malls].[43]

Gluck pointed out that unless Flint could propose a better project than the suburban malls, there was no point in doing anything.

This time the Downtown Development Authority (DDA) took the lead. After consulting with the city and with the foundation, the DDA set out to do something different with the City Center Plaza scheme. With the aid of a $3.8-million foundation grant, the DDA decided to buy most of the downtown properties needed for the proposed City Center Plaza. The DDA—representing merchants in the downtown area—voted in March 1983, to purchase eighteen buildings in the downtown area, even though neither the DDA nor the city had settled on a completed plan for City Center Plaza. A confident Mayor Rutherford dismissed suggestions that buying the property before the plans were worked out was risky. He boldly guaranteed that the plaza project would not fall through.[44]

What was the role of the foundation in downtown retail area revitalization? The foundation initially intended to support the City Center Plaza idea by providing funds for the purchase of properties that would then become part of the development project. Foundation president William S. White asserted that the foundation would put up $4 million to $5 million for land acquisition, but it would not finance construction of the shopping mall.[45] The foundation initially gave the DDA $3.8 million for the project's land costs. At this point in 1983, plans for City Center Plaza envisioned a construction project encompassing several downtown city blocks. The DDA used the foundation grant to purchase eighteen of the twenty-seven buildings required in the plan. Nine property owners held out, refusing to sell to the DDA-foundation team for various reasons. Some owners felt they were not offered enough money for their properties, while others could not sell because of legal disputes or conflicts among multiple part-owners of single properties. The foundation's support for the DDA-city hall plan virtually guaranteed that resistance by a small band of downtown merchants opposed to the City Center Plaza idea would be fruitless. The DDA promised to help merchants relocate to other downtown sites if they so desired, and most went along with the idea.

Ironically, the City Center Plaza preparations accelerated the demise of the downtown merchant community. Shortly after agreeing to sell to the DDA, several downtown businesses found that they could not find suitable sites to which they could relocate. Most of those who wanted to stay downtown said they would be forced either to move to the suburbs or go out of business altogether. Several expressed bitterness at what they called city hall's lack of concern for their needs. They felt they were being kicked out of downtown, with little or no help offered to relocate. Despite the huge number of vacancies in the city, few found properties with which they were satisfied.[46] Most of the disgruntled merchants who had trouble relocating did not own their business space, but rented space in downtown buildings. The DDA was only required to buy the properties, and did not have to buy out the leases of tenants. These businesses ultimately were forced out to make room for a project that had yet to be planned concretely.

By August 1983, the DDA had acquired twenty-three of the twenty-seven properties in the area slated for the planned City Center Plaza. The other four were purchased by the foundation directly, at a cost of $442,000. All were marked for demolition to make room for the new project. The DDA said demolition would not begin until the developer was selected, though Rutherford expressed a desire to see the buildings torn down as soon as they were all acquired.[47] Despite his insistence that he wanted to increase parking spaces downtown and to provide the developer with a cleared piece of land suitable for an early start on construction, the mayor may also have had electoral concerns on his mind.

Rutherford was up for reelection in November 1983. Although he had demonstrated considerable ability to get major capital projects built during his administration, the impact of these projects on the local economy was less than expected. He may have wanted to get as far ahead on Center City Plaza as possible prior to the election. He could then claim the plaza as the catalyst that would make AutoWorld (then under construction) and the Hyatt Regency Hotel (already complete and opened) really take off. Ultimately, Rutherford lost the decision about demolishing the downtown properties, and he lost the election as well. This had little impact on the plans for City Center Plaza, which had developed sufficient momentum to continue without a political shepherd.

ROUSE TO THE RESCUE: A "FESTIVE MARKETPLACE"

Behind-the-scenes in the fall of 1983, the city, the foundation, and the DDA discussed the selection of a developer for the project. The city opened a dialogue with James Rouse, the acclaimed developer who built Baltimore's successful Inner Harbor and Boston's Quincy Market, about the possibility of his firm doing a project in Flint. In August 1982, Rouse told the *Chicago Tribune* that he was considering doing a commercial project in Flint,[48] and in late September 1983, Rouse's Enterprise Development Co. was hired by the DDA to build a project downtown. According to the initial announcement Enterprise was hired to do preliminary studies and planning for the project,[49] but the firm was confirmed as the project developer soon thereafter.

Rouse's firm was touted as the developers of successful "festive marketplace" projects in numerous other cities, including Norfolk, Virginia, and nearby Toledo, Ohio. Flint decision-makers liked what they saw in Enterprise's previous work, and hoped to replicate the formula for success in downtown Flint. Rouse's firm specialized in waterfront development projects, having created successful attractions in New York, Santa Monica, Milwaukee, and Philadelphia, in addition to those already mentioned. At the time his company operated fifty-seven urban and suburban shopping centers in the United States and in Canada.[50]

Part of the deal to lure Rouse was the commitment of $1 million by the Mott Foundation to Rouse's Enterprise Development Foundation, which assists in financing and planning community-based, low-income housing and rehabilitation projects. Mott Foundation president William White was allegedly impressed with Rouse's foundation developments.[51] There were some preliminary discussions of a Rouse foundation housing effort in Flint, but those ideas never materialized.

The selection of Rouse as the developer effectively ended the grandiose notions of a retail project encompassing several blocks of downtown Flint. City officials immediately began talking of a smaller version of the project, to be nestled on the bank of the Flint River between the Hyatt Regency Hotel and Auto World. Officials still hoped to attract a major department store to anchor the project. Though financing for the project was not yet in place, officials expected to fund the festive marketplace much as they had done for Auto World, namely through federal funds, DDA tax-increment financing, and private sources including CRI (which invested in Auto World) and perhaps even Enterprise Development itself.

Enterprise sought to replicate its past successes in Flint. In an interview with the *Flint Journal* during the planning stage, Michael S. McCall, a development manager for Enterprise, claimed that Flint's festive marketplace would probably contain many of the same features of Rouse developments in other cities. McCall observed that the markets "commonly feature colorful buildings with lots of windows and skylights; dozens of small, primarily locally owned, specialty shops and food booths; interior courtyards where people are entertained by roving musicians . . . and restaurants overlooking water or carefully designed parks."[52] McCall added that designers would study Flint's history to create a facility that would relate to the community in a unique way. McCall was confident they could build a financially successful marketplace in Flint.

Enterprise's motivation for success in Flint can be summed up in one word: *profit*. But the financial relationship between the city, the foundation, and Enterprise was rather complex. It was standard operating practice for Enterprise to take at least part ownership in its development projects. In Flint, the Rouse firm did not put down a penny of its own money for construction, but it was promised a cut of any profits earned in the future. As part of its agreement to do the project, Enterprise Development and the Enterprise Foundation received a $4-million loan from the Mott Foundation, which they jointly invested in the festive marketplace project. In return for their participation, the Enterprise groups were promised a substantial management fee, plus reimbursed expenses and a cut of any profits from operations or from any eventual sale of the property.

"The city has everything to gain and nothing to lose," said Mayor Rutherford. He also noted that the foundation sorely wanted Rouse to build the plaza because of his reputation, and that desire led to what he agreed was a good deal for the developer. The city had no real choice about accepting the deal, a tacit acknowledgment that foundation money was the force behind this project.[53] Mott Foundation officials justified their heavy investment by pointing to Rouse's experience with this type of project. That experience was seen as a virtual guarantee of success. The Enterprise groups intended to operate and to maintain the Flint marketplace much as they did their successful properties in Boston, New York, Philadelphia, and elsewhere.

In Toledo and Norfolk, Enterprise received 50 percent of the proceeds without any investment, and the Rouse companies hold 100 percent ownership in both cities. In Flint, 90 percent of the ownership was held by CRI, the same investor that lined up private funds for Auto World and for the Hyatt Regency Hotel. According to the contract, Enterprise was to be paid a management fee equal to 17.6 percent of the debt service on the project, plus an amount equal to any lease payments payable to the DDA for the marketplace site. That rent was to be paid only if there was sufficient cash flow to make the payments. Rent not paid immediately was to be added to a rental balance to be paid later, with interest. Additional incentives based on a percent of gross receipts, management fee, and gross cash flow were added to sweeten the deal for Rouse. The bottom line was that the Enterprise groups were to split 50–50 all the net proceeds from the project with the city, the DDA, and the investment partners. The foundation loan was to be repaid over twenty years as the second mortgage on the property.[54]

Once the marketplace ball was rolling, the city played only a supporting role in the project. It agreed to provide parking for the facility, to take care of road changes and improvements around the marketplace, and to establish a $1.5-million loan program to help new businesses get started in the development. It also was the conduit for federal and state grants eventually allocated for the project. The city's grant application was approved by HUD in late December 1983, and the city received $3.5 million for the plaza project. Of all the grants Flint received from HUD, this one had seemed to be the least likely to come through. HUD determined grant eligibility through a formula that centered on the amount of pre-1940s housing in a city, weighting applications from older, deteriorating cities more heavily. In the early 1980s Flint had carried out an aggressive urban renewal and slum clearance program that demolished hundreds of older homes in the city. This wholesale demolition made Flint technically ineligible for the Urban Development Action Grants (UDAG).

But political contacts prevailed over bureaucratic formulas. New mayor James A. Sharp had a key meeting with HUD assistant secretary Stephen Bollinger at a conference at Harvard University in early December. He urged the agency to take Flint's slum clearance program into account. This request, coupled with lobbying by Senator Riegle, Representative Kildee, Rep. Carl Purcell (R-Plymouth), and Foundation president White helped win the grant approval. Another factor was the strong relationship Jack A. Litzenberg, Flint's community development director, had with key UDAG program officials. He worked closely with them on earlier HUD-funded projects, and thus had more influence than a first-time applicant might have had.[55] That grant brought the total received by the city under the UDAG program to $31 million from 1979 through 1983, and stamped the festival marketplace as a "go."[56]

As the politicians worked in Washington, Rouse himself worked in nearby Baltimore to sell the project to Flint businesspeople. He met with a dozen Flint merchants and residents who went to Baltimore for a two-day workshop at Enterprise's expense. The delegation toured Rouse's Baltimore Harborplace project, and were exposed to a steady stream of reasons why a festive marketplace would work in Flint. Rouse cited the huge market within 50 miles of Flint as an untapped source of revenue. He compared Flint to Toledo and to Norfolk, where smaller festive marketplaces had opened recently. Even though the Toledo example was struggling, with annual sales of only $15 million, the Norfolk project soared to popularity, generating $60 million in sales its first year. Rouse produced figures showing that his projects in Boston, Baltimore, and Norfolk rank among the highest sales per square foot of any retail developments in the country, despite the fact that none has a major department store as a retail anchor. The folks from Flint were sold. Leroy Nesbit, vice chairman of the Flint Convention and Tourist Bureau, remarked that

> The Flint project will be an attraction for local folks as well, as long as the city and the developer think we are a part of it. . . . It is important to get local people involved in planning this project like we are today.[57]

Rouse understood this, and made a serious effort to solicit local input. He also used the local media to generate public support for the project. In a large page-one interview with the *Flint Journal*, Rouse revealed his formula for urban shopping area success. He detailed the evolution and success of his projects in Boston, Baltimore, and Norfolk, emphasizing the fact that all draw customers from out of town. The developer revealed that the Norfolk Waterside marketplace produced $450,000 in new tax revenues for the city, when only $150,000 was expected. Rouse predicted that the combination of his project and Auto World would be a smash hit. He estimated that the development would attract one-third of its customers from beyond the Flint metropolitan area.[58] No mention was made of the struggling marketplace in Toledo, just a few miles south of Detroit.

Rouse must have seen the writing on the wall, for Jacobson's department store decided not to build an anchor store for the project. The developer pointed to the success of his other projects that were not anchored to a department store. This scaled down the demolition required for construction to begin, as DDA members refused to tear down buildings without plans to build in their place.[59]

At the same time, the foundation gave the DDA another $115,000 grant to help cover Enterprise's expenses. Though still involved in planning only, Rouse's firm had already received $235,000 as an advance, in addition to the latest cash infusion.[60] But the foundation was confident that the Rouse development would succeed and upped its financial commitment to $9 million. Expressing his faith in the idea, White said,

> We have visited quite a few Rouse projects and those projects are some of the most exciting, quality urban entertainment and retail centers in the country. . . . We expect what he's planning for Flint will be just as exciting and just as good.[61]

White believed the marketplace was the missing element that would bring the existing elements—Auto World, the Hyatt Regency Hotel, and the University of Michigan-Flint campus—together.

With hype and planning running at top speed, the project manager Michael S. McCall announced the official name of the development at the end of February: Water Street Market. He also announced that Piper Realty had been selected as the local leasing agent. McCall estimated that Water Street Market would have space for sixty businesses, about half of them food-related.[62] This last figure received a cool reception from the Flint Planning Commission, however. The commission produced a list of objections to the project that included

traffic patterns and parking changes;

a riverside terrace that was considered a waste of land and a possible encouragement to loiterers; and

the absence of substantial retail developments in the marketplace.

One commissioner quipped, "It doesn't look to me like a place to go shopping, but a place to go eating." He and other commissioners had been under the impression that the original intent was to create a facility to compete with suburban shopping areas.[63] But the Planning Commission's role was to make sure the project complied with the zoning ordinance, not to make judgments on the potential success of the development. The commission's objections were ignored.

WATER STREET PAVILION: END GAME

Construction began in early April 1984. In June a snag in the financing emerged, but a $6.7-million cash advance from the foundation smoothed things over. An HUD requirement prompted Enterprise to ask for the advance. HUD refused to release any of the $3.5 million UDAG for the project until it received assurances that the project was fully funded. Enterprise asked the city for an advance, but the city refused. The foundation stepped in to resolve the impasse. HUD officials had not required such an assurance in the previous Flint UDAG projects, and attorneys for the project speculated that the requirement was different because different HUD officials were involved in processing the marketplace grant. Under the original agreement, the city's "full faith and credit" were pledged, subject to the sale of $6.7 million in tax-increment bonds in the autumn of 1984. But Enterprise could not wait for the money, and the developer also wanted to collect the UDAG in the spring. City officials refused to sell the bonds early because the city would have had to pay interest for a longer period of time.[64] The foundation bridge was repaid after the city sold the tax-increment bonds in the fall.

The final cost of construction was $29.6 million, according to figures provided by Flint's economic development administrators:[65]

Source	Amount
State of Michigan	$ 3.62 million
Federal UDAG (HUD)	$ 3.50 million
Tax Increment Bond (City)	$ 7.20 million
Downtown Development Authority	$ 2.25 million
Private Investors	$ 3.00 million
Mott Foundation	$10.00 million
Total Cost	$29.57 million

The federal government contribution was small compared to the HUD awards for other Flint projects. And the $3 million from private sources was proportionally far less than the other major capital projects done in Flint. But the foundation really wanted this project done, since it contributed more to this than to all other local projects except Auto World, which received $14 million. But Auto World was a $68 million project, far larger than this retail project.

The project name was changed in June from "Water Street Market" to "Water Street Pavilion" because of a large glass pavilion that dominated the structure. Designers also argued that the term *market* gave a slightly misleading impression of what the project was.[66] This was the final name for the development project.

The first sign of trouble for the project came when prospective tenants looked into acquiring space in the pavilion. They found the rental rates much higher than they were used to paying downtown, and even higher than space in nearby large, suburban shopping malls. Enterprise defended the high rates, saying that merchants could expect sales two or three times greater than if they were located in a regular shopping mall. While Enterprise could not guarantee sales figures, it based its numbers on its experience at other marketplaces that it operated. Merchants countered that $35 per square foot was ridiculous and was far more than they could afford. The project manager said the rents were different depending on the merchants, but they were virtually the same as rents at Enterprise's Portside development, which opened in Toledo in May of 1984.[67]

As with the AutoWorld experience, Water Street Pavilion operated for only a few months. Opened in 1985, the facility housed food booths, boutiques, and other shops. Customer traffic never reached projected targets, and the whole facility fell into foreclosure in 1986. The city of Flint took possession of the property, and it sat vacant until 1992, when the University of Michigan-Flint reached agreement with the city to take over the property and to integrate it into the adjacent campus. The university bookstore, some campus offices, and a food court brought the Water Street Pavilion back to life, though in a different guise than was originally intended.

CONCLUSION

Luring shoppers to the downtown area was a central part of the revitalization strategies in both Omuta and Flint. Neither city succeeded in this area. Though the two cities had the same overall goals, they went about achieving them in different ways. Both retail revitalization efforts can be labeled "copy-cat" policy-making, since Omuta and Flint imitated existing ideas that were already proven successes. However, Omuta copied other cities' projects—Fukuoka City and earlier Community Mart program grant recipients—directly, while Flint hired successful private developers and consultants who replicated their own ideas for Flint. The Japanese approach was somewhat more problem-driven. Omuta's efforts at imitation were made by the local stores themselves, assisted by the city government and by the local chamber of commerce. Throughout the revitalization process, the city worked with the Omuta merchants. Flint's efforts were spearheaded by the foundation, FACI, and the city government. These organizations were not closely tied to the retail business, and their ultimate product—Water Street Pavilion—did not incorporate existing downtown stores into its plan. As a result, when the project was completed the local merchants were reluctant to move in.

Financing for the two cities reflected institutional differences between Japan and the United States. Omuta and Flint used public financing to leverage private capital investment, though the channels through which public funds were accessed differed. Omuta's government access was through overwhelmingly bureaucratic channels, while Flint gained its HUD grants through political influence. In Omuta's case, it was more important that program applications were completed properly. Local representatives in Tokyo played no role in the grant application and selection process. Though application formalities were important in Flint as well, lining up political support—at both the state and federal levels—was more important. In Washington, Flint's congressional representatives set up meetings with, and accompanied the mayor and local officials to visit, HUD officers.

Both revitalization efforts relied heavily on private sector funds, although in Omuta private funding came from the small store owners through their local retailers' associations. Private capital in Flint came from larger sources, some of which were not local. The foundation and syndicated venture financiers were crucial participants in the financing package. In addition, Omuta refurbished the retail environment surrounding existing downtown stores. Flint created new retail space that was used for boutiques and for upscale specialty stores.

Why did Omuta's merchants participate more than their counterparts in Flint? Flint's retailers did not really enter the process until the final stages of the Water Street project were well underway. There are two possible explanations, one cultural and one structural. The cultural explanation maintains that Japan's consensus-oriented decision-making norms prompted local leaders to include as many interested parties as possible. Through the practice of *nemawashi*, or "root bundling," project leaders conferred with all of the relevant players ahead of time, making sure they were included in the project-planning process. This way, project leaders got all their "ducks in a line" behind them, and they could count on local support and coordination throughout the implementation process. Surprise opposition to the project was unlikely, given this consultation and coordination system. Obviously this was lacking in the American case, where top-down planning dominated by a developer created dissension and ultimate failure.

The structural explanation concerns the funding for the project. Most of Omuta's funding came from within the community, while Flint's investors were from outside the city. This gave Omuta's merchants a larger stake in the project and prompted them to be more involved. Flint's merchants had no stake in the Water Street Pavilion project, and they remained peripheral throughout as a result. In addition, the Japanese bureaucracy's ability to coordinate the numerous parts and people involved is a significant institutional difference. Flint realistically had no option other than a top-down developer-centered project because bureaucrats in America generally do not get as involved in local affairs as their Japanese counterparts.

Finally, though participants in both cities planned large multi-use retail facilities for the downtown area, Omuta never built such a project, while Flint did. As in the case of theme parks, the systemic oversight forces that prevented construction in Omuta seem to have helped it avoid a large capital-intensive mistake; the lack of such institutional checks in Flint allowed the construction of a costly facility that quickly became a white elephant in the heart of the city.

CHAPTER 5

INDUSTRIAL PARK SURPRISES

Omuta and Flint needed to create jobs in order to spark economic revitalization. To lure new firms into the city, both sought to provide attractive facilities in which such firms might locate. This chapter compares the development of industrial park facilities in Omuta and Flint. Each city built several industrial parks in the late 1980s and early 1990s, and the similarities are worth noting. The most obvious similarity is that these efforts have not significantly changed the employment situation in either community. Both are still primarily company towns, with the old, large firms still providing a large percentage of available jobs. Mitsui companies in Omuta and General Motors (GM) in Flint have been the focus of local efforts to lure companies to the area. Both have served as bait to attract new jobs, most of which have been with firms related to the big corporations in town.

None of the parks in either city were particularly innovative, and all competed directly with other parks in their respective regions. Incentives for firms to move in were fairly standard, as were the facilities provided and the types of firms that opted to rent space. Industrial parks in both cities are the domain of city hall bureaucrats, along with some participation from local firms. Politicians play almost no role in the process, primarily because the projects are overwhelmingly local and require technical knowledge rather than political clout.

The goals that Omuta and Flint had for the industrial parks were identical: more jobs for residents and diversification of the local economic base away from their historic reliance on one industry. Neither city created many jobs through its industrial park projects. And the historically dominant firms—Mitsui and GM—served to attract firms to the new facilities, thus doing little to diversify the local economy. Why did both cities opt to build industrial parks as part of their revitalization strategy? The supply-side response explanation seems to work well for both communities. In Omuta, the national government was willing to fund new industrial parks. In Flint, the state government and the private sector were predisposed to new industrial park construction. Both cities were situated in regions already well endowed with industrial park facilities, but both still managed to build several new industrial parks, paid for mostly with national government funds.

In this policy type, Flint scored a decisive success while Omuta chalked up a mediocre performance. This is significant because it suggests that policy copying and supply-side decision making can work. In this case, Omuta's bureaucrats devised a safe but uninspired project. In contrast, Flint's political nature prompted it to take risks and to play an entrepreneurial game that ultimately paid big dividends. This outcome reinforces the idiosyncratic nature of urban revitalization: sometimes it is better to be lucky than good. Flint was in the right place at the right time, and it ended up landing a significant GM assembly facility as a result.

Omuta's Industrial Parks

The three industrial parks in Omuta are the Omuta Product Distribution Center (Omuta Butsuryû Senta), the Omuta Central Industrial Park (Omuta Chûo Kôgyô Danchi), and the Omuta Technopark Inland Industrial Park (Omuta Teknopâku Nairiku Kôgyô Danchi), each of which is slightly different in its focus and composition. All were small—less than ten hectares each—and were thus not big gambles for the city. What follows is the story of each park.

Omuta Central Industrial Park

Omuta's Central Industrial Park is a 7.5-hectare facility built on land acquired from the The Mitsui Mining Group (Mitsui Kôzan), of which Mitsui Coal was a part. Its development is a metaphor for Omuta's movement away from coal starting in the mid-1980s. It was also a good example of how cities go about luring firms to such facilities. The park was built on the site of the oldest mine shaft entrance in Omuta, part of a large vacant parcel of land that was fairly polluted with coal residue.

The plan for the park, first formally proposed in 1988, was conceived and produced entirely by officials in city hall.[1] The site was a fairly obvious choice for an industrial park, since the pollution in the ground and the close proximity to the old Miike Railroad—part of the old coal transit infrastructure—made the land unsuitable for residential use. It was also close to the main Omuta train station, used for both freight and passenger transit, which made it a convenient site for commercial use.

In late 1989, the city signed an agreement to purchase the land from Mitsui Mining in the spring of 1990. Prior to finalizing the sale, the city wanted time to conduct a geologic study and measurements to make sure the land was usable. Anticipating a favorable outcome to the study, city hall officials announced a tentative plan for the site. Most of the land would be devoted to industrial facilities, but the city also planned to add a major road through the development and some public green space as well. The public park was to serve as a memorial to the coal industry, preserving some of the artifacts from Omuta's past including such items from the coal era as part of the mine shaft entrance and a stretch of conveyor belt. One side of the site fronted on a residential section of town, which concerned planners. To avoid jeopardizing already low property values, the city proclaimed its intention to attract low pollution-emitting firms such as food producers and garment or textile companies, if at all possible.[2]

The geologic survey was completed and everything checked out by late February 1990, when the city announced plans to build the park. In March, the city's Land Development Corporation (a public, nonprofit corporation) bought the land from Mitsui Mining. Mitsui was eager to sell the land because of the long-term restructuring the firm was undergoing, but it still wanted to make a profit on the sale. The city paid a slightly higher price than it wanted to ($500 per *tsubo*, a Japanese unit of measurement roughly thirty-six square feet), but overall the land transaction went smoothly. The Land Development Corporation borrowed the money for the purchase from the national Public Business Finance Corporation (Kôei Kigyô Kinyû Kôkô), a public-sector finance outfit run by the Ministry of International Trade and Industry (MITI). The loan amount was $30,000, at 4.8-percent interest.[3] Omuta received no grants from the national or prefectural level for this project because it was too small to qualify for such financing. Such financial aid was available, but only for projects larger than ten hectares.[4]

City hall officials spent the spring and summer of 1990 planning the physical layout of the industrial park and searching for tenant firms. In November they produced a concrete plan for the facility, along with news that they had lined up four firms willing to move in upon completion: Kyushu Sankô (headquartered in Osaka), a manufacturer of fine clothing; Japan Look (headquartered in Omuta), another manufacturer of fine clothing; Omuta Taihô Industries (headquartered in Osaka), a molded plastics producer; and a frozen foods producer from central Japan whose name was not divulged at the time for unknown reasons.

The process of luring these four firms into the industrial park is typical of the process involved in all of Omuta's industrial park facilities: all had some prior connection to Omuta that facilitated the deal. Kyushu Sankô was a new venture of Sankô Clothing, a small (capital value $1.4 million in 1992) clothing maker from the Kansai area. The president of Sankô was searching for a site in Kyushu for a new factory. The president of Japan Look, an acquaintance of Sankô's president, introduced Sankô to Omuta city hall officials in 1990. They worked out a deal, and Sankô was the first firm to agree to move into the park. Part of the deal involved Japan Look moving in too, so park planners scored a two-for-one deal.[5] But Japan Look reneged on its commitment in the spring of 1991. Citing lower sales and higher employee costs than expected, the local firm was forced to cancel its planned move into the new facility.[6]

Omuta Taihô Industries manufactured molded plastics for the electronics industry. Despite the name, the company was located in Fukuoka City, fifty miles north of Omuta. Omuta Taihô Industries was a subsidiary (*kogaisha*) of the larger Taihô Industries, of Osaka. The president of the smaller firm was an Omuta native. When the company sought a site for a second production facility, Omuta officials convinced him to build it in his hometown.[7] Park planners worried that they would not soon fill the space reserved for Japan Look, but in 1992 the parent Taihô Industries claimed the site. They built a new plastic form production facility adjacent to their subsidiary.

Yayoi Foods, headquartered in Shizuoka Prefecture, was also searching for a new site in Kyushu. They contacted Fukuoka Prefecture's industrial promotion office in Tokyo. The Tokyo office put Yayoi in touch with Amagi City, a small farming community in central Fukuoka Prefecture also suffering from a decline in population. Yayoi representatives visited Amagi but were not impressed. Since they were in the area, they contacted several nearby cities—Omuta among them—to schedule site visits and tours. They chose Omuta over Amagi for three reasons. First, the labor in Amagi was not reliable. Too many citizens considered themselves full-time farmers and part-time factory workers, which meant that they scheduled their lives according to the growing seasons. Second, agricultural labor did not have the technological training and experience that Yayoi Foods desired. Omuta, as an historically industrial city, had few farmers and sufficiently skilled industrial workers. Third, Yayoi representatives found Amagi too charming—its sleepy pastoral character was too boring for the salarymen in the firm. Omuta had a surplus of night life and drinking establishments that better met Yayoi's expectations. It was an easy

decision, and Yayoi opted for Omuta.[8]
Prior to its opening in 1992, park planners filled the final vacancy in the facility. Asahi Seiki, a local producer of—and maintenance provider for—vacuum machines sought a new site and ended up choosing the industrial park. As of 1992, the park housed four firms in just over 5 hectares of space. These firms employed 295 full-time workers.[9] The park is a successful facet of redevelopment in Omuta. The city successfully built and filled the park in four years, and managed to attract firms from relatively clean industries (low pollution emitters) while creating jobs for city residents. Though only 25 percent of the jobs were completely new hires, the park prevented two local firms looking for new quarters from moving elsewhere. Omuta's image as an industrial community—often cited as something residents want to change—even worked to its advantage. Omuta was able to beat out more rural towns in the competition for skilled factory production jobs.

OMUTA'S PRODUCT DISTRIBUTION CENTER

The Omuta Product Distribution Center is one of the few revitalization schemes in Omuta that predates the Shiotsuka administration. But it did not become a reality until well after Shiotsuka was elected mayor. The project languished for more than a decade for one reason: the inability to come up with a suitable site. As originally conceived, the project was supposed to be a jumping-off point for regionally manufactured items bound for Asia. While a romantic and perhaps geographically sensible idea, given Kyushu's proximity to the Asian mainland, it never achieved this goal. It did, however, become a successful industrial park in the early 1990s.

The idea first surfaced in a 1979 Omuta Chamber of Commerce and Industry report entitled "A Plan for Modernizing Commerce in the Omuta Area."[10] The need for some product distribution facility was acknowledged, but no specific ideas were proposed. Momentum increased slightly when a 1983 Chamber of Commerce report listed it as a higher priority,[11] and it became a stand-alone entity in 1985, when the Chamber of Commerce conducted a survey on the demands and resources for such a facility in the community.[12] As a result of this study, Omuta city officials and the Chamber of Commerce established the Product Distribution Center Promotion Liaison Committee (Butsu Ryû Sentâ Suishin Renraku Kyôgikai). This organization was charged with securing a site, planning the physical structure, and organizing private sector firms to move into the facility.

Lack of agreement on a site prevented the project from moving forward smoothly, however. To avoid haggling with Mitsui, the planners chose a site that was not on Mitsui land. Further inland and closer to the expressway interchange, the desired site was privately held farmland. But no amount of pressure would convince the farmers to sell their property, so the committee was forced to search for a second-choice site.[13] This is the second case in Omuta where farmers were able to block a project by refusing to part with their land. The city had plans for widening and improving one of the major roads leading to the harbor area that were indefinitely delayed by private land owners who refused to sell. Omuta could have seized the land, claiming eminent domain, but city hall officials were reluctant to do so.[14] There was plenty of idle land in Omuta, so starting an open conflict over land was not a strategically smart idea. But each time the city wanted to acquire land, it was forced to wrestle it away from Mitsui, a task that always proved to be difficult.

In 1988 city officials searched for sites on Mitsui property. Though in the spring of 1988 it was public knowledge that the city wanted a parcel of land from the Mitsui Aluminum refinery on the southwest side of town,[15] they were unable to reach a purchase agreement until March 1989.[16] The impasse was caused by Mitsui Aluminum's financial difficulties: the company was dissolved at the end of March 1989, and its parts were either spun off into private subcontractors or merged into other Mitsui firms (e.g., Mitsui Metal Smelting, which had several facilities in Omuta).

This project was financed under the national Special Regions Small and Medium Enterprise Policy (Tokutei Chîki Chûsho Kigyô Taisaku, Rinji Sochi-hô, a law that expired in December 1991). Under the law, 80 percent of the total project cost could be financed interest-free, and the loan had to be paid back in no more than twenty years. The agreement called for Mitsui Aluminum to sell the 36.5-hectare property to the Omuta Land Development Corporation, which then sold the land to a public non-profit management company created by the firms that moved into the facility. The total project cost was $90 million, and included not only the land but a usable office building and other structures totaling about 29,700 square meters of space.[17] Again the Land Development Corporation borrowed money for the purchase from the national Public Business Finance Corporation. The loan amount was just over $55 million, at zero-percent interest this time, with the firms moving into the facility ($24.1 million) and the city and the prefecture ($7.5 million) covering the remainder of the cost.[18] Muramatsu Tarô, chairperson of Mitsui Aluminum, came to Omuta in early April for a signing ceremony with Mayor Shiotsuka, which started the project in motion.

Though the land appropriation was handled by the government, luring firms to the new facility was largely a private sector affair. In April 1988, the Omuta Chamber of Commerce started advertising for tenants for the new facility.[19] The reason for the delegation of this responsibility to the Chamber of Commerce is unclear, but it certainly was a significant decision. The Chamber of Commerce is well connected in the local business community, although it has few contacts outside the immediate Omuta area. Though the Chamber of Commerce successfully lured firms into the facility prior to construction, most of the committed firms were local. This meant that the number of jobs created by the center was perhaps not as great as it might have been.

By the time the land deal was completed, the Chamber of Commerce had lined up twenty-five firms that wanted to move in, almost enough to fill the facility. Only five of these were from outside Omuta.[20] Why was the project so popular among smaller local firms? The incentive package offered to move in was quite generous. All participants were given a 3-year 100-percent tax break on buildings and equipment, and a subsequent 6-year 50-percent tax break on the same.[21] Firms still had to pay property taxes, but these were negligible, given the fact that the site could not be used for anything but industrial purposes. The pollution in the ground, from its years as an aluminum smelting factory, was too high.

Ownership of the center was set up in an interesting way. The companies were organized into two cooperatives, based on the type of business they did. Of the twenty-five companies, ten belonged to the Omuta Freight Transportation Cooperative (Kyôdô Kumiai Omuta Kamotsu Yusô Sentâ) and fifteen to the Omuta Industrial Park Cooperative (Omuta Kôgyô Danchi Kyôdô Kumiai). The latter group was made up primarily of small firms in heavy industries, mostly involving some type of steel working. Seven of the firms were Mitsui subcontractors (shita-uke), though none worked for Mitsui full-time. Ownership of the center was held by these two cooperative umbrella organizations on behalf of the companies, although the companies provided all the capital. All common facilities were owned on a cooperative basis, with firms paying their proportional share. Facility maintenance fees were paid through the cooperatives, proportional to the size of firm. Water purification (postuse) was paid monthly according to use.[22]

The job creation impact of the center was moderate. A total of 894 people were employed in the center, an increase of 161 jobs over precenter employment levels.

Though most of the firms that moved into the center voiced an intent to hire even more employees, the nationwide economic slowdown in the early 1990s made this difficult. The center did add a new building in 1992 and found eight more firms to fill it. All were local, one was a Mitsui subcontractor, and one was a Mitsui subsidiary spun off as part of the company-wide rationalization. The job impact of those firms was light: a total

of 290 people were employed in the center, an increase of 98 jobs over precenter employment levels.

The Omuta center was completed and officially opened in April 1992.

Omuta Technopark Inland Industrial Park

The Omuta Technopark Inland Industrial Park was only in its earliest
planning stages when this research was conducted in 1992–1993, but it
looked to be an overwhelmingly top-down project with strong financial
and administrative support from the national level. The park was apparently modeled on successful projects in Kumamoto Prefecture, just south
of Omuta. This facility was to be built just one mile from the Omuta interchange on the main north-south Kyushu Expressway, which would provide ideal access to all parts of Kyushu and beyond. It was to be a large
project—66.5 hectares—with a projected goal of about two thousand new
jobs created.

The project was done under the auspices of the MITI Energy Resource
Agency (Shigen Enerugî-cho), which did not seem like a logical organization to develop an industrial park. But Omuta's history as a center of coal
production, coupled with the fact that the actual project administrator was
the Regional Promotion and Facilities Corporation (Chiiki Shinkô Seibi
Kôdan), a public corporation overseen by MITI, made it a somewhat logical choice within the MITI organization.

No local funds were used in the planning and implementation of this
project. The park cost the city nothing, and the project did not even appear
in the city's budget. Even though the city was committed to helping find
tenants for the facility once it was built, all funding came from MITI, via
the Regional Promotion Facilities Public Corporation. The corporation
floated bonds that were to be used to buy and prepare the site and to build
the infrastructure required for industrial use.[23]

The corporation spent most of 1991 studying the prospects of this
industrial park. Site searches, basic needs studies, facilities planning
options, site suitability studies, and other reports were prepared.[24] Though
some Omuta residents expressed concern that the site was too far from the
city center (6 miles outside of the downtown area), there were two important reasons for choosing that location—in addition to the proximity to the
expressway. First, planners believed it would catalyze development in a
largely agricultural part of Omuta. This would encourage residents to
give up farming and to move to jobs nearby in other industries. Second,
there was ample clean water available from rivers and streams abutting
the site. Park planners knew that high technology manufacturing firms
needed large amounts of clean water, which Omuta's downtown parks

could not provide. Nearby Kumamoto Prefecture had been quite success-ful in luring high-value added manufacturers to its clean water-rich industrial parks, and Omuta sought to replicate that formula. According to a report issued in June of 1991, the corporation hoped to attract firms in the automobile, food production, wood products, retail, and furniture industries.[25]

In January 1992, MITI expressed concern that all environmental and water use studies be completed as soon as possible. For unexplained rea-sons, the agency wanted to pay for the park in the 1992 budget year, and thus pressure was put on the city to hurry through the various studies required.[26] A possible explanation for the MITI pressure was the concern about losing bureaucratic turf in Omuta. For decades, MITI had been a lead-ing agency in the conduct of Omuta's affairs. MITI encouraged domestic coal use among heavy industry during the coal heyday (pre- and postwar), and MITI administered the series of nine Special Coal Area Assistance poli-cies during the three decades of rationalization of the Miike Coal industrial complex. With the end of the coal era, MITI was in danger of losing regional decision-making influence. But a switch from rationalization to revitaliza-tion and promotion gave MITI a fresh, enhanced role in the region.

However, MITI's desire for rapid progress was hamstrung by the sys-tem of heavy oversight and regulation favored by environmental and agricultural interests. The number of required studies piled up faster than the city—acting as the national government's agent—could carry them out. At the beginning of 1992, the city still had not produced studies on the availability of water for industrial use; the yet-to-be-constructed facilities required by government regulation to handle industrial discharge and runoff; the process of getting agricultural area promotion exemptions from standard national project procedural regulations; and a study of the effect that such a facility would have on groundwater and water used for agriculture.[27] The regulations of other agencies prevented this project from progressing rapidly, despite MITI's urgings and backing. Omuta's Waterway Division (Suido Kyoku), Agriculture, Forestry, and Fisheries Section (No Rin Sui-ka), Public Works Section (Doboku-ka), and Pollution Policy Section (Kôgai Taisaku-ka) all had overlapping duties to fulfill before the park could proceed. Nine months later, in the fall of 1992, the required studies were finally completed and the process of finding tenants for the planned industrial park officially began.

LURING FIRMS BEYOND THE PARKS

The process of luring corporations (*kigyô yûchi*) to Omuta began in 1980, well before the three projects just described were up and running.

Between 1980 and 1992, the city counted thirty-three successful cases of kigyô yûchi, most of which were achieved after 1986.[28] Thirty of the companies were involved in some sort of manufacturing, with seven in metals and/or ceramics, five centered on plastics production, five producing clothing, five in chemicals and fertilizers, and the remainder in service, food processing, or light manufacturing industries. Though thirty-three firms sounds impressive, the effect these companies have had on local employment statistics is marginal at best. Thirteen firms were already in existence in Omuta in some form, while twenty companies actually moved to Omuta from somewhere else. Only seven of the firms were Mitsui subsidiaries, but if one adds up Mitsui suppliers, the firms spun off from Mitsui concerns, and subsidiaries—all the firms related to Mitsui and/or doing business with Mitsui concerns—the number grows to twelve. Firms related to Mitsui account for just over one-third of all kigyô yûchi in Omuta.

How did Omuta go about luring firms to the area? Several strategies were used: word of mouth among corporate groupings, advertising in Japan's major urban centers, and introductions set up by prefectural offices in Tokyo and Osaka were the most successful approaches.

It is notable that tax breaks and other fiscal incentives are not listed among the strategies Omuta used. Tax credits, exemptions, and deferments were given to firms creating jobs in Omuta, but these incentives were not a significant factor in firms' decision-making processes. This is due to the nature of the tax system in Japan's unitary structure, which limits local flexibility. Formally, localities are free to manipulate taxes however they want, as long as they notify the Ministry of Home Affairs (MOHA). In reality, locally controlled taxes can only be raised and lowered within a range approved by the MOHA. Local governments are given a maximum and a standard tax rate, and they must demonstrate need and solicit permission to deviate from the standard.

Reed distinguishes between long- and short-term fiscal flexibility. Japanese local governments have plenty of short-term flexibility but little long-term flexibility.[29] Short-term flexibility is a mechanism for effecting sound financial management. Sound local financial management has been the overarching concern of Japanese central government officials in the postwar era.[30] Taxes can be raised to deal with temporary problems, such as the decline in revenues caused by the "oil shock" of 1973–1974. That crisis caused local corporate taxes to be raised to the maximum rate for a period of five years nationwide. Taxes rarely need to be lowered in response to short-term conditions.

Long-term tax increases—such as for a new welfare program—are discouraged by the MOHA. But local governments enjoy a great deal of discretion for lowering taxes for specific purposes. Promoting local businesses and attracting new industry is an obvious use for this power. However, cities cannot jeopardize their fiscal health in the process, so tax breaks are limited in principle. Cities seek other means for increasing long-term flexibility, namely maximizing central grants and borrowing. Neither of these options allows much long-term flexibility, however, and both incur considerable oversight and interference from higher levels of government.

Local government borrowing is dominated by bureaucrats, and is quite far removed from the electorally motivated affairs of politicians. Much local borrowing is done through the fifteen public units (*kôdan*), of which the Regional Promotion and Facilities Corporation mentioned earlier is one. According to Johnson, the *kôdan* are the heart of the public enterprise sector. They invest huge sums provided by the Fiscal Investment and Loan Program (FILP, described in the previous chapter), primarily in large-scale public works and construction projects. Kôdan enjoy a high degree of independence: while Japanese public corporations (kôsha) and public finance corporations (kôko) must submit their annual budgets and business plans to a Diet vote, kôdan are only subject to the approval of their supervising ministers.[31]

The effects of this system are both positive and negative. On the positive side, cities must practice conservative fiscal management. Japanese cities do not—indeed, cannot—go bankrupt, since the monitoring agencies will not allow them to take on too much debt. On the negative side, Japanese localities have one less effective tool with which to lure firms. Instead, localities must compete for companies on other criteria such as proximity to markets and resources, infrastructure, cost of living, and availability of trained workers.

Word of mouth among corporate groupings was the most successful way of luring firms to Omuta. Eight of the firms were either wholly or partially owned Mitsui subsidiaries. Four more were spin-offs from Mitsui, which cut loose numerous branches that were not performing well economically. These became independent companies that stayed in Omuta, many still doing business with Mitsui and occupying space in Mitsui facilities. Another four firms were introduced to Omuta by someone in Mitsui, and were lured to Omuta by the promise of contract work with the large corporation.

Omuta also used another type of corporate networking that may have contributed to this limited success in this area. City officials contacted Omuta natives living in Tokyo and Osaka, and invited them to seminars. The officials solicited the natives' opinions on how Omuta might improve its image and attract firms from outside Kyushu. As part of these seminars, city officials distributed Omuta promotional materials and solicited help from the former residents in spreading the good word about Omuta. In the Tokyo seminar, the focus was on Omuta natives who were higher-level executives in several Mitsui concerns, including Mitsui Mining and Mitsui Tôatsu Chemical. Omuta's efforts in Osaka centered on small manufacturing enterprises with Omuta connections.[32] It is hard to tell whether these efforts had any effect on firms' decisions to create jobs in Omuta, and local officials were noncommittal on this point.[33]

The second major group of firms lured to Omuta were companies actively looking for new sites that heard about Omuta and made initial inquiries at city hall. Five firms fell into this category. Omuta made a concerted effort to publicize its willingness to welcome new firms within its borders. The city mounted an extensive publicity campaign that included a promotion video, color pamphlets and brochures, large seminars in Tokyo and Osaka, and direct mass mailings to firms all over the country. The seminars were expensive, costing about $17,000 per session. Each seminar attracted roughly 250 firms, of which perhaps ten were seriously interested in Omuta. Though the city ran several seminars, no firm came to Omuta as a result of this technique.[34] Omuta also invited representatives from the Tokyo offices of major Kyushu corporate and government offices to Omuta—all expenses paid—to publicize the city as a business opportunity. Officials explicitly targeted those individuals responsible for matching firms with new sites for factories and offices. In 1988, for example, they brought representatives from the Tokyo offices of Kyushu Electric Power Co., Fukuoka Bank, Mitsui Bank, and the Fukuoka prefectural office in Tokyo. The goal was not to lure these firms to Omuta, but to convince these influential strategists to recommend Omuta as a place for other companies to locate.[35] City officials faced a dilemma over advertising as a method of attracting jobs to Omuta. It was a high-cost method of garnering marginal benefits, but they remained committed to pursuing firms that way.

Omuta also ran an annual seminar in Tokyo and Osaka conducted by Teikoku Databank, the largest corporate information database in Japan. Omuta bought data on firms from Teikoku Databank, and sent invitations to healthy target firms in certain regions it hoped might be interested in relocating. Some firms attended the seminars, and some were even lured to make site visits to Omuta. As with their independent seminars, no firms have moved to Omuta as a result of these efforts. The city did not cancel these seminars, however, and was even forced to run such sessions in Fukuoka City. Competition among localities to attract firms to industrial parks became so fierce in the late 1980s and early 1990s that Fukuoka firms were being stolen away by Kumamoto and Saga prefectures, also located in Kyushu.

Competition to lure companies to areas outside Tokyo and Osaka was fierce. The intense competition among localities for firms resulted in part from the surplus of industrial park space constructed in Japan nationwide in the 1980s and early 1990s, though not especially in Omuta. Many localities sought to grab a piece of the expanding Japanese economic pie, and the central government agencies encouraged them to prepare sites for firms willing to move. The expansion of industrial park space is a good example of supply-side economic development without regard for the zero-sum nature of the game. MITI encouraged localities from Hokkaido to Okinawa to build industrial parks to attract firms. It provided funding through various instruments and programs, including the Regional Promotion and Facilities Corporation and the Technopolis program. The result of this central government encouragement was a rise in the amount of available industrial park land nationwide.

In 1991 the total amount of industrial park space nationwide was 1.3 billion square meters in 2,976 facilities. Despite the fact that Japan's economy began to cool off in 1990, industrial park construction continued unabated for several years after the slowdown. By 1992 there were 1.5 billion square meters of space in 3,269 industrial park facilities.[36] The combination of a slowing economy and new industrial parks created a surplus of vacant space in some parts of Japan. Nationally, the effects of this excess were minimal. Only 2.3 percent of the total facilities designed for industrial use lay vacant in 1991, and that number rose to 3.3 percent in 1992.

But variation was greater from region to region and by locality, and some areas experienced serious debt crisis (by Japanese standards) as a result of overextending themselves to create industrial parks they could not fill.[37] Among prefectures, Hokkaido was hardest hit in this regard, with 6 percent of its industrial park space lying vacant in 1992. Most of this was in one large project, the Tomakomai Eastern Industrial Park, started in 1991 and located in the paper-making city of Tomakomai on the south coast of Hokkaido. Kyushu fared worse than the national average as well, with 4.2 percent of park space unused in 1992. Northern Kyushu did well, with only 2.9 percent of industrial park space sitting vacant, but the situation in southern Kyushu was worse than in Hokkaido, with 7.3 percent of park space unused.[38]

The data provided by MITI seems to be overly optimistic, and may not reflect reality. This assessment is based on the portrayal of Omuta in the data. Among the three Omuta facilities included in the data, the Inland Industrial Park is listed as having no available space. Yet at the time this survey was done, the Inland Industrial Park had not even been built. There was no evidence of corporate commitments to move into the facility, and no one at city hall could explain the fact that the MITI data were so inaccurately reported. It may be safe to assume that the real figures for available unused industrial park facilities are somewhat higher.

Either way, it is clear that Omuta was on the back end of the industrial park boom, and that it was encouraged to enter the industrial park competition by both lateral and vertical pressures. Laterally, hundreds of other localities around Japan were building industrial parks, most well before Omuta entered the game. Vertically, the national government—MITI, in particular—offered incentives and subsidies to build such facilities. Omuta, being a skilled and experienced player in the subsidy application arena, applied and successfully received aid in this policy area.

The impact of these industrial park efforts and general kigyô yûchi was minimal. Several hundred jobs were created over a ten-year period, but these were dwarfed by the cutbacks Mitsui made in its work force. As with Omuta's theme park and retail revitalization projects, a fiscally conservative effort with close government oversight prevented the city from taking significant risks. At the same time, the oversight and reliance on proven ideas prevented Omuta from discovering a new way to spark growth.

FLINT'S INDUSTRIAL PARKS

Flint's efforts to build industrial parks aimed at economic diversification started in the mid-1970s. GM cut back its car production in response to the oil crisis of 1973–1974, and workers in Flint were hit hard. In response, the city sought to diversify its economic base—while preserving its status as a center of American manufacturing—by building sites for new and expanding firms.

The industrial park experience in Flint is an excellent demonstration of path dependent policy-making. It went as follows: there was an acknowledged need to do something to combat economic decline. The city commissioned feasibility studies to examine the possibility of building new industrial parks, even though there was plenty of unused industrial park space in the county at the time. The studies noted the existence of ample vacant industrial park space, but predicted that Flint could successfully support more industrial park space if certain conditions were met. Flint successfully sought federal funds to pay for the industrial parks, putting up less than half the money itself. And what it did contribute it raised through local bond issues. With construction underway, the city hired professionals to sell the facilities to interested businesses. In the end, the parks were only marginally successful. In return for the $27-million total investment in the projects, only seven hundred jobs were created. Economic diversification was not achieved, since the best draw to the new industrial facilities was the parks' proximity to GM. Most of the park space built since the first oil crisis was occupied by GM suppliers and subcontractors.

The two largest and most celebrated industrial parks built in Flint in the last two decades are the Bishop Airpark and the St. John Industrial Park. Bishop Airpark is a 50 acre, city-owned, class A industrial park located next to the city's Bishop Airport (southwest of the city center).[39] St. John Industrial Park is a hundred-eighty-acre, city-owned, class A industrial park. It is located northeast of the city center, adjacent to the Buick City factory complex. The rest of the chapter will focus on these projects.

Following the 1973 oil crisis, local administrators started preaching the benefits industrial park development and local economic diversification as ways to cushion the city against the jolting ups and downs of the auto industry. In the summer of 1974, the Genesee County Economic Development Commission conducted a survey of local firms to determine the state of economic diversification and to learn the needs and wants of local businesses. Genesee is a small county, dominated politically, economically, and demographically by the city of Flint. It found that more than 90 percent of the county's 222 non-GM manufacturers employed 75 or fewer workers, and about 72 percent employed 25 workers or fewer. In contrast, GM had, at times, more than 76,000 workers on its payroll locally.[40] The total number of workers in small firms was not provided, but even a generous calculation with the figures provided puts the number of small-firm employees around 8,500.

According to the *Flint Journal*, the most common complaint voiced by the firms was that they felt isolated from similar firms, an issue the Development Commission took as an indication of a demand for industrial parks. The paper claimed that such parks usually group firms in related fields together, though this does not seem to be the case in many American industrial parks. Several other survey questions suggested, in the Development Commission's opinion, a demand for industrial park space. More than 45 percent of the firms responding to the study said that if they were going to move, they would prefer an industrial park. Twenty-seven percent actually expressed a preference for some other type of location than that which they occupied at present. The study concluded that industrial parks could meet the needs of more than 70 percent of local manufacturers, if they decided to move. Flint firms seemed to move frequently: In the three years prior to the survey, nearly 10 percent of the firms relocated; only 3 percent were brand-new firms.[41]

Despite this less-than-convincing evidence that Flint needed new industrial parks, Flint's Department of Community Development hired Zuchelli, Hunter and Associates, to do an analysis of the demand for

industrial park land in the area. At the same time the department commissioned the Detroit office of Coopers and Lybrand to create a preliminary marketing study for the St. John Industrial Park, suggesting that the
city fully intended to go ahead with the parks regardless of what the market study concluded. Zuchelli, Hunter and Associates, a Baltimore firm,
played an active part in Flint's redevelopment planning. In addition to the
industrial park study, they were also hired as the predevelopment packager for Riverfront Center, the $32-million Hyatt Regency convention cen-
ter begun in the late 1970s. Donald Zuchelli also served as the acting head
of Flint Area Conference, Inc. (FACI) at one point, where he put together a
study team of architects, financial experts, exhibit designers, and attendance experts to create a master plan for AutoWorld.[42]

The Zuchelli, Hunter and Associates report on the market for serviced
industrial land in Genesee County is objective in its assessment of the
industrial park situation Flint faced. They stated up front that in early 1976,

> the amount of land zoned for industrial use in Genesee County
> is considerably more than necessary to service the market for
> several years into the future. However, the location of much of
> this land and the lack of availability of adequate roads, utilities
> and linkages place the majority of the industrially zoned real
> estate outside the mainstream of current market demand. Much
> of the existing supply of industrially zoned real estate has been
> on the market and moderately priced for many years.[43]

Their data demonstrate that roughly 12,500 acres were zoned for
industrial use in Genesee County, of which approximately 3,000 was actually in use. Of that 3,000 acres, only 178 acres was located in planned
industrial parks. Of the 9,500 acres of unused land, only 650 acres had
paved approach roads, adequate sewer, water, gas, and electric service
and could be considered "on-line" and ready for construction without
extensive preparatory construction.[44]

Viewed in terms of the number of industrial parks, Flint looked saturated. In 1976 there were already ten industrial parks in Genesee County,
in varying stages of development and marketing. Only one park was
within the city of Flint. Nine of the others were in townships (and one
town) south of the city, in Burton, Flint and Mundy townships, and
Fenton, while one was to the north in Morris Township. Most were initiated in the early or mid-1960s. In the three parks begun after 1970, a total
of only twelve acres had been sold, in parcels of one to three acres.[45] Plenty
of land was available, but little of it was sufficiently developed to attract
new industrial investment.

Only one of the Genesee County parks—the facility in Fenton—was "certified" by the state of Michigan. It was one of twenty-two certified industrial parks south of Lansing, the state capital. In an effort to standardize the term *industrial park*, the Michigan Department of Commerce adopted a set of standards for qualified developments to be known as "Certified Industrial Parks." Landowners were still free to call their acreage anything they chose, but only those meeting certain requirements received state certification. The state adopted criteria, established by the Michigan Industrial Developers Association, which assigned a score to a particular property based on utilities, transportation access, facilities, and special park features. Certified parks could be rated A, B, or C, depending on their point totals.[46] All certified parks were 40 acres or larger, zoned for industrial use, and equipped with fully paved streets and sanitary sewer systems. These were all large parks ready for immediate industrial use. Beyond the state's "Certified" designation, the Detroit Edison electric power company further classified industrial parks as "Qualified" (a minimum of ten acres with proper zoning, utilities, and infrastructure in place and ready for use), "Other" (platted and zoned, but not meeting more of the requirements), and "Planning" (future parks likely to be designated as Certified or Qualified).[47] Except for the Fenton park, all of the other Genesee County industrial parks fell into the Other category because of their lack of infrastructure.

The Zuchelli, Hunter and Associates report found other indications of a weak demand for industrial park space, particularly in the way in which existing park space was being used: while some industrial park space is always taken over by commercial, warehousing and distribution, and retail businesses, the ratio of manufacturing to these other functions was atypically low in Genesee County. The report attributed this anomaly to the absence of medium-size manufacturing concerns in Flint. Such medium-size firms—manufacturing products for regional or national markets—form the backbone of most parks. Such firms are usually independent of other industries. The manufacturing concerns in Flint area parks were mostly small manufacturers, dependent on the large (automobile) manufacturing operations.[48]

Though the report acknowledged a sizable inventory of available industrial park space in 1975, it offered guardedly optimistic conclusions about the region's ability to absorb newly created space in the ensuing decade. Basing their predictions on the space absorption rates of the 1960s, and dismissing the slow growth of the early 1970s as an anomaly, the report predicted a gradual increase in local demand for industrial space that would be driven by a strengthening national economy. Putting an even more positive spin on the situation, the report concluded that these estimates could be increased sizably as the result of public actions at the state, local, and/or national levels which stimulate business recovery and improve the comparative advantage and marketability of Michigan and Flint for industrial location and expansion. Also, a more optimistic recovery of the automobile industry could have additional positive spin-off benefits in small- to medium-sized manufacturing establishments. . . .[49]

Flint did not benefit from the national recovery as the consultants hoped, but the two new industrial parks were not totally disastrous development projects like AutoWorld and Water Street Pavilion. Instead, they achieved modest job creation. Unfortunately for Flint, they did not spark any diversification of the local economy. Instead, they fell into the same pattern of industrial space use exhibited by all of the other local parks: most space was either used by small firms related to the automobile industry, or by commercial and retail businesses.

The following section describes the development of Bishop Airpark and St. John Industrial Park. Following that, I address the question of why Flint went ahead with the construction of these two facilities.

BISHOP AIRPARK

In contrast to most of the revitalization projects in Flint, Bishop Airpark, the smaller of the two industrial park projects, evolved smoothly and rapidly. This was in part due to the fact that it was a small project, but it was also easily developed because it was built in a previously undeveloped area of the city. In particular there were no old buildings to buy and raze as there were for other projects, including the St. John Industrial Park. But as with many other projects, the origins of the idea are unclear. This project seems to have started more informally than most. Whereas other redevelopment efforts were openly debated in the media and recorded in Mott Foundation documents, the first mention of Bishop Airpark was in the summer of 1975, when it was announced that financing for the project was apparently assured.

In June of 1975, the United States Commerce Department's Economic Development Administration (EDA) offered Flint $240,000 via a Title X grant (reserved for labor intensive projects) to develop a proposed $800,000-industrial park at Bishop airport.[50] Sen. Don Riegle announced the award.[51] In response, the city and county each decided to contribute money to the project. The Personnel Committee of the Genesee County Board of Commissioners voted $107,000 in federal job money toward the project, while the Finance Committee of the Flint City Council recommended that the city contribute $131,500 from its own federal job budget—in addition to $237,000 in city money—toward the project. The job money from the city and county came from the United States Labor Department under the Comprehensive Employment and Training Act (CETA). The remainder of the city money came from Flint's public improvement fund. The Flint Airport Commission, the local organization that runs the airport, promised another $75,000.[52]

Political support for the airport industrial park was fairly strong, even though the city council was split on the project. The county Board of Commissioners gave strong support to the project, as did the mayor of Flint, Paul Visser, and the Flint city manager, Daniel Boggan Jr. The Flint City Council was the only local institution divided on the issue. Three dissenting council members opposed the use of the city's CETA funds for the airpark development. They said it took away money that could create summer jobs for youths and continue other job programs that the city had already funded. One member argued that the money should go to help deteriorating central city neighborhoods rather than to economic development on the periphery of the city. But the city manager replied that there was still some money left over for jobs. He argued that the Bishop Airpark would be a serious step toward diversifying the local economy.[53]

Other objections arose at the next city council meeting in early June. One member opposed spending the money because he said there were no firms that seemed interested in putting their operations near the airport. He instead suggested they use the money to widen certain city streets. This project prompted a debate about whether the council should focus on long- or short-range goals. The vote in favor of the airpark project indicated that most of the council members believed the council should approve projects that are more long-range and that do not benefit a particular council member immediately and directly. Despite the objections, the full city council approved the funds—$368,500—at a meeting the following week.[54] This decision was not necessarily the rational one from each council member's perspective, since the immediate benefits to their respective districts and constituents were far from clear. But the council apparently felt some obligation to address long-term economic issues, even though there was no short-term political payoff.

Officials at the county level argued persuasively in favor of the airpark project. Dr. Rodney L. Boyes, a member of the Genesee County Economic Development Commission (EDC), called the airpark crucial for local economic diversification. The commission predicted that a thousand jobs would be created by a new light manufacturing facility next to the airport. The commission also argued that mostly federal money would be spent, and that all city funds would be returned in two years in the form of property taxes. The Flint City Council gave the go-ahead for an application to be submitted to the U.S. Economic Development Administration, with the proviso that Flint would take any grants awarded only if the city could come up with its share of the money first. The project was not a high priority for city. County EDC officials said the EDA was willing to contribute $300,000. The EDA suggested that the city apply for the money, something it did not do unless it was pretty sure a project would fly.[55] In addition, the recommendation by the mayor and city manager apparently carried some weight in the council's decision-making process.

Later that summer, the Flint Airport Commission realized it could not meet its $75,000-commitment to the airpark project. Already committed to the park, the Flint City Council voted to approve an $11,000-grant and a $64,000-loan to make up the difference.[56]

The city council chose Samborn, Steketee, Otis, & Evans, an engineering, architecture, and planning firm to design Bishop Airpark. Headquartered in Toledo, Ohio, the firm already had an office in Flint with forty employees, and had been there since 1969. They were paid $31,600 for the design work. There was some council dispute over the use of outside firms for the engineering, architecture, and planning of this and other projects. Dissenting council members maintained that sometimes local firms were weighted more heavily in the contract award process, and sometimes they were not.[57] Though there were calls for consistency in the selection procedure, the debate ultimately had little effect on the way in which consultants and specialists were chosen.

A ground-breaking ceremony was held on October 17, 1975. Construction took longer than expected because of the use of CETA workers on the project. CETA workers were not experienced construction workers. They were people who had lost jobs as a result of the GM plant closings. The CETA money was a form of labor retraining, providing them with on-the-job training as they worked on a real project.[58] This made the work go more slowly, but also was an investment in area workers for the future.

Construction continued through all of 1976. By February of 1977 the park was completed except for some finishing touches. Bishop Airpark received a class A certification from the state of Michigan. In addition to the normal features of a certified industrial park—water, sewer, and other utility services and paved streets—the development also had direct access via a taxiway to airport runways. It was also within easy reach of major interstate freeways and a railroad line.

The next step was marketing the project. To market Bishop Airpark, the city council designated it as an industrial development district, allowing property tax breaks as incentive. State law allowed a maximum 50-percent tax break for twelve years. GM got such tax breaks regularly. But property tax breaks are only offered to property owners. Since the city owned the park and opted to lease it to firms willing to move in as tenants, this perk did not offer much incentive to lure companies to the new industrial park. Flint was only able to offer tax breaks on property improvements made by tenant firms. Immediately after the park was completed, the city estimated that industrial development in the facility would total $5.25 million, about one-third of the total estimates when the park was funded in 1975.[59] Thirty-five of the 50 acres was platted for industrial use. The rest became roads and taxiways.

The city planned to hire a land marketing expert, using a state economic development grant. Jobs for the Unemployed was the battle cry that got the project politically supported, funded, and built initially, and airpark construction did produce some jobs for local workers. But long-term job gains proved to be more difficult. The city had no marketing strategy for selling the park, so it hired someone to handle the job. Jack C. Hutchinson was hired to head the Flint/Genesee Corporation for Economic Growth. This public, nonprofit firm was funded mainly with state money, with contributions by the city and county tacked on. It represented the first effort to sell businesses on expanding in—or locating to—Flint. Hutchinson was a community salesperson, hired to fill Bishop Airpark and St. John Industrial Park. He was a certified industrial developer, hired after a nationwide search. Before going to Flint, he worked for the Middle Tennessee Industrial Development Association, where he brought $700-million worth of investment to that area. Flint first offered the job to two other candidates, both of whom took other positions.[60]

Bishop Airpark started to accumulate tenants soon after it was completed. By the end of 1979, nine of the nineteen slots in the facility were filled. Six firms had already moved into the airpark, with another three also expressing interest. Instead of leasing space, the city decided to sell land to firms willing to locate there. This allowed Flint to offer property tax incentives, thereby making the facility even more attractive. Despite its billing as an ideal site for light manufacturing, most of the Bishop Airpark tenants were either in service or distribution industries. Only a couple of tenants actually assembled or made products in the airpark. Most were firms that moved to Flint from another location in southeast Michigan. The original eight tenants were

- National Furniture Distributors, Inc., formerly of Grand Blanc, Michigan. They bought 1.88 acres, built a warehouse and office complex, and employed 20 workers;

- Flint Ceilings and Partitions, Inc., a local firm, bought 1.77 acres and had about 75 employees;

- Computers Diversified, Inc., originally from Livonia, bought 1.88 acres. They provided bookkeeping services for businesses all over Michigan and had roughly 20 employees;

- Davis-En-Tech, originally from Detroit, bought 2.35 acres and erected a $700,000 building there. The firm, a plastic injection molding operation, employed about 75 people;

- Zantop International Airlines, one of the largest air freight operations in the world, bought 14 acres on which it built an office, terminal, and apron for its aircraft. Initially it employed about 15 people in serving its customers, mostly GM plants;

- Murray Wyman, an air freight operator based in Pontiac, Michigan, bought 5.5 acres and built a small terminal and office space;

- Clarklift Inc., of Flint, bought 3 acres. The firm moved its forklift sales and service business to the airpark;

- R&S Electronics, of Detroit, purchased 1.88 acres. The business, which makes electronic components mostly for the auto industry, erected an office, warehouse, and assembly plant;[61]

The ninth tenant, Comcast Corporation, known locally in Flint as "Cablevision," was lured to the airpark with the help of federal funds. The city applied for and received a $105,000-Urban Development Action Grant (UDAG) that it turned over to Comcast to help defray the cost of a roughly $1-million office and warehouse at Bishop Airpark. The firm matched the grant with a $943,000-commitment to build a facility on 3.5 acres of land. Comcast's expansion resulted in 20 new jobs added to the 75 people it employed locally already. Sixty construction jobs—ten of which were CETA jobs—were also created. The city estimated at the time that it would earn an additional $29,000 in annual property taxes. Comcast was asked to repay the UDAG money to the city at 6-percent interest over twenty years.[62]

Bishop Airpark was a reasonably successful endeavor for Flint, especially when compared to the large, capital-intensive fiascoes that preceded it. Federal funds were used in each step of the development process, from initial market demand assessments through planning, construction, and marketing of the industrial park.

St. John Industrial Park

While Bishop Airpark was built despite the fact that it was not a high priority for some city of Flint officials, the St. John Industrial Park was started in 1975 because it was the city's top priority. Compared to the airpark's $1-million price tag, the $26-million St. John project was a much more serious undertaking. It required more local fiscal and political commitment, and the city supplied both in generous measure.

The St. John project was built in the St. John Street neighborhood of Flint, one of the oldest residential areas, and one of the most blighted and depressed in the city. The idea for an industrial park in that location came out of the city's participation in the federal urban renewal program of the late 1960s. Flint had been clearing the St. John area since an urban renewal program was adopted for that section of the city in 1970. Ten years before that, the city's master plan had recommended industrial use for the old residential neighborhood. More than half of the St. John area was cleared with federal urban renewal program funds, and the continuation of the clearance had the city council's highest priority.[63]

The project was launched toward completion in February of 1975, when the city received a federal EDA grant of $1.6 million for the development of an industrial park in the St. John area. The city applied for the grant in October of 1974, after receiving a request from the EDA to do so. The grant approval was announced by the office of Sen. Robert P. Griffin (R-Mich.).[64] But the grant was contingent on the city matching the amount with local money. The city asked the foundation for the matching funds, and the foundation agreed. This initial $3.2 million was used to build streets, install utilities, and make other changes in the 140-acre site to make it a certifiable facility according to the Michigan standards for industrial parks.

Converting the St. John project from an old urban renewal project to a new community economic development project caused some delays in the process. Under the old-style renewal programs, there were often problems between the city and the federal government. Delays in receiving federal funds became legendary. Even though the new community development block grant programs of the 1970s sought to smooth these procedural rough spots, the switch caused problems for Flint this time around.

One of the big changes touted by the Department of Housing and Urban Development (HUD) as an improvement over past policy was that money earmarked for cities under the new program would now go directly to cities as revenue-sharing programs, instead of to cities and urban counties as categorical grants, as had been the standard procedure under the preceding Model Cities program. In the switch from the old to the new, HUD reallocated some funds, giving more money to Flint under the Community Development Act and taking some funds away from Genesee County (which had been receiving money through the Model Cities program). In the first year of the program, Flint received $1.6 million more than the city anticipated under the previous categorical disbursement system.[65] This meant that it had to come up with the money to match that grant, or be forced to return it to HUD. Fortunately, the foundation was willing to provide the matching funds.

But the situation between Flint and Genesee County became problematic for the St. John project, since for the previous five years the county had operated several social services projects in Flint under the old Model Cities system. HUD decided that more federal money should go directly to city officials, and should not pass through the county apparatus. This angered county officials.[66] At the same time, the city had to apply for more money to get the new funds. Reapplication meant a new review by citizens, and by council, county, and state approval. This left the city's programs that were dependent on federal funding—including the city's program to buy land in the St. John area—without funding temporarily while the city jumped from one federal program to the other. Flint asked the regional HUD office in Detroit for an advance on the pending funds, which the HUD office granted.[67]

The city continued to buy out residents of the St. John area throughout 1975 and 1976. The park was a large public gamble. City property purchases effectively removed that property from the tax rolls temporarily, while the city prepared to resell it for redevelopment. Unlike Bishop Airpark, which was prepared for industrial use in less than two years, the St. John project took much longer. The city eroded its own tax base in the short-term, in an effort to improve that tax base in the long-term. In addition to the EDA and foundation money, the city initially chipped in an additional $2 million through rehabilitation bonding.[68] This number eventually rose to $10.5 million, more than the city spent on any other single project.[69] The bulk of this money was spent buying out St. John residents. Flint officials contended that they maintained a fairly generous buyout program for those remaining in the area. They certainly paid more than the state. Both the city and the Michigan Department of State Highways and Transportation ran buyout programs for area residents: the city bought land for the St. John project, while the state bought land for the new state highway. In the fall of 1976, one resident testified in city council hearings that the city bought her neighbor's house for $28,000, while the state bought her identical house located next door for only $18,000.[70]

The difference between the city and highway department compensation packages was due to the difference paid in relocation benefits and not usually because of the differences paid for the property itself. A relocation payment was an amount given in addition to the price paid for the house and was intended to help the owner-occupant and tenants find other housing. Both the city and state buyout programs were financed mostly with federal money. A federal uniform relocation law, signed in 1971, was supposed to make relocation payments for all federally sponsored projects generally the same. Unfortunately for some of the St. John area residents, this did not happen. Different federal agencies, such as HUD, which funded urban renewal and the community development programs, and the Federal Highway Administration, which funded the state's highway efforts, paid different amounts and had different methods for computing relocation payments.[71]

To complicate matters further, local governments had some discretion in choosing methods of figuring relocation payments, according to local and HUD officials. Both the highway department and the city were required to relocate residents being displaced by the new projects into safe, sanitary housing at least comparable to what they left behind. But the definition of "comparable" introduced a large fudge factor into the equation. The highway department said it checked the local housing market and made direct comparisons of available housing for sale. It then referred displaced persons directly to those homes for sale. Highway department officials defended their procedures, asserting that they administered the law fairly and as Congress intended. Flint's Department of Community Development operated under a different set of rules. The city agency developed its own schedule to figure relocation benefits, using a square footage method to determine how large a home the displaced family needed and what price range was allowed:

> Up to 900 square feet, a relocatee can [receive] from $15,500 to $23,900. From 901 square feet to 1,200 square feet, the range is $17,500 to $29,000. For a home 1201 to 1,600 square feet, a relocatee can pay $18,500 to $31,900. And from 1,601 to 2,000 square feet, the range is $19,800 to $37,000.[72]

Contrary to the highway department's system, a relocatee did not receive total benefits until after they found another home. Relocation experts contended that the large spread in each square footage category encouraged people to spend up to their limits in their search for new housing.[73]

While the city continued to purchase property in the area, it commissioned the accounting firm of Coopers and Lybrand's Detroit office to do a marketing study of the St. John Industrial Park. The goal of this study was provide the site planning team with generalized design constraints for the project, to identify the specific industry groups toward whom marketing efforts should be directed, and to identify the level of demand for industrial land in the Flint area. The report produced the following somewhat obvious conclusions:

- A considerable marketing effort backed by specific inducements will be required if a reasonable level of land use is to be achieved in St. John;

- The delays already experienced may make an already difficult marketing situation virtually impossible;

- The regional industrial park market was already highly competitive. The recession of 1973–1975 caused a virtual halt in land sales in the 18 Certified Class A parks surveyed;

- The majority of developers interviewed incorporated both local and national promotion efforts into their marketing strategy. Those who only marketed locally maintained that the minimal results obtained from national marketing did not warrant the expense;

- Favorable financing terms and tax benefits are required incentives to market the park successfully.[74]

The bulk of the report was based on interviews with other industrial park managers in Michigan.

The report also made recommendations regarding the types of industries that should be targeted in the marketing effort. The authors ranked industries based on six criteria: relationship to the auto industry, environmental impact, job creation potential, growth potential, wage level, and degree of labor skill required. The major concern in this exercise was to suggest nonpolluting industries that could diversify Flint's economy. The study concluded that the following ten industries would be the best targets for Flint's St. John marketing effort:

miscellaneous plastic products
corrugated fiber boxes
porcelain electric supplies
switchgear and switchboards
electrical components
semiconductors
canvas

ophthalmic goods
service industry machinery
printing trades machinery

The report acknowledged that practical considerations might make it impossible to attract any of these preferred industries to the St. John facility, but that these did represent the industry groups that would provide the greatest benefits to Flint.[75]

The Coopers and Lybrand report told Flint what all localities doing economic development projects—industrial parks, in particular—wanted to hear: industrial diversification was possible, and there were industries somewhere that could help improve the local economy. The report pushed Flint into the intense competition for clean, job-producing growth industries, a competition Flint would not win.

With all the area property purchased and the marketing study in hand, the city broke ground for the St. John project in late June of 1977. Of the 250 acres in the St. John area, fifty were set aside for the construction of the state highway, and the rest were to be split between Buick and whatever small- and middle-size firms the city could attract.

By 1980, Bishop Airpark was humming while the St. John project was struggling. Though 90 percent of the infrastructure facilities were completed, 100 of the 180 acres zoned and prepared for industrial use were still available. Flint's economic development coordinator, Patrick J. Martin, remained upbeat about the park, saying it usually takes a decade to fill such a facility.[76] The companies located in the park during its first three years of operation were:

- Buick Motor Division, which bought 60.5 acres at $32,230 per acre. Buick used the space for a marshaling area for new cars and for auto haulaway firms;

- Major Oil Co., which bought 12 acres at the north end of the park and built an oil reclamation plant. This sale was not officially part of the industrial park at first because city officials thought the property, the site of an old landfill, was not suitable for building;

- Berlin & Farro Incineration, Inc., bought about 1.5 acres and used the land to store trailers. This local firm was controversial—it had been accused of polluting its old site in nearby Gaines Township with highly toxic and suspected cancer-causing materials. The company wanted to buy more land, but the city would not sell unless the firm agreed to a long list of promises and conditions;

- Ignition, Inc., bought 1.2 acres for a small facility;
- Security Federal Credit Union bought nearly three acres to serve its customers, mostly Buick employees;
- Universal Electric Construction Co. purchased six acres on which it built a large office-warehouse and shop facility.[77]

As the list of early tenants indicates, Flint failed to meet the goals of economic diversification and pollution-free industry set out in the Coopers and Lybrand report.

At the same time, however, rumors swirled that Buick officials were possibly interested in buying nearly all of the vacant land in the park, a report that Buick neither confirmed nor denied. The *Flint Journal* reported speculations that Buick was considering a "minitechnical and experimental center, possibly even with a small test track."[78] In fact Buick had something much bigger in mind, and internal company politics turned the St. John project from a struggling facility into a successful project, proving yet again that Flint's fortunes rose and fell at the whim of GM.

In 1981, GM faced its worst economic situation since the Great Depression. Sales of new cars were falling, and profits were declining to postwar record lows. The company was forced to scale back capital improvement plans, which included canceling some construction plans in Flint. Buick had planned to modernize production in a new facility to be built in Genesee Township, in a deal assembled by the city of Flint, but that plan was scrapped late in the game despite the fact that the city already had UDAG funds in hand for the project.[79]

Jones and Bachelor describe the corporate events that ultimately led to a boom for the St. John facility: In an effort to streamline the company, top GM officials planned to partially consolidate production of several divisions in one Assembly Division plant. This meant that the Buick Division would lose control of some of its assembly operations. Lloyd Reuss, head of GM's Buick Division, assembled a team of his top executives to explore the possibility of restructuring Buick operations within the existing facilities, thereby retaining control of Buick's own production. The Buick team incorporated the Japanese *kan-ban* system into its restructuring plan, proposing a "just-in-time" inventory system much like that used by Japanese automakers.

The economic decline at the time meant that GM was relatively short of capital, and the Buick proposal required a smaller capital investment than the plan for a new Assembly Division plant. Reuss's team won the internal competition and was given the go-ahead to develop their proposed Buick City concept. At first, Buick City was a mixed blessing for Flint. Though the plan called for a $235-million corporate investment in the old Flint Buick Assembly plant, it also meant the end of the Flint Fisher body plant, since body assembly would be merged with final assembly in the new facility. The merger would cost the city 3,600 jobs, since only 5,000 workers would be retained at the new Buick City.

But Buick City fostered an entirely new set of relationships between GM and its suppliers. The kan-ban system was more demanding of suppliers. It meant that such firms would have to deliver smaller lots of parts on time and more frequently and that the quality of those parts would have to be much higher than was previously demanded. Jones and Bachelor write:

> Buick also made it clear that it expected supplier firms that were granted long-term arrangements to locate in the Flint-Southeast Michigan region. In announcing Buick City, Lloyd Reuss claimed that "right now, we know we can source 99 percent of our parts within a 300 mile radius, 93 percent within 200 miles, and 83 percent within 100 miles." Three hundred miles is about a day's transit distance. "In the years ahead, we will encourage our suppliers to locate closer to Flint. . . . Ideally, we would envision a ring of nearby suppliers delivering parts directly to the assembly line, with no inventory floats at all."[80]

Buick worked directly with the local government to attract suppliers to the area. The automaker gave the city financial and operating information on various supplier firms, which provided the city with an advantage over other localities trying to lure firms to their own facilities.

The St. John project provided immediately available land for suppliers wishing to move to Flint. Jones and Bachelor comment that it seemed "natural" to link the St. John facility with the emerging Buick City concept.[81] Given the city's lack of success in attracting other industry, city officials were happy to have Buick serve as a magnet for firms willing to move into the largely vacant industrial park.

Suppliers snapped up the remaining acreage quickly, for example, Kasle Steel Corp., of Dearborn, bought a 10-acre site, with an option on an additional 8.5 acres, on which it built a $7.5-million plant to convert steel coils to flat blanks for use in body panel production. Mayor Rutherford and Community Development director Jack Litzenberg met with Kasle's owners and explained how the city's EDC could offer tax-exempt industrial development bonds along with a 50 percent property tax abatement for up to 12 years. Kasle paid $25,000 per acre, and that money went back into the city's community development program to help finance other economic activity. Kasle president Leonard Kasle told the *Flint Journal* that they decided to open a Flint operation because the Buick contract required steel to be delivered every four hours. Although that could have been done from Dearborn, transportation problems could have interrupted the delivery schedule.[82]

CONCLUSION

Why did both cities opt to build industrial parks as part of their revitalization strategy? Copy-cat policy-making norms and institutional incentives provide a good explanation for the behavior of Omuta and Flint. Both saw other localities building facilities to lure firms into their communities, and this drew them into competition with surrounding communities. Neither city was particularly innovative in its efforts to entice new companies into town, instead creating basic industrial facilities with standard benefits packages and incentives.

The supply-side response explanation seems to work well for both communities. In Omuta, the government was willing to fund new industrial parks. In Flint, the government and the private sector were predisposed to new industrial park construction. Both cities were situated in regions already well endowed with industrial park facilities, but both still managed to build several new industrial parks, paid for mostly with national government funds. In addition, industrial parks were relatively cheap to build. Both cities used money other than their own whenever possible. The public sector dominated the industrial park development process. Flint looks more fragmented than Omuta in the sense that Flint cobbled together grants to build an industrial park program that did not cost the city much.

This chapter demonstrates the idiosyncratic nature of urban revitalization efforts. Copy-cat policy-making is sometimes sufficient to catalyze a successful redevelopment project, as long as other factors fall into place. The success of Flint's St. John Industrial Park is not the result of local project innovation. It is a complex convergence of several unrelated factors coming together at the same time. The "garbage can model" best summarizes this success: problems, solutions, leadership, and windows of opportunity float around in a policy primeval soup, and change that results from their convergence is essentially random.[83] The point here is that copying *can* lead to success. Building yet another industrial park in Michigan paid off for Flint because it was in the right place at the right time with the right political leadership. The faith that policy imitation can be successful will lead to its perpetuation at the local level, thus reinforcing the tendency of localities to copy rather than to innovate. Since industrial park space is basically a commodity, the key to success in this policy type is the accurate forecasting of demand for park space on the part of the city. Omuta did a better job of realistically predicting demand on the region. Flint did a terrible job of forecasting demand, but the city was saved from another redevelopment flop by GM's decision to add production capacity by building Buick City. As with their other revitalization strategies, Flint took on more risk than did Omuta. However, in this case the risk paid off for the American city: Buick selected Flint as the site for Buick City, a decision that kept hundreds of jobs from leaving the Flint area. Omuta did nothing as daring, since its industrial park efforts were minor and conservative by comparison. Flint's industrial park efforts went through political channels while Omuta's efforts were overwhelmingly bureaucratic. This supports the characterization of Japanese politics as more bureaucratic and American politics as more political.

CHAPTER 6

CONCLUSION

How do Japanese and American cities go about the task of urban revitalization? How do these efforts compare with one another? In this chapter I answer these questions and point out a paradox illustrated by this comparative case study. I also suggest that the Japanese system may be somewhat better for a city than the American system.

JAPANESE-STYLE URBAN REDEVELOPMENT

Omuta's redevelopment efforts started with a reliance on government funding for the projects and the focus of local actors on governmental and quasi-governmental players and permission. The Japanese government played a larger role in Omuta's revitalization efforts than the American government did in Flint's. The earliest efforts to manage Omuta's decline came from the national government in the form of six laws targeting the coal industry. Government officials used these laws to generate a series of coal policy aid packages that helped provide a softer landing for Omuta and for the other cities dependent on the coal industry. This was a stereotypical example of the government targeting and supporting a specific industrial sector, something the United States government does far less explicitly. Governmental involvement in the post-coal era efforts continued, with coal policy bureaucrats shifting their emphasis accordingly and providing funding opportunities for coal

169

industry research and development and for economic diversification through industrial parks and tourism promotion.

A second, though related, aspect of Omuta's redevelopment that stood out was the risk aversion built into the process, exemplified by the delayed implementation of the GeoBio World idea, the largest planned project in the city's policy arsenal. The Japan Development Bank (JDB) carefully scrutinized several iterations of the GeoBio World plans, ultimately rejecting all of them as unlikely to generate a profit for the investor and the city. As a public finance corporation capitalized with public funds, the bank provided much tighter oversight than any investor—public or private—did in Flint. The Japanese system appeared to be more reserved than the American system in its willingness to fund speculative and risky projects. By taking a more hands-on approach to local economic development efforts, national institutions created more approval hoops for Omuta to pass through. Such hoops produced more veto points at which time projects could be killed. By taking the plan evaluation responsibility away from the local level, bank officials added an objective voice to the process. From an institutional perspective, this produced a more conservative policy apparatus, a finer idea filter. Omuta ultimately secured financing for GeoBio World because the city sought funding in an era in which, in retrospect, Japanese banks were quite loose with their capital. The late 1980s and early 1990s were a time for banks to lend money in a somewhat reckless manner, which resulted in a mountain of bad debts and calls for more disciplined lending practices.[1] GeoBio World squeaked through at the tail end of the speculative "bubble" economy.

This close oversight by the JDB was both a good and bad thing for Omuta and for other struggling cities. Close supervision and scrutiny hindered Omuta in implementing what turned out to be an expensive bad idea that failed. Such an oversight apparatus might have prevented Flint from attempting AutoWorld. On the other hand, the inherent conservatism of the bank probably stifled innovation and creativity. New ideas would be viewed skeptically from an investor's perspective, and the city was constrained in its ability to finance projects on its own. Japanese cities had far less fiscal freedom than their American counterparts, which meant they could assume less risk. They also could never accumulate the huge debts of United States cities and could never approach bankruptcy even in the worst of times.

The final notable difference is the primacy of bureaucrats in the redevelopment process, rather than politicians. The mayor was the only politician who played a significant part in Omuta's revitalization effort, and he was a former Ministry of Construction official. The bureaucratic dominance in this policy area made technical know-how more important than political clout. In particular, participants in the process repeatedly stressed the need to understand how the government grant allocation system worked. Bureaucratic primacy in an area of potentially politically lucrative pork-barrel projects seems odd and goes against some accepted views of Japanese politics.[2] Nevertheless, the bureaucrats dominated redevelopment policy in Omuta.

AMERICAN-STYLE URBAN REDEVELOPMENT

In contrast to the Japanese side, the three most distinctive features of American-style urban redevelopment were the predominance of politicians in the process; the crucial role played by local private sector interests; and the explicit intent of federal grant programs to leverage private capital, thereby encouraging private business to undertake urban redevelopment efforts.

Politicians served two functions in Flint's redevelopment efforts. First, at the local level they rallied support for ideas and brought all the local ducks into line. The mayor was the prime mover in this effort, and he was quite successful in building and maintaining local support for what turned out to be a collection of pretty bad ideas. Mayor Rutherford was a good salesperson, and he truly believed in his product. He had no malicious, evil, or greedy intent; he just listened to his consultants and put his support behind the wrong ideas.

At the national level, local congressional representatives successfully lobbied federal agencies and thus were credited with bringing $65 million in federal aid to Flint. The city probably would have received a large amount of national money even without the political support, because Flint's socioeconomic conditions were compelling and its situation was more dire than most. But Flint's representatives capably made their presence felt in Washington, and dutifully arranged meetings and escorted Flint officials to sessions at which they presented and defended their project ideas. Even though the projects were ultimately unsuccessful, the politicians succeeded in helping to win funding for their constituents.

The main private sector institution in Flint that differed radically from anything in Omuta was the Mott Foundation. It contributed almost $50 million to large projects in the city's revitalization effort, in addition to thousands of dollars in smaller program and project donations. Most cities the size of Flint do not have a large patron philanthropic foundation in residence, which made Flint something of an outlier even among American cities. The foundation cultivated a unique public-private partnership that helped to develop and finance many of Flint's larger projects, including the St. John Industrial Park, Bishop Airpark, AutoWorld, Water Street

Pavilion, the riverfront campus of the University of Michigan-Flint, River Village, Windmill Place, the Hyatt Regency Hotel, and Riverbank Park. It often provided the seed money to fund feasibility studies and planning efforts for these projects. Foundation president William S. White said the foundation supported these and other economic redevelopment efforts because he believed they would create new jobs, which in turn would cure many of Flint's problems.

At the height of its focus on economic development in 1983, the foundation allocated nearly $10 million—about one-third of its philanthropic outlay for that year—to projects in Flint.[3] In 1992 the foundation was still paying for the AutoWorld fiasco, allocating another $3.8 million to purchase revenue bonds issued to complete the financing of AutoWorld.[4] Despite the numerous failed projects in Flint, the foundation did not stop contributing money to the cause of Flint's revitalization. Their strategy did change, however, and the foundation increased the number of smaller grants it awarded for small business economic development and for poverty relief programs at the grassroots level. The foundation continued to fund feasibility studies and analyses of local conditions for prospective projects and ideas.[5] Though it spent a lot of money on projects that did not pan out, the foundation did not abandon Flint, and instead continued to voice support for community revitalization schemes backed up by foundation grants.

Finally, the federal government's Urban Development Action Grant (UDAG) program pushed local government to work with business interests in the pursuit of economic growth. It used relatively small amounts of public money to leverage private investment in industrial, commercial, and neighborhood development. This emphasis on private leadership in revitalization efforts provided strong incentives for developers to get into the economic renewal business. Once national corporations like the Rouse Corporation learned the formula for winning grants, it was a relatively easy matter for them to sell their idea to struggling localities and thus continue to ride the wave of success. Cities that wanted a piece of the lucrative UDAG pie were forced, in turn, to rely on these experienced players in order to win federal grants. Over half of Flint's $65 million in federal funds came from the UDAG program, including the largest grants for Buick City ($11.9 million) and AutoWorld ($8.6 million).

THE CENTRAL QUESTION ANSWERED

Why did Omuta and Flint pursue what, in retrospect, appeared to be bad policy ideas? Why did they implement revitalization projects that ultimately failed to meet their goals? Why and how did Omuta avoid bad policy decisions more adeptly than Flint? Supply-side policy-making was a strategy used by both cities. They copied—or at least tried to copy—successful ideas from other communities, and they were encouraged to do so by various institutional features of their respective governmental systems.

WHAT THEY DID

Both cities tried to use proven policies to address their economic woes, although few of their efforts produced positive results. Even though a few jobs were created in each community, they were far from able to offset the massive job losses caused by the downsizing and restructuring of the primary employers, Mitsui and General Motors (GM). Redevelopment efforts in both places failed to stem the decline in population and failed to diversify the local economy away from the historically dominant industries. Omuta and Flint worked from strategically similar positions: both went after projects that focused on quality of life improvements, tourism, and new job creation.

One might count the refurbishment and improvement of existing public facilities—parks and a library, hospital, and community center in Omuta; and parks and a university in Flint—as minor successes because they added to the quality of life in each city. At the same time, however, large tracts of land sat vacant or unused, blighted by years of pollution-intensive industry in Omuta and by urban decay and decline in Flint. These chronic problems were battled but not remedied by revitalization efforts in both cities.

Different strategies emerged from distinctly different institutional structures. Although these strategies focused on similar goals—attracting new firms to the community, promoting tourism, and improving quality of life in the community to retain remaining residents and to entice people (and companies) to move there—the way they went about attaining these goals differed significantly. The Japanese system prompted Omuta to do three things that made its outcome look better than Flint's. Two of these systemic features are structural and one is cultural. First, it forced greater oversight on Omuta's larger projects. There were more veto points in the Japanese decision-making system that made it harder for bad policy ideas to come to fruition. Second, the norm of inclusive decision-making—embodied in the practice of *nemawashi*—brought more people into the decision process at the local level. Whereas Flint's redevelopment efforts were overwhelmingly dominated by local elites, Omuta's projects tended to be far more inclusive. This meant that projects brought to fruition in Omuta were more widely supported than those in Flint. Finally, the fiscal constraints built into the Japanese system forced Omuta to take a more conservative approach toward redevelopment. This helped it avoid making really bad policy decisions. In contrast, Flint's emphasis on private sector resources allowed it to take huge financial risks that ultimately did not pan out.

Why They Did What They Did

What explains this lack of innovation? The local redevelopment strategies in each country are remarkably similar because the institutional structure in both nations pushes cities to replicate successful projects from other communities, rather than encouraging them to innovate new solutions appropriate to their own specific problems. Supply-side government programs that reward local compliance with national government programs, a heavy reliance on private sector consultants interested in replicating their own past successes, and a local tendency to copy other cities' successes all caused Omuta and Flint to choose redevelopment efforts that faced strong odds against them from the beginning.

Policy copying is the normal method of policy-making for localities in Japan and in the United States. Replicating ideas in other policy areas is a good idea because it seems to work—copying another city's pollution control statute, social welfare program, or other policy innovation often produces the same positive result for the copiers as it does for the idea's originator. Water fluoridation, education finance innovation, and various local welfare programs demonstrate this.[6] However, these policy areas are all positive-sum games. Such ideas can be replicated repeatedly, with no decline in the benefits gained by the copiers. Every city and town in the nation could fluoridate their water, and everyone drinking that water would benefit. The payoff would only start to diminish when localities build multiple, redundant fluoridation systems.

But this model of copy-cat policy-making is inappropriate for economic development policy, since such programs tend to produce a zero-sum (or negative-sum) game outcome.[7] Being first matters. And though the next few localities to implement a program may profit, subsequent copycats will experience diminishing returns. In fact, if several adjacent localities copy each other and build a concentration of one type of project, they may create a negative-sum game. Take the proliferation of amusement parks (or industrial parks, or gambling casinos, the current American craze) as an example. The first community to build an amusement park reaps some reward for its innovation, since it is the only facility of its kind in the region. But if the towns on either side of it also build amusement parks, supply exceeds demand and everyone suffers from the overcapacity of available amusement park space—including the innovator who built the first amusement park. In such situations it is irrational for localities to approach economic development from a diffusion perspective, since unless they innovate they will always be on the downside of a curve and always be losing.

Beyond the basic similarity of copy-cat policy-making, however, the institutional differences between Japan and the United States account for the different outcomes observed in the two cities: Omuta latched onto some big ideas that local leaders were unable to bring to fruition, while Flint implemented several grand schemes that quickly became notorious failures. Three interconnected institutional structures dictated this difference in outcome.

Governmental Oversight

First, Omuta operated in an environment of more strict intergovernmental oversight than did Flint. Japanese national officials were more involved in Omuta's redevelopment efforts than American national officials were in Flint's efforts. Omuta was not given national grant money until the details of a project plan were approved. Flint received national grant money based on a broad conceptual proposal, and it was then free to use it under less scrutiny. Such grants were used to leverage private financing for revitalization projects.

Public versus Private Funding

Public versus private project financing was a second salient structural difference between Omuta and Flint. Public funds paid for a higher percentage of Omuta's projects. This money came from both directly controlled ministerial budgets and from a variety of public corporations established to implement ministerial policy pronouncements. In contrast, Flint's redevelopment efforts relied more heavily on private sector financing. Private philanthropy, in the form of the foundation, and private venture capital sources provided most of the money used for redevelopment in Flint. The effect of this difference was that Omuta's planners and financiers operated with great public accountability. Flint's planners and financiers were accountable primarily to the sources of their capital, though they did receive some public money that served to leverage the private investment. This lack of broad accountability on the American side, coupled with the weaker oversight provided by the American governmental structure, made it easier for Flint to implement risky project ideas.

A recent study of private foundations and their impact on health care reform provides some conclusions that are equally applicable to the foundation's role in Flint's revitalization efforts. Weissert and Knott found that

America's major foundations come to the policy arena with good intentions and means. They want to do good, and they operate under few constraints and with little accountability. Furthermore, their ideas are highly regarded by policymakers and others in the policy process, and they often provide "public interest venture capital."[8] They are in a position to encourage risk-taking and innovation—project failure is unlikely to lead to a loss of jobs for foundation leaders, even though they are notoriously unwilling to act boldly. Instead they act rather timidly, rarely pushing the policy frontiers.

These comments accurately describe the foundation and its position in Flint's revitalization policy-making process. It wanted to do good, operated under few constraints, and spoke boldly in public of new initiatives. Yet it acted rather timidly in pushing policy to new areas and ideas, instead opting to support proven winners and to previously successful policy options. Despite this reality, local policymakers held the foundation in high regard for its continued efforts in the right direction.

Bureaucrats versus Politicians and Consultants

The final institutional difference of note was the role of bureaucrats and politicians in the revitalization process. In Omuta, bureaucrats were more important than politicians; in Flint, politicians were more important than bureaucrats. More specifically, the application process for national grant money operated primarily through bureaucratic channels in Omuta and through political channels in Flint. Technical expertise and project know-how were more important in Omuta, while political connections and support were more important in Flint. This institutional feature further buttresses the pattern of oversight already created by the two structural features just noted. Politicians are concerned with bringing national expenditures to their district. Such pork barrel projects have electoral repercussions. They are generally not concerned with the minutiae—or the viability—of projects. Though Japanese politicians have a similar interest in pork, Omuta's national representatives were bringing home the bacon in other policy areas. Urban redevelopment was the purview of bureaucrats, who were quite interested and involved in the details of the proposed projects.

The Source of Bad Ideas

What are the likely sources of bad ideas? There are two different causes of bad policy ideas. One is copy-cat policy-making in a zero-sum system. The second is the norm of supply-side policy-making, the tendency to take on solutions provided by others rather than thinking through the problem and taking the responsibility for designing the best possible solution for that problem regardless of whether ideas are old or new or whether they come from within or from outside. The amusement park comparison is a case of copy-cat policy-making. Both cities simply tried to copy ideas for promoting tourism from other localities. The key to avoiding bad policy-making in this instance was for someone on the outside of the process to make a judgment about whether the project was a good gamble or not. There was such an outsider in Japan; no such player existed in the U.S. case.

Supply-side policy-making applies to the comparison of downtown shopping center revitalization. Here copy-cat policy-making matters less than carefully thinking through the problem. Thinking through such a project is difficult. The Japanese do it better because of bureaucratic capability and a custom of bottom-up participation. Neither of these features would have helped in the amusement park (copy-cat policy-making) case.

Both of these are difficult situations, so their "success"—or their ability to avoid stupid mistakes—really depends on some good government performance. The Japanese governmental system performed better than its American counterparts. Industrial parks do not depend on good government per se. They rely more on common sense and luck. Omuta had the first; Flint had the second. No city should need expensive outside studies to conceive ideas for industrial parks. Rather, narrow surveys of who would be likely to move in are all that are required. Cities can easily do these on their own.

STRENGTHENING THE CAUSAL LINK

How closely does the presence of copy-cat policy-making vary with policy success and failure? If the theory is correct, copied redevelopment efforts should be successful if imitated early on in the life of the idea, or early on the diffusion curve. But well-worn revitalization ideas adopted by these cities should be failures if the area is saturated with similar projects. Conversely, innovative ideas should correlate positively with success. Innovation is a necessary, though not sufficient, factor for a revitalization project to succeed.

Success is defined differently for each project, since each project comes with a different set of stated goals. Projects aimed at tourism promotion are judged on their ability to draw visitors to the community and on their ability to provide jobs for local residents. Projects aimed at creating jobs and luring new firms to the area are evaluated on their success in these areas. Success or failure in these endeavors should also be determined relative to the cost of the project. An expensive project that generates few jobs is not a rousing success. I did not provide a precise measure of success for comparing these projects against each other. Instead, I evaluated the effect of these projects on Omuta and Flint and rated them accordingly.

Figure 6.1 places the projects discussed in the preceding three chapters along a continuum in terms of relative success or failure, with the degree of cost (or benefit) to the community figured into the evaluation. "Failure with cost" denotes a project with significant financial costs that was an absolute failure: it failed to meet any of its goals, and it caused investors—whether public or private—to incur a heavy financial debt. At the other end of the spectrum are projects classified as "success with high benefits." These projects met or exceeded their goals; these projects turned out better than expected. In the middle of the spectrum are projects termed *no effect or not implemented*. These are projects that made it through the planning stages but were not actually constructed or otherwise brought to fruition. They are not cost free, since planning projects does take time, money, and human effort. However, these costs are generally low relative to the cost of actually implementing the projects, and they are thus treated as virtually costing nothing. The final two categories, midway between failure and no effect, and success and no effect, represent projects that are middling versions of the extreme positions.

As figure 6.1 suggests, Omuta's revitalization efforts cluster toward the middle of the spectrum, while Flint's projects reside at the extremes. Most of Omuta's projects that actually were implemented fall in the "success with marginal benefits" category. The *shôtengai* redevelopment efforts brought some shoppers back to the downtown area, though not many. The industrial park efforts were marginally successful in that they created some jobs and filled the park sites. However, a substantial number of the firms that took sites were already in Omuta to begin with, and these did not increase their employment markedly. All of these marginally successful projects were either small- or medium-size efforts. Omuta's largest effort, GeoBio World, did fail. On the other hand, because there were so many other existing theme parks in the region, the delayed decision to build it—forced on the city by the JDB, which would not finance the project—may well have saved the city and any investors a lot of money. The Matsuya department store nonproject is evaluated in a similar fashion. Had it been built, it would have competed directly with similar facilities in nearby Kurume and Fukuoka City.

What does this clustering in the middle range mean? This suggests a general trend in Japanese policy-making that warrants further study: urban revitalization policy-making in Japan is better suited to effecting incremental improvements in local socioeconomic conditions. In baseball

Figure 6.1: Relative Success and Failure

	Success with High Benefit	Moderate Success with Benefit	No Effect or Not Implemented	Moderate Failure with Cost	Failure with Cost
Omuta		Shotengai Redevelopment Industrial Parks		GeoBio World	
Flint	Industrial Parks				Water St. Pavilion AutoWorld

terms, the Japanese system is better suited to hitting singles, to hitting for average, than it is to hitting home runs. There are no home runs in Omuta's redevelopment policy lineup, but there are no big strikeouts either.

In contrast, Flint's redevelopment efforts were either big hits or big misses. The only exception to this statement is the Bishop Airpark, a small industrial park that falls in the "success with marginal benefits" category for the same reasons as its counterparts in Omuta: it was occupied by local firms, and few new jobs were created. AutoWorld and Water Street Pavilion, however, were large, high-profile, costly projects that quickly became huge white elephants. Buick City and the St. John Industrial Park were also large projects that were clear home runs. They created or saved a large number of jobs for local residents, and they successfully attracted new firms to Flint. Innovation was notably absent in the two failed projects. Consultants plugged Flint into off-the-shelf successful redevelopment formulas, and the projects went nowhere. Buick City was a huge coup for the city because it stopped GM from moving even more jobs out of the city than it already had. The St. John project benefited from the events surrounding Buick City, though there was really no innovation involved in its evolution. In fact, the St. John project languished until GM decided to build Buick City. The St. John facility was a success with great benefits, though it attained this success largely by being in the right place at the right time.

ALTERNATIVE EXPLANATIONS

The St. John Industrial Park story is an example of an alternative explanation for success; luck and geographic positioning explain more of its success than do innovation and/or copy-cat policy-making. Other cases defy my copy-cat policy-making and policy diffusion hypotheses, indicating that urban redevelopment is a complicated topic that resists simple explanation. Why did Omuta and Flint go after what, in retrospect, were bad policy ideas? Other explanations are available to answer this question, from both a success and failure perspective.

It is possible that there is a lack of good ideas—or a surplus of bad ideas—floating in the system. When is a good idea more likely to be generated or selected? I found no study that answers this question directly in the Japanese politics literature, but we can infer some possible answers from other areas of political studies. Aberbach, Putnam, and Rockman argue that politicians are more likely than bureaucrats to articulate ideals in the United States, though they claim the American system is exceptional when compared to the various European countries: the worlds of bureaucrats and politicians overlap much more in the United States than they do in

Europe.[9] Despite the fact that Japan is not included in their analysis, Japan fits this characterization as well, though probably not to the extent that the United States does. If anything, Japanese bureaucrats are more involved in policy-making than their American counterparts. Though their four images of bureaucrats and politicians suggest new ideas should come from politicians rather than bureaucrats, their evidence shows that American bureaucrats are in a position to provide ideas as well.

In Japan, however, empirical evidence supports the notion that politicians are more likely to come up with an innovative good idea than bureaucrats are. Two of the most innovative—and widely known—revitalization schemes in Japan were conceived by politicians in Kyushu. Chikami Toshiyuki, mayor of Kurume City, is credited with coming up with the "Technopolis" strategy of regional information capitals that has been implemented in Japan. Chikami's idea was picked up by the National Industrial Structure Council in 1980, and by the late 1980s a network of smaller cities across Japan were designated to spearhead the extension of new information technology and research to the society at large.[10] Hiramatsu Morihiko, governor of Oita, came up with the idea of one village, one product (*isson, ippin*) to focus local energy in one unified direction.[11] His program has also been copied by many localities, and eventually was supported by national government grants.

Calder supports this idea with evidence from national level policy-making. He asserts that "Japanese conservative policies have been creative, first and foremost, because Japanese conservative politicians have been insecure and hence preoccupied with stabilizing their own positions."[12] It makes sense that politicians should want to make good policy in order to secure victory in the next election. They bestow benefits in order to win votes. Bureaucrats excel at maintaining stability through routine policy channels. Politicians—other than the mayor—were notably absent from Omuta's redevelopment policy process. Perhaps their participation might have stimulated more innovative program ideas and pulled revitalization efforts out of the bureaucratic policy routine. Further study of other Japanese cities—especially successful cases—might shed some light on this alternative possibility. Omuta may simply be an outlier in this regard.

On the American side, politicians were involved in the successful projects. Specifically, Flint's mayor Rutherford played a skillful game of negotiation to entice GM into Buick City (and the GM suppliers into the St. John project). This seems to support the "politicians come up with (or at least sponsor) innovative ideas" hypothesis. However, politicians—including the same mayor Rutherford—also were instrumental in bringing the AutoWorld and Water Street Pavilion ideas to fruition. This may be only part of a complex answer to the question of where innovative ideas come from.

Paradoxical Findings

Two paradoxical observations come out of this research. First, a city can succeed (with a project) and still fail (to reverse the city's decline). Both cities tallied successful projects, but neither was able to ease the socioeconomic pain of its residents. This suggests that the whole of urban revitalization can be less than the sum of its parts (viz., specific projects).

Second, a city can fail (with a whole series of projects) and still succeed (by not making a bad situation worse). Omuta fits this description. The key to these two paradoxes is context: what happens to GM and Mitsui overpowers whatever Flint and Omuta do. Sometimes a city is just (un)lucky.

Which System is Better?

It is rare to find a city that tries something truly innovative and succeeds at it, and the process that leads to success is highly idiosyncratic and difficult to predict. Some stories of successful revitalization have been told, however.[13] If replication of these successes elsewhere only produces diminishing returns, then perhaps we need to study the failures and develop better redevelopment policy processes from them.

This is a study of two cities in desperate need of revitalization. Both made concerted efforts to stimulate their economy. Flint spent heavily on several risky projects, while Omuta spent more conservatively. Both communities tried to copy successful projects from other localities. Why was public policy in the development area so much worse in Flint than it was in Omuta? The American institutional structure allowed Flint to implement what, in retrospect, were foolish policy ideas. In particular, the foundation, private sector consultancy, and the federal grant system are responsible for the policy direction taken by that city. Though the foundation was undoubtedly well intentioned, its lack of accountability to anyone other than itself was problematic. Prominent consultants sold previously successful reputations and ideas to officials in both cities. However, consultants were actively involved in the federal grant process in the American system. Furthermore, once grants were awarded to Flint, there was little federal oversight or evaluation of the proposed projects. These factors combined to produce a structure of institutionalized irresponsibility where the salient actors operated with great autonomy and little accountability. Though consultants are active in Japan, they are not part of the grant application process because it is a much more technocratic—and far less political—affair. Moreover, national government oversight is more detailed and involved in the Japanese system. There is less autonomy and more accountability built into the Japanese system. Omuta's redevelopment efforts were less disastrous than Flint's because the national institutional structure minimized the city's ability to try policy ideas that rapidly resulted in failure. The American system permits risk to excess, while the Japanese system probably does not permit enough risk-taking on the part of localities. Which system is preferable? Though neither situation is desirable, the Japanese is better for the community. After trying hard to revitalize, neither city has progressed very far. But at least Omuta is not saddled with the abandoned projects and massive debt that Flint must bear. After all their efforts, Flint is in worse shape than Omuta.

CHAPTER ONE: NO MIRACLES HERE

1. Peter Eisinger, "Do the American States Do Industrial Policy?" *British Journal of Political Science*, No. 20: 509–535 (October 1990). Paul Brace, *State Government and Economic Performance* (Baltimore: Johns Hopkins, 1993).

2. Economic restructuring refers to the largely market-driven process by which certain industries lose their comparative advantage and thus are forced to close or relocate. Although new industries may simultaneously be emerging in other parts of the nation, the effects on the localities that suffer the loss of one or more primary employers is devastating. Population exodus, loss of tax base, and the general breakdown of the local socioeconomic system are common results of economic restructuring. This process of decline is commonly known as "hollowing out" in the local economy.

3. A book by Ross J. Gittell, *Renewing Cities* (Princeton: Princeton University Press, 1993), addresses this question in four medium-size American cities. An earlier volume of case studies is Dennis Judd and Michael Parkinson, eds., *Leadership and Urban Regeneration: Cities in North America and Europe* (Beverly Hills: Sage Urban Affairs Annual Reviews, 1990).

4. Timothy K. Barnekov, *Privatism and Urban Policy in Britain and the United States* (Oxford: Oxford University Press, 1989).

5. Timothy J. Conlan, *The New Federalism: Intergovernmental Reform and Political Change from Nixon to Reagan* (Washington, DC: Brookings Institution, 1988).

6. Ichirô Ozawa, *Nihon Kaizô Keikaku* (A plan for remodeling Japan) (Tokyo: Kôdansha, 1993).

7. The terms *policy* and *policy-making* refer to the development and pursuit of strategies aimed at revitalizing a city. Though "policy" often connotes national-level decisions, I use it to describe local—at times in conjunction with the

185

state/prefecture and nation—government action. Thus, urban redevelopment policy is the activity on the part of government to help depressed or declining cities rebound and to improve local socioeconomic conditions.

8. See, for example, Sven Steinmo, Kathleen Thelen, and Frank Longstreth, eds., *Structuring Politics: Historical Institutionalism in Comparative Analysis* (Cambridge: Cambridge University Press, 1992); and R. Kent Weaver and Bert A. Rockman, eds., *Do Institutions Matter?: Government Capabilities in the United States and Abroad* (Washington, DC: Brookings Institution, 1993).

9. Peter Hall, *Governing the Economy: The Politics of State Intervention in Britain and France* (New York: Oxford University Press, 1986), p. 19.

10. G. John Ikenberry, "Conclusion: An Institutional Approach to American Foreign Economic Policy," in Ikenberry, David A. Lake, and Michael Mastanduno, eds., *The State and American Foreign Economic Policy* (Ithaca, NY: Cornell University Press, 1988), p. 226.

11. Paul E. Peterson, *City Limits* (Chicago: University of Chicago Press, 1981).

12. On Lowell, see Gittell, *Renewing Cities*, pp. 65–93. For more detail on Oita, see Ezra Vogel, *Comeback* (Tokyo: Charles E. Tuttle, 1985), pp. 114–119, 122–23.

13. This definition is taken from James G. March and Herbert A. Simon, *Organizations* (New York: Wiley, 1958), pp. 174–175.

14. Edward M. Gramlich, "Intergovernmental Grants: A Review of the Empirical Literature," in Wallace E. Oates, ed., *The Political Economy of Fiscal Federalism* (Lexington, MA: Lexington Books, 1977), p. 222.

15. Conlan, *New Federalism*.

16. Martha Derthick, *Uncontrollable Spending for Social Service Grants* (Washington, DC: Brookings Institution, 1975), pp. 106–9.

17. Eisinger, "Do the American States Do Industrial Policy?"; Brace, *State Government and Economic Performance*; David Osborne, *Laboratories of Democracy* (Boston: Harvard Business School Press, 1988).

18. Osborne, *Laboratories of Democracy*, pp. 154–161, 165–170.

19. Steven R. Reed, *Japanese Prefectures and Policymaking* (Pittsburgh: University of Pittsburgh Press, 1986), p. 29.

20. Ronald P. Dore, *Shinohata: Portrait of a Japanese Village* (New York: Pantheon, 1978), p. 238.

21. Reed, *Japanese Prefectures and Policymaking*, p. 38.

22. Robert A. Dahl, *Who Governs? Democracy and Power in an American City* (New Haven: Yale University Press, 1961).

23. Gittell, *Renewing Cities*, pp. 157–58.

24. John W. Kingdon, *Agendas, Alternatives, and Public Policies* (Glenview, Ill.: Scott, Foresman, 1984), p. 122.

25. See Reed, *Japanese Prefectures and Policymaking*, p. 48; Masatoshi Yorimitsu, "The Decline and Renaissance of the Steel Town: The Case of Kamaishi," in

Kuniko Fujita and Richard Child Hill, eds., *Japanese Cities in the World Economy* (Philadelphia: Temple University Press, 1993), pp. 203–223; Jack L. Walker, "The Diffusion of Innovations among the American States," *American Political Science Review* 63:880–899 (1969); and Virginia Gray, "Innovation in the States: A Diffusion Study," *American Political Science Review* 67:1174–85 (1973).

26. This is in reference to welfare policy in Japan. See Richard J. Samuels, *The Politics of Regional Policy in Japan: Localities Incorporated?* (Princeton: Princeton University Press, 1983), p. 90.

27. The idea that bureaucratic organizations change operating procedures when they learn from past mistakes (or decisions), and that their inclination in any case is to do things according to a "standard operating procedure," is borrowed from Graham T. Allison, *Essence of Decision: Explaining the Cuban Missile Crisis* (Boston: Little, Brown, 1971).

28. See Douglass S. North, *Institutions, Institutional Change, and Economic Performance* (New York: Cambridge University Press, 1990), pp. 92–106. North employed the notion of path dependence to explain the survival of societies and economies that are characterized by consistently poor performance. Once institutions exist, the cost of changing or going against those institutions is higher than the cost of following those previously developed pathways. Though the institutional paths may have been developed to deal with a historically obsolete issue, they continue to exist long after their utility has expired. Path dependence is used to explain a wide range of institutional structures, from the practice of common law to the odd layout of a typewriter keyboard (Paul David, "Clio and the Economics of QWERTY," *American Economic Review* 75:332–337).

29. Robert E. Cole, *Strategies for Learning: Small-Group Activities in American, Japanese, and Swedish Industry* (Berkeley: University of California Press, 1989), p. 44.

30. Ibid., pp. 45–46.

31. Robert L. Crain provides an example of a successful policy diffusion area in "Fluoridation: The Diffusion of an Innovation among Cities," *Social Forces* 44:467–476 (June 1966).

32. In "The Diffusion of Innovations among the American States" Walker looked at eighty eight policy areas where the diffusion of innovations had positive effects.

33. This is more likely in a unitary system, but it happens in federal systems as well. See John C. Campbell, *How Policies Change: The Japanese Government and the Aging Society* (Princeton: Princeton University Press, 1992).

34. Franklin James, "Urban Economic Development: A Zero-Sum Game?" in Richard D. Bingham and John P. Blair, eds., *Urban Economic Development* (Beverly Hills: Sage Publications, 1984), pp. 157–174.

35. Mark Schneider and Paul Teske, *Public Entrepreneurs: Agents for Change in American Government* (Princeton: Princeton University Press, 1995), p. 7.

36. Chalmers A. Johnson, *MITI and the Japanese Miracle: The Growth of Industrial Policy, 1925–1975* (Stanford, CA: Stanford University Press, 1982), pp. 19–20.

37. Kurt Steiner, *Local Government in Japan* (Stanford, CA: Stanford University Press, 1965), p. 166.

38. Michio Muramatsu , "Center-Local Political Relations in Japan: A Lateral Competition Model," *Journal of Japanese Studies* 12:307 (1986).

39. Ibid., p. 308.

40. Ibid., pp. 320–323.

41. Samuels, *Politics of Regional Policy in Japan*, pp. 90–91.

42. Reed, *Japanese Prefectures and Policymaking*, pp. 158–159.

43. Eisuke Sakakibara, "The Japanese Politico-Economic System and the Public Sector," in Samuel Kernell, ed., *Parallel Politics: Economic Policymaking in Japan and the United States* (Washington, DC: Brookings Institution, 1991), pp. 52–53.

44. Peterson, *City Limits*.

45. Chalmers Johnson, *Japan's Public Policy Companies* (Washington, DC: American Enterprise Institute for Public Policy Research, 1978), p. 16.

Chapter Two: A Tale of Two Cities

1. Paul E. Peterson, Barry G. Rabe, and Kenneth K. Wong, *When Federalism Works* (Washington, DC: Brookings Institution, 1986), p. 99.

2. Ibid., pp. 100–101.

3. Peterson, *City Limits* (Chicago: University of Chicago Press, 1981); Clarence N. Stone and Heywood T. Sanders, *The Politics of Urban Development* (Lawrence: University Press of Kansas, 1987); Stone, *Regime Politics: Governing Atlanta, 1946–1988* (Lawrence: University Press of Kansas, 1989).

4. Ross J. Gittell, Renewing Cities (Princeton: Princeton University Press, 1993), p. 8.

5. Robert Dahl's *Who Governs?* (New Haven: Yale University Press, 1961) is a good example of this type of research.

6. Some scholars consider Japan's high growth to be a post-World War II phenomenon. However, rapid heavy industrial growth started late in the nineteenth or early in the twentieth century. For an explanation of this debate, see W. G. Beasley, *The Rise of Modern Japan* (New York: St. Martin's, 1990).

7. By 1987, top-grade bituminous coal from the Miike mine was selling for $128/ton, versus $41/ton for imported coal. This was primarily due to the fact that extraction costs overseas were so much lower than in Japan. But the rise in the strength of the yen vis-à-vis the dollar also hurt the competitiveness of domestic coal. See: Fukuoka Prefecture, *Conditions in Coal-Producing Regions of Fukuoka Prefecture* (Fukuoka-ken Santan Chiiki no Genjô), (Fukuoka, Japan: 1992), p. 5.

8. The story of MITI's decision to manage the decline of the coal industry is an interesting one. The ministry had a difficult time balancing the demands of coal users for cheaper coal on the one hand, and the demands of the declining coal industry for an easing of the burden of rationalization on the other. In

addition, there was considerable pressure from environmentalist groups calling for the burning of cleaner, less sulfur-laden coal. Two good explanations of this interest group struggle are Richard Samuels, *The Business of the Japanese State: Energy Markets in Comparative and Historical Perspective* (Ithaca, NY: Cornell University Press, 1987); and Laura Hein, *Fueling Growth: The Energy Revolution and Economic Policy in Postwar Japan* (Cambridge: Council on East Asian Studies, Harvard University, 1990).

9. See: City of Omuta, *An Overview of Omuta* (Omuta no Gaikyô), December 1992.

10. See: National Census Data for Omuta.

11. City of Omuta, *Citizens Lives* (Shimin no Kurashi), annual statistical publication.

12. Sôrifu Shakai Hoshô Seido Shingikai Jimukyoku, ed., *Social Security Statistical Yearbook* (Shakai Hoshô Tôkei Nenpô) (Tokyo: Hôken, 1993), p. 91.

13. For examples see "A Tale of Two Auto Towns," *Newsweek*, April 1, 1974; "Hard Times in the Heartland," *Time*, December 7, 1981; and "The Uneven Burden of Today's Recession," *US News and World Report*, March 1, 1982.

14. Ronald Edsforth, *Class Conflict and Cultural Consensus: The Making of a Mass Consumer Society in Flint, Michigan* (New Brunswick: Rutgers University Press, 1987), p. 97.

15. For a detailed history of the politics of class conflict in Flint, see ibid.

16. U.S. Bureau of the Census, *County Business Patterns.*

17. For a more explicit description of Japanese local government structure, see Kurt Steiner, *Local Government in Japan* (Stanford, CA: Stanford University Press, 1965); and Steven R. Reed, *Japanese Prefectures and Policymaking* (Pittsburgh: Pittsburgh University Press, 1986), pp. 22–43.

18. Reed, *Japanese Prefectures and Policymaking*, p. 25.

19. Ibid.

20. *Zaisei Tôkei*, Ministry of Finance Shûkei-kyoku Chôsa-ka, 1992.

21. This formula is set by the MOHA, and is applied to all local governments nationwide. At present, the Omuta assembly has 44 directly elected members, representing a population of just over 150,000.

22. Interview with Muto Yasukatsu, Planning and Promotion Section Chief, Omuta City Hall, December 22, 1992.

23. Omuta City, *Citizens' Lives* (Shimin no Kurashi), annual statistical publication, 1979–1989. In 1979 there were 5.5 kilometers^2 of public park area within city boundaries. By 1989 that number had increased to 6.3 kilometers^2.

24. In the United States, there is some anecdotal research that suggests this is true. See Joel Garreau, *Edge City: Life on the New Frontier* (New York: Doubleday, 1991).

25. "Summary of the Six Laws Relating to Coal" (Sekitan Kankei Roppô no Gaiyô). Internal document received from Fukuoka Prefecture's Regional Development Division, Coal Mining Area Development Section.

26. The current program is functionally the "ninth coal policy", but it is not called that because it is intended to be the final iteration in the series. According to one Fukuoka Prefecture official, simply calling it the "ninth coal policy" would imply an intention to make a tenth, eleventh, and so forth. This is the government's way of communicating the termination of this industry rationalization policy series. (Interview with Sato Seiji, Coal Mining Area Development Section Chief, Regional Development Division, Fukuoka Prefecture, May 27, 1993.)

27. Hein, *Fueling Growth*, p. 230, 248.

28. Samuels, *Business of the Japanese State*, pp. 108–124, 131.

29. John C. Campbell, *How Policies Change: The Japanese Government and the Aging Society* (Princeton: Princeton University Press, 1992), p. 353.

30. Kyushu Trade and Industry Bureau, *Present Conditions of Kyushu Coal Production Areas* (Kyushu Santan Chiiki no Genkyô) (Fukuoka, Japan: Kyushu Tsûsho Sangyô Kyoku, 1992), pp. 13–14.

31. Shiotsuka made this clear in public comments and in statements to the press.

32. *Nikkan Kôgyô Shimbun*, April 21, 1989.

33. *Nikkei Sangyô Shimbun*, November 9, 1988.

34. *Nikkan Kôgyô Shimbun*, April 4, 1989.

35. Interview with Nishimura Satoru, Omuta City Assembly official, May 24, 1993.

36. Interview with Goto Kanichi, Director, Research Division, Kyushu Bureau of International Trade and Industry, MITI, February 16, 1993.

37. "Overview of the Coal Area Promotion Policy," n.p., January 1993. Information provided by the Kyushu Bureau of International Trade and Industry, MITI.

38. The city slogan, *Sekitan mo aru toshi* (The city that also has coal) symbolizes this goal. This slogan received wide play in the local newspapers.

39. In the first six years of his administration, the population continued to decline, though at a slower rate, and there were few new jobs created in Omuta.

40. Interview with Muto Yasukatsu, December 22, 1992.

41. Interview with Nishimura Satoru, May 24, 1993.

42. This point is developed more fully in chapter 1. See Ronald Dore, *Shinohata: A Portrait of a Japanese Village* (New York: Pantheon, 1978), pp. 236–241; also Kent Calder, *Crisis and Compensation: Public Policy and Political Stability in Japan* (Princeton: Princeton University Press, 1988); and Eisuke Sakakibara, "The Japanese Politico-Economic System and the Public Sector," in Samuel Kernell, ed., *Parallel Politics: Economic Policymaking in Comparative Perspective* (Washington, DC: Brookings Institution, 1991).

43. See for example, Local Financial Affairs Association (Chihô Zaimu Kyôkai), *How to Understand Local Independent Projects* (Kore de Wakaru Chihô Tandoku Jigyô) (Tokyo: Local Financial Affairs Association, 1992). Though the title implies independence, the book is an overview of all the major national government

programs that allocate money for urban economic redevelopment. It contains the enabling legislation and examples of completed projects—including color photographs—funded by the various programs. See also Planning Section of the Ministry for Local Autonomy, *Tandoku Jigyô Handobukku* (*Independent Project Handbook*) (Tokyo: Dai-Ichi Hôki Publishing, 1993); Mitsuo Yokota and Kenji Ebata, *Kôkyô Shisetsu Zaigen Benran* (Public Facility Finance Handbook), (Tokyo: Gyôsei, 1993).

44. "Summary of the Six Laws Relating to Coal" (Sekitan Kankei Roppô no Gaiyô). Internal document received from Fukuoka Prefecture's Regional Development Division, Coal Mining Area Development Section.

45. *Asahi Shimbun*, October 31, 1989; *Yomiuri Shimbun*, March 10, 1990.

46. *Mainichi Shimbun*, December 21, 1990.

47. *Mainichi Shimbun*, December 3, 1991.

48. *Asahi Shimbun*, March 5, 1991.

49. Reported in all the major papers that same date.

50. "Overview of the World Coal Technology Center Facilities Plan Study Report," Omuta City, March 1992.

51. Held in 1992 and 1993, both were called the "Active Coal Forum in Kyushu."

52. "Overview of the World Coal Technology Center Facilities Plan Study Report," Omuta City, March 1992.

53. Interview with Muto Yasukatsu, December 22, 1992.

54. An example of this is the Technopolis strategy, a seed program for stimulating high-tech research, development, and production in rural areas. See Sheridan Tatsuno, *The Technopolis Strategy: Japan, High Technology, and the Control of the Twenty-First Century* (New York: Prentice-Hall, 1986); and Ezra F. Vogel, *Comeback, Case by Case: Building the Resurgence of American Business* (Tokyo: Charles E. Tuttle, 1985), pp. 121–124. Neighboring Oita Prefecture's "One Village, One Product" (*Isson, Ippin*) strategy is another example of a development idea picked up and disseminated by the national government. Of course, some localities borrowed the idea directly from Oita, but the national government was still willing to fund the policy dissemination.

55. Interview with Usui Mitsuhiro, Director, Regional Planning and Research Department, JDB, August 3, 1993.

56. Mark Gelfand, *A Nation of Cities: The Federal Government and Urban America, 1933–1965* (New York: Oxford University Press, 1975), chapter 6.

57. *Flint Journal*, December 9, 1984.

58. This is a controversial observation based only on the two cases presented here. It is not necessarily true in other cities and policy areas. Some Japanese policy areas are far more politicized than others. Construction and agriculture are highly politicized, for example, while industrial policy is more bureaucratic. See Sakakibara, "The Japanese Politico-Economic System and the Public Sector," in Kernell, *Parallel Politics*, Budget politics also appears highly

politicized. See Muramatsu Michio, "Center-Local Political Relations in Japan: A Lateral Competition Model," *Journal of Japanese Studies* 12:303–327 (1986).

59. Reed, *Japanese Prefectures and Policymaking*, p. 29, supports this statement. Richard Samuels tempers this comparison, however. He points to the duplication of programs in the Japanese system—caused by *tatewari gyôsei*, the vertically fragmented system of administration—as evidence of room for creativity. See Samuels, *The Politics of Regional Policy in Japan: Localities Incorporated?* (Princeton: Princeton University Press, 1983), p. 247. Duplication does exist in both systems, as it does in Western European nations. But Reed asserts that the epidemic of duplication in the United States is far worse than the instances of duplication in Japan. Japan is comparatively centralized and orderly, for example, the case of rampant social service spending without oversight depicted by Martha Derthick would be unimaginable in the Japanese system. See Derthick, *Uncontrollable Spending for Social Service Grants* (Washington, DC: Brookings Institution, 1975).

60. Eric H. Monkkonen, *America Becomes Urban: The Development of United States Cities and Towns, 1780–1980* (Berkeley: University of California Press, 1988), pp. 148–151.

61. "Program Profile: Urban Development Action Grants," City of Flint internal document provided by the Office of Economic Development.

62. Ibid.

63. Robert E. Cole, *Strategies for Learning: Small-Group Activities in American, Japanese, and Swedish Industry* (Berkeley: University of California Press, 1989), p. 44.

64. "Glitzy Development Ending; Subtle Period Taking Over," *Flint Journal*, August 21, 1985.

65. *Flint Journal*, March 7, 1972; July 23, 1974.

66. Data provided by Department of Community Development, Flint City Hall.

67. Five million dollars came from an Army Corps of Engineers flood control project on the Flint River. The remainder was HUD grant money for urban revitalization projects.

68. *Flint Journal*, May 2, 1973.

69. Minutes of the FACI, Board of Directors Meeting, August 12, 1987.

70. John R. Wilson, FACI, Chairman. Notes from address delivered June 4, 1985. Wilson was the general manager of GM AC Spark Plug Division, located in Flint.

71. James S. Sheaffer, "Report to the Board and Members of the Flint Area Conference, Inc.," October 1, 1981.

72. See Gittell, *Renewing Cities*. He offers Lowell, Massachusetts, and Jamestown, New York, as examples of cities that successfully redeveloped without conforming to national program ideas.

73. The concept of path dependence is borrowed from Douglass C. North, *Institutions, Institutional Change, and Economic Performance* (New York: Cambridge University Press, 1990), chapter 1.

74. Interview with Nancy Jurkiewicz, Special Operations Coordinator, Flint Department of Community Development, March 8, 1994.

75. Data provided by the Department of Community Development, Flint City Hall.

76. Ibid.

77. Interview with Frederick Kump, Economic Development/TIFA Manager, Flint City Hall, March 8, 1994.

78. Interview with Frederick Kump, March 8, 1994.

79. Interview with Richard King, Economic Development Administrator, Flint City Hall, March 8, 1994.

80. The Charles Stewart Mott Foundation, "1983 Annual Report," p. 39.

81. Interview with Richard King, March 8, 1994.

82. Michael J. Rich, *Federal Policymaking and the Poor* (Princeton: Princeton University Press, 1993), pp. 43–49.

83. Interview with Frederick Kump, March 8, 1994.

84. Data provided by the Department of Community Development, Flint City Hall.

85. *Flint Journal*, August 6, 1986.

86. *Flint Journal*, June 9, 1991.

87. Steven P. Dandaneau, "Ideology and Dependent Deindustrialization: A Study of Local Responses to Flint, Michigan's Social and Cultural Decline from a Critical Theory Perspective," Ph.D. diss., Brandeis University, 1992, p. 436.

88. Ibid.

89. Ibid., p. 431.

90. Ibid., pp. 436–437.

91. *Flint Journal*, July 10, 1991.

92. Dandaneau, "Ideology and Dependent Deindustrialization," p. 443.

93. Ibid., pp. 448–449.

94. Ibid., p. 464.

95. See foundation annual reports, which include a list of projects funded each year. The foundation stopped funding large projects requiring substantial capital investment, instead opting to fund smaller projects aimed at improving quality of life, social welfare, and small business opportunities.

96. Data provided by Frederick Kump, as of October 1993. This number does not include tax abatements for GM suppliers or related businesses.

97. George F. Lord and Albert C. Price, "Growth Ideology in a Period of Decline: Deindustrialization and Restructuring, Flint Style," *Social Problems* 9:155–169 (May 1992).

98. John R. Logan and Harvey L. Molotch, *Urban Fortunes: The Political Economy of Place* (Berkeley: University of California Press, 1987).

Chapter Three: A Tale of Two Theme Parks

1. John W. Kingdon, *Agendas, Alternatives, and Public Policies* (Boston: Little, Brown, 1984), p. 1.

2. Interview with Ishii Kan, Planning Research Section Chief, JDB, Fukuoka branch, July 23, 1993.

3. *Nishi Nihon Shimbun,* September 14, 1989.

4. *Nishi Nihon Shimbun,* February 11, 1989.

5. Ibid.

6. *Nishi Nihon Shimbun,* November 25, 1989.

7. Chapter 2 contains a detailed explanation of the movement for a coal R&D facility.

8. Explained by Hoshioka Morihiko, the first president of Navel Land, in an interview in *Yomiuri Shimbun,* September 28, 1989.

9. Interview with Sakaguchi Toshihide, Planning Section Chief at Navel Land, May 12, 1993; and Navel Land, report, "The Development of Navel Land Up to Now," (Neiburu Rando Ima Made no Keika), April 1993.

10. *Nishi Nihon Shinbun,* January 30, 1990.

11. Interview with Sakaguchi Toshihide, May 12, 1993.

12. Navel Land, report, "The Development of Navel Land Up to Now, April 1993.

13. *Mainichi Shimbun,* June 21, 1990.

14. Interview with Sakaguchi Toshihide, May 12, 1993.

15. *Mainichi Shimbun,* June 21, 1990.

16. *Gendai Yôgo no Kiso Chishiki* (Tokyo: Jiyû Kokumin-sha, 1990), p. 481.

17. Chalmers Johnson, *Japan's Public Policy Companies* (Washington, DC: American Enterprise Institute for Public Policy Research, 1978), pp. 123, 131.

18. Interview with Sakaguchi Toshihide, May 12, 1993.

19. Interview with Ishii Kan, July 23, 1993.

20. Interview with Usui Mitsuhiro, Director, Regional Planning & Research Department., JDB headquarters, August 3, 1993.

21. Interview with Ishii Kan, July 23, 1993.

22. Ibid.

23. *Nishi Nihon Shimbun,* September 27, 1990.

24. Interview with Ishii Kan, July 23, 1993.

25. Interview with Shiotsuka Kôichi, Mayor of Omuta, June 21, 1993.

26. Interview with Ishii Kan, July 23, 1993.

27. *Flint Journal,* June 22, 1980.

28. Interview with former Flint mayor James Rutherford, April 8, 1991.

29. *Flint Journal,* June 22, 1980.

30. Interview with James Rutherford, April 8, 1991.

31. *Flint Journal*, June 22, 1980.

32. Ibid.

33. Ibid.

34. Interview with James Rutherford, April 8, 1991.

35. *Flint Journal*, March 11, 1981.

36. *Flint Journal*, June 22, 1980.

37. Zuchelli, Hunter & Associates, Memorandum Re: Analysis of the Market for Serviced Industrial Land in Genesee County, January 19, 1976.

38. *Flint Journal*, June 22, 1980.

39. *Flint Journal*, January 22, 1978.

40. *Flint Journal*, November 23, 1980.

41. Ibid.

42. *Flint Journal*, June 9, 1977.

43. Ibid.

44. *Flint Journal*, January 22, 1978.

45. *Flint Journal*, June 22, 1980.

46. Interview with James Rutherford, April 8, 1991.

47. *Flint Journal*, June 9, 1977.

48. *Flint Journal*, January 22, 1978.

49. *Flint Journal*, June 22, 1980.

50. *Flint Journal*, June 17, 1980.

51. *Flint Journal*, June 22, 1980.

52. *Flint Journal*, June 17, 1980. James Rutherford echoed this opinion in an interview on April 8, 1991.

53. *Flint Journal*, June 17, 1980. A tax increment bond is a tool for deferred financing from tax revenues. In tax-increment financing, a taxation district is formed and property assessments in that area are frozen—for accounting purposes—at a base year level. Any increases in property taxes after the base year are funneled to a special fund that is used to pay off the bond issue. Existing city tax dollars are thus not used to fund a project.

54. Ibid.

55. Ibid.

56. *Flint Journal*, June 23, 1980.

57. Ibid.

58. Ibid.

59. Interview with James Rutherford, April 8, 1991.

60. *Flint Journal*, June 23, 1980.

61. Ibid.

62. *Flint Journal*, July 30, 1980.

63. *Flint Journal*, August 29, 1980.

64. Ibid.

65. *Flint Journal*, May 1, 1982.

66. *Flint Journal*, March 20, 1981.

67. *Flint Journal*, March 26, 1981.

68. *Flint Journal*, April 10, 1981.

69. *Flint Journal*, March 26, 1981.

70. *Flint Journal*, June 8, 1981.

71. FACI Newsletter, "In Depth," November 1981.

72. Ibid.

73. Ibid.

74. *Flint Journal*, March 3, 1982.

75. *Flint Journal*, April 6, 1982.

76. Editorial, *Flint Journal*, April 30, 1982.

77. *Flint Journal*, May 1, 1982.

78. *Flint Journal*, May 2, 1982.

79. Ibid.

80. *Flint Journal*, November 23, 1980.

81. *Flint Journal*, January 22, 1978.

82. *Flint Journal*, July 9, 1982.

83. *Flint Journal*, July 19, 1982.

84. *Flint Journal*, October 14, 1982.

85. Data provided by the Department of Community Development, Flint City Hall.

86. *Flint Journal*, June 22, 1980.

87. *Flint Journal*, June 23, 1980.

88. Interview with James Rutherford, April 8, 1991.

89. *Flint Voice*, April 30–May 13, 1982.

90. *Flint Journal*, August 7, 1984.

91. *Flint Journal*, January 20, 1985.

92. *Detroit Free Press*, November 23, 1995.

93. *Flint Journal*, March 22, 1983.

94. This is pure speculation. I tried to confirm or deny this notion in interviews at all three firms, but no one would comment on the possibility.

95. See Douglas Ostrom, "The Flip Side of FILP: Japan's Public-Sector Institutions and Economic Policymaking," *Japan Economic Institute Report* 21A (May 27, 1994). Ostrom lists ten finance corporations, including the JDB, the Export-Import Bank of Japan, the Finance Corp. of Local Public Finance, and the Small Business Finance Corp., and thirty-seven public corporations. This larger second group is made up of agencies with much more narrow purposes. Examples include the Employment Promotion Projects Corp.; the Japan Sewerage Works Agency; Japan Private School Promotion Corp.; Water Resources Development Corp.; and New Energy and Industrial Technology Development Organization.

CHAPTER FOUR: DOWNTOWN RETAIL RENEWAL

1. Carol S. Weissert and Jack H. Knott, "Foundations and Their Impact on Health Care Reform." Paper presented at the American Political Science Association annual meeting, Chicago, 1995.

2. Omuta Ginza Street Shotengai Promotion Association, "Omuta Ginza Area Shotengai Activity: Model Project Report" (Omuta-shi Ginza-chiku Shotengai Kassei-ka: Moderu Jigyô Hôkokusho), March 1987, p. 6.

3. Interview with Omuta mayor Shiotsuka Kôichi, June 21, 1993.

4. "Omuta Ginza Area Shotengai Activity: Model Project Report," March 1987, pp. 14–16.

5. Interview with Tajima Tetsuya, General Affairs Section Manager, Omuta Chamber of Commerce, May 12, 1993.

6. Interview with Ono Takeshi, Commerce & Industry Promotion Section Consultant, Omuta Chamber of Commerce, May 12, 1993.

7. Interview with Gotô Kanichi, Director of Research Division, MITI Kyushu branch office (Chôsaka-cho, Sômu Kikaku-bu, Kyûshû Tsûsan Kyoku), February 16, 1993.

8. Ibid.

9. *Nishi Nihon Shinbun*, "93-oku-en Kake Fukugô Biru Kensetsu," April 15, 1989.

10. "Omuta Ginza Area Shotengai Activity: Model Project Report," March 1987, p. 40.

11. Interview with Tajima Tetsuya, May 12, 1993.

12. Information provided by Omuta Chamber of Commerce, *Model Project Chronology* (Moderu Jigyô Jisshi Keika), March 1987.

13. "Omuta Ginza Area Shotengai Activity: Model Project Report," 1987, p. 161, "Section Plan, by *Shôtengai*."

14. Interview with Tajima Tetsuya, May 12, 1993.

15. Information provided by Omuta Chamber of Commerce, *Model Project Chronology* (Moderu Jigyô Jisshi Keika), March 1987.

16. Interview with Tajima Tetsuya, May 12, 1993.

17. Information provided by Omuta Chamber of Commerce, Model Project Chronology (Moderu Jigyô Jisshi Keika), March 1987.

18. Ibid.

19. Interview with Mutô Yasukatsu, Vice Director, Omuta Planning and Promotion Section (Fuku-Kachô, Omuta Kikaku Shinkô-ka), December 22, 1992.

20. "Omuta Ginza Area Shotengai Activity: Model Project Report," March 1987, p. 201.

21. Chalmers Johnson, *Japan's Public Policy Companies* (Washington, DC: American Enterprise Institute, 1978), p. 21.

22. Information provided by the Omuta Chamber of Commerce, "Financial Procurement Methods" (Shikin Chôtatsu Hôhô ni tsuite) document, February 1991.

23. "Omuta Ginza Area Shotengai Activity: Model Project Report," March 1987, p. 201.

24. Ibid.

25. *Nishi Nihon Shinbun*, "Miyamae-dori Seibi ga Kansei," April 22, 1988.

26. Interview with Tajima Tetsuya, May 12, 1993.

27. Interview with Ono Takeshi, May 12, 1993.

28. *Mainichi Shinbun*, "Shian Bashi ga Atarashiku," October 22, 1989; "'Kamaboko' Arcade Kansei," October 5, 1989.

29. *Mainichi Shinbun*, "Modan na Akêdo Kansei," December 7, 1990.

30. *Yomiuri Shinbun*, "Shiro Kichô ni Akarui Mûdo," December 8, 1990.

31. Unpublished data provided by the Omuta Chamber of Commerce.

32. *Nishi Nihon Shinbun*, "93-oku-en Kake Fukugô Biru Kensetsu," April 15, 1989.

33. *Yomiuri Shinbun*, "Yôto Betsu Biru 4-tô Kensetsu," December 1, 1990.

34. *Yomiuri Shinbun*, "Fukyô de Saikaihatsu Keikaku Minaosu," December 5, 1992.

35. Ibid.

36. *From the Omuta Chamber* (Omuta Kaigi-sho da Yori, Chamber of Commerce monthly newsletter), January 11, 1993.

37. *Nishi Nihon Shinbun*, "Omuta, Yoshino-chiku ni Naitei," June 2, 1989.

38. *Flint Journal*, "Flint Details Downtown Plaza Plans," March 17, 1978.

39. Ibid.

40. Ibid.

41. *Flint Journal*, "Bigger Plaza Plan Emerging Downtown," January 20, 1980.

42. Ibid.

43. *Flint Journal*, "Downtown Flint Plaza Ideas Get Praise," March 22, 1983.

44. *Flint Journal*, "City Buying Key Parcels for Plaza," March 23, 1983.

45. *Flint Journal*, "Mott Foundation to Guide, not Fund, Plaza Construction," March 24, 1983.

46. *Flint Journal,* "Merchants in Way of Planned Mall Say New 'Homes' Downtown Scarce," April 9, 1983.

47. *Flint Journal,* "Most Buildings Acquired for Planned Downtown Plaza," August 25, 1983.

48. *Flint Journal,* "City Buying Key Parcels for Plaza," March 23, 1983.

49. *Flint Journal,* "DDA Hiring Rouse Firm for Plaza Plans," September 30, 1983.

50. Ibid.

51. Ibid.

52. Ibid.

53. *Flint Journal,* "Plaza Developer Given Big Share of Revenues to Take on Flint Project," October 30, 1983.

54. Ibid.

55. *Flint Journal,* "Downtown Delight," December 23, 1983.

56. Ibid.

57. *Flint Journal,* "Rouse Plugs Downtown Flint's Potential," December 1, 1983.

58. *Flint Journal,* "Urban Centers 10 Years in the Making"; "Rouse Says Mall to Open by July '85," January 27, 1984.

59. *Flint Journal,* "Mall Demolition May Be Scaled Down," January 11, 1984.

60. Ibid.

61. *Flint Journal,* "Marketplace Decision Called Good News for City," January 27, 1984.

62. *Flint Journal,* "Flint Marketplace Finally Gets Name," February 28, 1984.

63. *Flint Journal,* "Downtown Mall Gets Cool Reception from Planning Panel," February 29, 1984.

64. *Flint Journal,* "Marketplace $ Advanced by Mott," June 12, 1984.

65. Data provided by the Department of Community Development, Flint City Hall.

66. *Flint Journal,* "Water Street Pavilion is New Name of Marketplace," June 12, 1984.

67. *Flint Journal,* "High Rent: Some Prospective Tenants . . .," August 21, 1984.

CHAPTER FIVE: INDUSTRIAL PARK SURPRISES

1. Interview with Ikeda Yûsuke, Omuta City Hall Economic Bureau, Industry Promotion Section, June 8, 1993.

2. "Raishun ni wa Yôchi Baishû e," *Asahi Shinbun,* December 26, 1989.

3. Internal data provided by the Omuta City Hall Economic Bureau, Industry Promotion Section.

4. Interview with Ikeda Yûsuke, June 8, 1993.

5. Ibid.

6. "Kôgyô Danchi no Shinshutsu Danren," *Nishi Nihon Shinbun*, April 22, 1991.

7. Interview with Ikeda Yûsuke, June 8, 1993.

8. Ibid.

9. Data provided by the Omuta City Hall, Industrial Promotion Section.

10. Omuta Chamber of Commerce, "A Plan for Modernizing Commerce in the Omuta Area (Omuta Chiiki Shôgyô Kindai-ka Chiiki Keikaku)," 1979.

11. Omuta Chamber of Commerce, "Omuta Area Product Distribution Base Plan (Omuta Chiiki Butsu Ryû Kyoten Keikaku)," 1979.

12. Omuta Chamber of Commerce, "Omuta Product Distribution Center Construction Study (Omuta-shi Butsu Ryû Sentâ Kensetsu Chôsa)," 1985.

13. Interview with Yamana Hiroaki, Omuta City Hall Economic Bureau, Industry, and Tourism Section, June 7, 1993.

14. Interview with Muto Yasukatsu, Vice Section Chief, Omuta Planning Division, Planning and Promotion Section, December 22, 1992.

15. "Kôgyô Danchi Kôzô ga Uki-Age," *Nikan Kôgyô Shinbun*, May 11, 1988.

16. "Omuta Product Distribution Center Overview," report prepared by Omuta City Hall Economic Bureau, Commerce and Tourism Section, n.d.

17. Ibid.

18. Internal data provided by the Omuta City Hall Economic Bureau, Industry Promotion Section. The city and prefectural contributions were only used for public road repairs and improvements.

19. "Kôgyô Danchi Kôzô ga Uki-Age," *Nikan Kôgyô Shinbun*, May 11, 1988.

20. "Omuta Product Distribution Center Overview," p. 2.

21. Interview with Yamana Hiroaki, June 7, 1993.

22. Ibid.

23. Interview with Ikeda Yûsuke, June 8, 1993.

24. "Fuyô e O-gata Kôgyô Danchi," *Yomiuri Shinbun*, February 6, 1991; "Overview of the Inland Large-Scale Industrial Park Development Project," Omuta Industrial Promotion Section internal document, n.d.

25. "Shi-ka Chiku wa Tekichi," *Asahi Shinbun*, June 14, 1991.

26. "Chakkô ____nirami Chosa Isogu," *Mainichi Shinbun*, January 25, 1992.

27. Ibid.

28. This list excludes firms in the Product Distribution Center. The firms in this center reinforce the trends observed in Omuta's kigyô yûchi in general. These trends are highlighted in the next section.

29. Steven R. Reed, *Japanese Prefectures and Policymaking* (Pittsburgh: University of Pittsburgh Press, 1986), pp. 27–32.

30. Interview with Ito Ren, Regional Development Division Director, Ministry of Home Affairs, July 9, 1993.

31. Chalmers Johnson, *Japan's Public Policy Companies* (Washington, DC: American Enterprise Institute for Public Policy Research, 1978), pp. 38–40.

32. "'Image-Up' e Tasai na Teigen," *Nishi Nihon Shinbun*, November 1, 1988;" Kigyô Yûchi mo Jinmyaku," *Yomiuri Shinbun*, November 19, 1988.

33. Interview with Muto Yasukatsu, December 22, 1992; Interview with Ikeda Yûsuke, June 8, 1993.

34. Interview with Ikeda Yûsuke, June 8, 1993.

35. "Omuta, Shutoken ni Uri-Kome," *Yomiuri Shinbun*, June 10, 1988.

36. Data received from MITI, Industrial Location Pollution Branch (Ritchi Kôgai Kyoku), Industrial Location Advisory Section (Ritchi Shidô-ka), May 1992.

37. "Toma Higashi, Saimu Chôka no Kiki," *Asahi Shinbun*, August 2, 1993.

38. Numbers based on data received from MITI, Industrial Location Pollution Branch (Ritchi Kôgai Kyoku), and Industrial Location Advisory Section (Ritchi Shidô-ka), May 1992.

39. The state of Michigan has a rating system by which it classifies industrial parks. I will explain the system in the next section.

40. "Industrial parks? Survey says area businesses prefer them," *Flint Journal*, January 5, 1975.

41. Ibid.

42. *Flint Journal*, June 22, 1980.

43. Zuchelli, Hunter & Associates, Memorandum Re: Analysis of the Market for Serviced Industrial Land in Genesee County, January 19, 1976, p. 1. This report was directed to Coopers and Lybrand and to the Flint Department of Community Development. It was apparently circulated in FACI to some extent, since I found a copy in the University of Michigan-Flint archives, where the personal papers of Gerald F. Healy, a prominent commercial realtor in Flint, are available to the public. Healy was a member of FACI.

44. Ibid., pp. 1–3.

45. Ibid., pp. 3–6.

46. Office of Economic Development, Michigan Department of Commerce, *Michigan Business Fact Sheet*, "Michigan's Certified Industrial Parks" (No. 6), n.d.

47. Detroit Edison, "Rating System for Industrial Parks in Southeast Michigan," n.d. This information was included in a 1982 letter from Detroit Edison to Gerald F. Healy.

48. Zuchelli, Hunter & Associates, Memorandum, Re: Analysis of the Market for Serviced Industrial Land in Genesee County, January 19, 1976, p.p. 7–10.

49. Ibid., p. 13.

50. "Economic Development Commission of Genesee County, 1975 Annual Report," pp. 5–6.

51. "Flint gets US $ for airpark," *Flint Journal*, June 18, 1975.

52. "Airpark financing apparently assured," *Flint Journal*, June 5, 1975.

53. Ibid.

54. "Boggan says work on airpark likely to start this fall," *Flint Journal*, June 11, 1975.

55. "Airpark benefits to Flint outlined by county official," *Flint Journal*, May 25, 1975.

56. "Council approves airport grant, loan," *Flint Journal*, August 7, 1975.

57. *Flint Journal*, August 19, 1975.

58. "Airpark project producing jobs now, and for future," *Flint Journal*, August 14, 1976.

59. "Bishop industrial park nearing completion," *Flint Journal*, February 6, 1977.

60. "Tennesseean takes over as 'salesman'," *Flint Journal*, September 8, 1977.

61. "Industrial park investment starting to pay off for Flint," *Flint Journal*, January 6, 1980.

62. "Granted—Cablevision to build and expand . . .," *Flint Journal*, July 4, 1980.

63. "Grant for industrial park hinges on matching funds," *Flint Journal*, February 11, 1975.

64. Ibid.

65. "HUD confirms Flint will get bonus money," *Flint Journal*, January 28, 1975.

66. Ibid.

67. Under the new regulations, the Detroit HUD office could approve such requests without routing them to Chicago and Washington as before. See "Grant for industrial park hinges on matching funds," *Flint Journal*, February 11, 1975.

68. "St. John project getting an official looking over," *Flint Journal*, April 6, 1975.

69. Data provided by the Department of Community Development, Flint City Hall.

70. "Payouts vary in renewal area," *Flint Journal*, September 28, 1976.

71. Ibid.

72. Ibid.

73. Ibid.

74. Coopers and Lybrand, "St. John Industrial Park Preliminary Definition of Marketing Parameters," January 25, 1976, pp. 1–2, 11, 16, 35.

75. Ibid., pp. 3–10.

76. "Industrial park investment starting to pay off for Flint," *Flint Journal*, January 6, 1980.

77. Ibid.

78. Ibid.

79. Bryan D. Jones and Lynn W. Bachelor provide an excellent description of the city's political maneuverings to keep the Buick expansion project in Flint in *The*

Sustaining Hand: Community Leadership and Corporate Power (Lawrence: University Press of Kansas, 1986), pp. 179–188.

80. Ibid., pp. 190–191.

81. Ibid., p. 192.

82. "New Buick suppliers to overflow park, officials predict," *Flint Journal*, August 18, 1983.

83. Michael Cohen, James March, and Johan Olsen, "A Garbage Can Model of Organizational Choice," *Administrative Science Quarterly* 17:1–15 (1972).

CHAPTER SIX: CONCLUSION

1. See Douglas Ostrom, "The Flip Side of FILP: Japan's Public Sector Institutions and Economic Policymaking," *Japan Economic Institute Report* 21A (May 27, 1994), pp. 9–10.

2. Eisuke Sakakibara, "The Japanese Politico-Economic System and the Public Sector," in Samuel Kernell, *Parallel Politics: Economic Policymaking in Comparative Perspective* (Washington, DC: Brookings Institution, 1991), pp., 50–79.

3. *Flint Journal*, November 26, 1984.

4. "Charles Stewart Mott Foundation 1992 Annual Report," p. 84.

5. Foundation president William White, in a letter dated March 27, 1987 to foundation Town Hall meeting participants, lists various studies funded by the foundation, including feasibility studies for a medical research facility and for a center for technology.

6. Robert L. Crain, "Fluoridation: The Diffusion of an Innovation among Cities," *Social Forces* 44:467–476 (June 1966); Beth Moncure Winn and Marcia Lynn Whicker, "Indicators of State Lottery Adoptions," *Policy Studies Journal* 18:293–304 (Winter 1989–1990); Lee Sigelman, Phillip W. Roeder, and Carol K. Sigelman, "Social Service Innovation in the American States: Deinstitutionalization of the Mentally Retarded," *Social Science Quarterly* 62:503–515 (September 1981). These last two articles focus on policy diffusion in the United States at the state level, but conceptually it is the same as diffusion at the local level.

7. Franklin James, "Urban Economic Development: A Zero-Sum Game?" in Richard D. Bingham and John P. Blair, *Urban Economic Development* (Beverly Hills: Sage Publications, 1984), pp. 157–174.

8. Carol S. Weissert and Jack H. Knott, "Foundations and Their Impact on Health Care Reform," Paper delivered at the American Political Science Association annual meeting, Chicago, 1995, p. 4.

9. Joel D. Aberbach, Robert D. Putnam, and Bert A. Rockman, *Bureaucrats and Politicians in Western Democracies* (Cambridge: Harvard University Press, 1981), p. 243.

10. Ezra Vogel, *Comeback* (Tokyo: Charles E. Tuttle, 1985), pp. 121–122.

11. Hiramatsu Morihiko, *An Idea from the Local Level* (Chihô kara no Hassô) (Tokyo: Iwanami Shôten, 1990).

12. Kent E. Calder, Crisis and Compensation: *Public Policy and Political Stability in Japan* (Princeton: Princeton University Press, 1988), p. 20.

13. Ross J. Gittell, *Renewing Cities* (Princeton: Princeton University Press, 1993); Masatoshi Yorimitsu, "The Decline and Renaissance of the Steel Town: The Case of Kamaishi," in Kuniko Fujita and Richard Child Hill, eds., *Japanese Cities in the World Economy* (Philadelphia: Temple University Press, 1993), pp. 203–223; Heywood T. Sanders and Clarence N. Stone, *The Politics of Urban Development* (Lawrence: University of Kansas Press, 1987).